THE UNDISCOVER'D COUNTRY

This collection of essays, drawing together new material from four countries, challenges many of the current trends in Shakespeare studies.

The discussions of Shakespeare's plays and poems in this collection, by a range of academics, practising psychotherapists and the theatre director Jonathan Miller, discover many kinds of reference beyond the text: intuitable meanings, symbolisms inspired by the dark – undiscover'd – side of human relations, and characterizations of individual and group identities. The authors – Philip K. Bock, M. D. Faber, Jonathan Miller, Ruth Nevo, Angela Sheppard, B. J. Sokol and Lyn Stephens – are especially interested in the dynamics of emotional life. They variously bring to bear on Shakespeare's texts knowledge of theatrical practice, social history, anthropology, theology, political history, art history and other disciplines.

The editor contributes an introduction which claims the importance of psychological and psychodynamic understanding for the progress of literary studies. The volume also contains a bibliography of psychoanalytic and psychological Shakespeare studies in English from 1979–1989, which will prove invaluable to those already familiar with the two previous ten-year bibliographies in the field.

B. J. SOKOL lectures in English at Goldsmiths' College, University of London. He has published recently on Sir Philip Sidney, Shakespeare, Jonson, Milton and Marvell.

THE UNDISCOVER'D COUNTRY

NEW ESSAYS ON PSYCHOANALYSIS AND SHAKESPEARE

Edited by B. J. SOKOL

'an association in which the free development of
each is the condition of the free development of all'

Free Association Books / London / 1993

Published in Great Britain in 1993 by
Free Association Books
26 Freegrove Road
London N7 9QR

A CIP catalogue record for this book is available from the British Library

ISBN 1-85343-197-4

Typeset from author's disc by Archetype.
Printed in Great Britain.

CONTENTS

ACKNOWLEDGEMENTS

My thanks are first and foremost to the authors of these essays. Acknowledgments are made to Routledge and to the author for kind permission to reprint Ruth Nevo's chapter, 'The perils of Pericles', originally published in her book *Shakespeare's Other Language* (1987), New York and London: Methuen. For permission to reprint Philip Bock's essay '"Neither two nor one": dual unity in *The Phoenix and Turtle*', originally published in the defunct *Journal of Psychoanalytical Anthropology*, my thanks are due to the author and to the present copyright holders, *The Journal of Psychohistory*.

I thank Jonathan Miller for permission to use his talk given to the Squiggle Foundation, London, on 11 March 1989. For the audio tape of this talk I thank The Squiggle Foundation to Study and Cultivate the Tradition of D. W. Winnicott, and its directors Alexander Newman and Nina Farhi. Transcription of the tape by Barbara Wells was made possible through the generosity of Lawrence Stein. For other typing assistance I am grateful to Pam Hooker. Thanks also to Clare Steward of the University of London Computer Centre for helping me with their Kurzweil Reader.

I wish also to thank the English Department of Goldsmiths' College and Marilyn Jones, Sacha Shaw and Pauline Ryall at the Goldsmiths' College Library. The staff of The British Library, the University of London Library, the Tavistock Institute Library, and Free Association Books have also been most helpful. I particularly wish to thank Ann Scott of Free Association Books and Anita Kermode for lending their great sensitivity and expertise.

Thanks finally to my teachers, my friends, and my wife who have suffered with me and taught me.

NOTES ON CONTRIBUTORS

PHILIP BOCK is Presidential Professor of Anthropology at the University of New Mexico.

M. D. FABER teaches literature and psychology at the University of Victoria, British Columbia, where he is Professor of English.

CHRISTINE LEVEY is the Automation Librarian for Goldsmiths' College, The University of London. She was previously a librarian dealing with Psychology, Life Sciences and Earth Sciences.

JONATHAN MILLER first qualified as a Doctor of Medicine but his subsequent career has encompassed many fields. He is an author, academic, television producer, television presenter, and opera and theatre director.

RUTH NEVO has lived in Israel since 1950. She was Head of the English Department at Hebrew University in 1970, appointed to the Renee Lang Chair in Humanities in 1982 and made a member of the Israel Academy in 1987.

ANGELA SHEPPARD is a psychoanalyst in private practice, and a member of the Canadian Psychoanalytic Society, Quebec English Branch.

JERRY SOKOL lectures in English at Goldsmiths' College, The University of London.

LYN STEPHENS is an analytic psychotherapist. She practices and teaches in London.

INTRODUCTION

An ulterior purpose of this collection of essays on Shakespeare by international academics, practising psychotherapists, and a writer/theatre-director is to illustrate the relevance of certain tenets of criticism, especially today. These tenets amount to no self-proclaimed school, and exclude no other principles or methodologies. Yet the following introductory remarks may seem a bit manifesto-like, for they will address powers and agencies for criticism often currently denied it by fashion.

In any event the 'tide' of fashion is turning. Trends in cultural institutions such as literary criticism do resemble tides in manifesting cyclical movements not controlled by individuals or groups; yet the metaphor is imprecise for these trends, unlike tides, never simply return to earlier phases. Certainly I do not believe Shakespeare criticism can ever again ignore the problems raised in its recent past. Intellect should seek to be informed, not trapped, by passionate movements: educated not swept away by received ideas. And although recently fashionable dogmas have placed restrictions, some would go so far as to say near 'taboos' (Frattaroli, p. 407), on certain kinds of critical discussion, there is neither need nor cause to ring the bell backward. There are still, as always, alternative voices, and much for those voices to comment upon. Like psychic repressions, cultural consensuses which exclude the 'other' are rarely as monolithic as they present themselves, and indeed are often self-compelled to leak suppressed meaning through exaggeration, inconsistency, flamboyance or fugue. One

century after the discovery of psychoanalysis, we should be warned
against the pathology involved in denigration of all but selected
forebears. The following essays have been assembled in full
awareness of recent scepticism, agnosticism, and even strictures in
English Studies. I believe they point forward to new openings, with
the proviso that if parts of the past are unacknowledged and
unincorporated into future visions the resulting repressions will
enfeeble and impoverish the new visions.

At a time when a major Shakespeare conference advertises itself
with the observation that 'many no longer believe in minds or
characters – or in Shakespeare as something other than author
position or cultural construct', the essays in this collection
unashamedly present discoveries of Shakespearian references to
common concerns of human minds, and of intuitable Shakespearian
characterizations of lively individual and group identities. This is
not to say that these essays do not benefit from the structural and
material insights of social history, anthropology, political history,
art history, analysis of dramatic construction, poetics and so forth.
I believe that no genuine contribution to an increased comprehen-
sion of literature excludes any other. Thus the essays in this
collection employ Freudian, Jungian, Kleinian, Winnicottian and
other psychological perspectives, and viewpoints inspired by all
the above mentioned cross-disciplines, and even by theology.

Despite this diversity all the authors collected here seem to me
to co-operate in an endeavour outlined recently by Edward Tayler
when he made a 'modest proposal' for a critical approach based on
the notion of works of literature being like living people. This,
according to Tayler's irony, is the 'simple-minded analogy, the
people-paradigm analogy that alone lends significance to our
reading and teaching' (1990, p. 46). We are well positioned today
to know how cramping a reductive, scientistic rather than
scientific, analogy may be, but Tayler's 'simple-minded' analogy is
for me just the opposite. Following this analogy, Tayler quotes J. V.
Cunningham on our relationship with art:

> the problem that is here raised with respect to literature is really the
> problem of any human relationship: Shall we understand another on his
> terms or ours? It is the problem of affection and truth, of appreciation

and scholarship . . . Now it is common experience that affection begins with misunderstanding. We see our own meanings in what we love and we misconstrue for our own purposes. But life will not leave us there, and not only on account of external pressures . . . We sit across the room and trace the lineaments of experience on the face of concern . . . The end of affection and concern is accuracy and truth, with an alteration but no diminution of feeling. (In Tayler, p. 46)

Psychoanalysis especially understands how drastically changeable within our relation to it is the living face of human love and concern, and in Tayler's view our relation to literature may be the same. The process of growth through reading, as through living, requires us to discover, question, and reformulate feelings.

What the psychoanalytic tradition has to offer to such a process is the support of its rich insight into how extremely deep affectional 'misunderstanding' runs: how vitally (comically) necessary our original affectional misunderstanding is, and how devastatingly (tragically) detrimental the inhibition of our growth beyond that misunderstanding must be.

This relates to a widespread feeling that psychoanalytic thought has a particular kinship with the work of Shakespeare. The perceived kinship may arise partly because Freud himself was inspired by his reading of Shakespeare when he first found courage to 'disturb the sleep of the world' (Frattaroli, p. 410; Gornick, pp. 105–6). But I believe the affinity arises more intrinsically because in Shakespeare's work, as in psychoanalytic work, there is a profound sense of how the unconscious processes that develop our capacities for love and concern underlie all other aspects of human life.

When Tayler proposes his 'simple-minded analogy' he thinks, albeit with due reservations, of John Milton's concept of a 'good book', one of those that are 'not absolutely dead things, but contain a potency of life in them to be as active as that soul whose progeny they are; nay they do preserve as in a vial the purest efficacy and extraction of that living intellect that bred them' (Milton, *Areopagitica*, in Tayler, p. 45). Almost all we are ever likely to know of Shakespeare's 'living intellect' is in his good books (the same is not true of Milton), and so I include no guesswork psychobiography of Shakespeare the Man in this collection.[1] But if not fanciful

Shakespearian biography, yet the idea of virtualized life stories does play an important role in the critical explorations collected here. (By virtualized I mean made to affect our inner or outer senses as if real – I mean deliberately emulating the effects of the real.)

Although it is not a logical equivalent, in insisting on the importance of life in Shakespeare's text I mean also to suggest movement away from the Shakespeare of constrained formalist criticism to a Shakespeare concerned with presenting through texts virtualized lives and identities. I am therefore following Tayler's analogy backward, from the life of the text to the life the text is about. I am encouraged in doing this, although I do not mean to address quite the same question, by a most challenging recent article by the psychoanalyst Elio J. Frattaroli, 'On the validity of treating Shakespeare's characters as if they were real people'. This argument in support of 'character criticism' is not at all naive, nor is its notion of 'as if' philosophically unsound. Frattaroli investigates the famous theoretical views of L. C. Knights, Norman Holland and others that have for some time outlawed, or labelled as irresponsibly indulgent, responses to Shakespeare characters 'as if' they were real. Within these views Frattaroli discovers fallacies and he applies newer ideas of A. D. Nuttall, Seymour Chatman, and particularly E. D. Hirsh as correctives. The key issue left, I think, is not if but how we may accept the distinction Nuttall makes: 'Of course [A. C.] Bradley never supposed for a moment that Hamlet was a real man. Knights's ill-made shaft misses both Shakespeare and Bradley, and falls on stony ground. But the stony ground, it must be confessed, received it with joy' (1983, in Frattaroli, p. 415). In what sense does Shakespeare's work portray humanity? I will propose a reply, drawn from psychoanalytic thinking, neither to displace nor replace Nuttall's concept of 'a new mimesis', nor Chatman's of a reader's aesthetic rights, nor Hirsh's assertion of the possibility of determining authorial intention and of the invalidity of textual 'semantic autonomy'. Nor does my reply depend on Frattaroli's way of extending these critics' concepts into the psychoanalytic realm, although I find fascinating his application to literary critical theory of a psychoanalytic epistemological model distinguishing empathic (primary) and conceptual (secondary) understanding (Frattaroli, pp. 416–17). Rather, with full acknowledgement of the cogency of these other positions, I will suggest another reply.

This reply is tentative and partial, as I believe all replies must be in response to questions of art and reality. It certainly does not suggest the absurdity that we can attempt to 'psychoanalyse' Shakespeare's characters. My view depends rather on the theory that psychic objects, and especially their dynamic relations in unconscious phantasy, profoundly affect all human perceptions and actions from the start of life. This theory derives from Melanie Klein, who wrote:

> The analysis of very young children has taught me that there is no instinctual urge, no anxiety situation, no mental process which does not involve objects, external or internal; in other words object relations are at the *centre* of emotional life. (Klein, 1952, p. 206; discussed in Segal, 1980, p. 168)

Some later psychoanalysts have gone further, asserting, like Harry Guntrip, that '*the significance of human living lies in object-relationships, and only in such terms can our life be said to have meaning, for without object-relations the ego itself cannot develop*' (1968, pp. 19–20, author's italics). Even if we stop short of accepting the argument that the origin of the ego must subsume all meanings the ego will encounter, it is possible to accept that the relations of internalized objects may play a great part in forming the representations, symbols and conceptualizations necessary for human meaning.

But if we accept the principle of the primacy of psychic reality, a principle meaning that object relations in phantasy not only have primacy in being the archaic reality for every human being, but also in being the definitive driving force in later living, the question of human meaning becomes very complex. For psychoanalytic observation of children and adults has indicated that there is a continuity between the infantile primitive self, only dimly, if at all, differentiated from its own first objects which bring to it nurture, anxiety and so forth, and the mature self, fully recognizing others who possess their own independent and intermixed drives, loves and hates. This continuity derives from a history of development involving repeated oscillations between affection, misunderstanding, disaffection, and learning. In this turbulent and never-ending internal drama there are many knots, so that for example a dynamic in phantasy similar to the one that allows the creation of ethical autonomy may also serve to destroy personal authenticity and morality. Such complications arise in accordance with the discovery that internalized objects are split into parts and projected out many times in the course of mental growth, and are often reunified and re-introjected – a process giving rise to our knowledge of wholeness and difference. External/internal and self/other distinctions fall in between learned and created things. Because subjectivity itself derives from continuous object relations, from internal stories or phantasies through which we repeatedly redefine ourselves and others, literature may even be a close cousin of what actually makes people real. The sense many viewers and readers have of the reality of Shakespeare's creations may arise, then, because these creations resemble radically real things: the dynamic internal objects with which we build reality.

The philosopher Richard Wollheim, discussing Klein's views of internalized psychic objects, expresses some doubts concerning the retrievability of their 'distinctive casual histories', yet states that in a certain sense internal figures 'lead lives' paralleling the mimetic lives of fictional characters (1984, pp. 126–7). Writing of the way internal objects are formally represented, Wollheim extends his comparison with fictional characters, with a proviso: 'the formal marks of internality reproduce, while greatly exaggerating, the marks of fictionality' (p. 128). He states four common charac-teristics in the modes of representation of internal and fictional characters:

1 radical incompleteness or indeterminacy of character, so that certain questions . . . do not arise;
2 deathlessness, or rather a permanent renewability of existence;
3 an unlimited power to attract to itself novel significance through expanded associations;
4 a relative imperviousness to reality-testing, or at any rate to any matching of a given figure against its external original. (p. 128, numbering added)

Characteristics 1, 2 and 4 seem to me to apply equally well to representation in fictionality and internality, but characteristic 3 seems to me very questionably applicable to fictionality. It seems to me this issue is related to hotly debated issues of literary theory: if fictionality is *not* marked by the exaggeration Wollheim attributes to the representation of internal objects, but is held none the less to permit unlimited interpretation, then the most extreme claims of hermeneutic nihilism are justified. However, this justification collapses if Wollheim is correct and fictional objects only to a slight degree share the supposed limitless significances of objects of unconscious processes. The justification collapses also, it seems to me, if there is some intuitive means whereby we may retrieve the 'casual histories' of internal objects, for then some form of validity testing by 'recognition' of interpretations of phantasy, and commutatively of fiction, would be possible. I am myself inclined to this latter alternative, and believe with Klein and many of her followers that unconscious phantasy resembles a story with considerable firmness of outline. This is a developmental story, beginning from the time when inner and outer objects are hardly distinguished at all, when the new-born baby internalizes the mother's breast before it can be conceived of as having external reality. Features of the tempestuous journey from that point to mature relationships have been narrated by Klein, Winnicott and others and are still, of course, being investigated (see, especially, Klein, 1957).

Following such a story implies far more than the mere use of a specialized terminology or jargon. The particular value of the psychoanalytic approach is that it can take us much further in certain enquiries than can 'common sense'. Yet paradoxically, application of psychoanalytic ideas makes a *difference* to literary studies, in my belief, precisely because these ideas are intelligible to what Richard Wollheim calls 'ordinary thought'. Much of the insight of psychoanalysis has come from studies of mental distress in neurotics, pre-verbal children and, more recently, psychotics. Faced with such difficult material, writers in Freud's tradition mostly follow his admirable model of lucidity, relying on the thought processes found in rationality and common sense rather than on any special kind of logic to assess unconscious phantasy. As Wollheim writes, 'I do not quite see how the defensive or regressive character of [even severe] fragmentation of the inner world can be appreciated unless it is recognized that the ground-rules of phantasy are provided in our ordinary thought' (1984, p. 129).

The mental meeting ground with phantasy is 'ordinary thought', but that leaves open the question of what sort of language to use when talking about archaic states of mind and very primitive kinds of thinking. When treating young children Melanie Klein often used a language of anatomical parts and functions and bodily sensations, and a number of analysts today follow this practice also with adults. But there is a trend now among some psychoanalytic practitioners to move away from giving interpretations in such 'symbolic' language to their adult patients, especially of phantasies concerning the aggressive and often violent 'part object relations' (Spillius, vol. 2, pp. 7–9). Instead they are inclined to diminish or delay uses of the language of 'archaic, anatomic' perception, because archaic phantasies are for adults 'now felt and thought in the patient's adult language' (Riesenberg Malcolm, p. 318).

But consulting-room effectiveness need not have any bearing on how literary criticism best employs psychoanalytic insights. As I've said, the 'as if' reality of Shakespeare's creations cannot justify in any way subjecting his imagined people (or groups) to attempted veritable psychoanalysis. Correspondingly, despite psychoanalytic practice, it would be absurd to avoid psychoanalytic terminology where it helps clarify and order critical discourse. Yet I believe that everything discovered by psychoanalysis has analogues in everyday thoughts and feelings (since it underlies these). It is through this circumstance that psychoanalytic concepts most usually manifest kinship with imaginative literature.

Of course literature has infinite variety and in its uniqueness can be very strange; like the perfect remembering of grammar in cases of amnesia, literature may allow communication beyond our ken. The archaic stories of unconscious phantasy may also seem very strange. For instance, Melanie Klein's findings about the first object of infancy, the maternal introject, include discoveries that babies usually experience such enjoyment and gratitude and pleasure at the breast that they internalize 'inner wealth [which] derives from having assimilated the good object so that the individual becomes able to share its gifts with others'; and yet in their first months babies in order to grow must also experience 'sadistic impulses directed, not only against the mother's breast, but also against the inside of her body: scooping it out, devouring the contents, destroying it by every means which sadism can suggest' (Klein, 1957, p. 19; 1935, p. 116). The great complexity of pre-verbal emotional life does not stop there either, according to Klein, but includes production of terrifying retaliating monsters, and of real, although pre-ethical and pre-linguistic, senses of responsibility and guilt. I sketch her findings partly to whet the appetites of new readers of Klein and her followers, but mainly to illustrate that the way archaic phantasy feels to infants must seem foreign to adult awareness, although it is logically comprehensible to it.

In most art, as in adult behaviour, phantasies are usually expressed through the 'acting out' gestures that are their safer quotidian analogues. I believe Shakespeare's mistakenly over-rational Duke Theseus refers to such expression when he somewhat dismissively comments that poets provide for their wildly imagined 'forms of things unknown', 'a local habitation and a name' (*A Midsummer Night's Dream*, V,i,14–17). Shakespeare has a great many ways of giving 'things unknown' local habitations and names. These are found not only in his dramatic settings and characterizations, which are obvious and important habitations and names (and even these are subdivided in many ways). Shakespeare's mimesis is extremely varied, and numerous types of apprehension are therefore possible and profitable even when one is dealing with a single work or genre, not to mention dealing across the wide range of his modes and styles. Thus there is predictably a great variety of method in the following essays.

The 'undiscover'd country' of human motivations is approached through the clarifying imperatives[2] of theatre by Jonathan Miller, whose talk, reproduced here, was presented to a psychoanalytically oriented audience at the same time as he was creating a new production of *King Lear*. He discusses the damaged human relationships in the play and the consequent exclusions from family and society[3] in terms of the drives motivating the play's characters, their implied spiritual states, and their personal and religious feelings. These he investigates in the light of poetic imagery, the political presuppositions of Shakespeare's age, aspects of social and economic history, art history, religious history, anthropological patterns and many other matters. To expose the emotional roots of the play – not pointing up to the cosmos but down to the soil of real human needs and anger and terrors – he properly considers, for example, political and theological contexts which would have appeared more clearly in Shakespeare's time than in ours. For even *King Lear*, which is perhaps the most poetic of Shakespeare's 'dramatic poems', cannot manifest a relation to the roots of emotional life unless a 'local habitation', a virtualized reality, is comprehended. Sympathetic historical understanding and emotional intuition combine to allow the director, rather as a stream of associations and transference allow an analyst, to interpret. Thus Miller demonstrates the kind of thinking a director uses to discover and make visible the Shakespearian motivations, characterizations and transforming relationships which are best portrayed on the theatrical stage.

To show how psychodynamic patterns may inform a different literary genre, I have included Philip K. Bock's very interesting essay on Shakespeare's non-dramatic poem, *The Phoenix and Turtle*. This poem is difficult and little studied. Its mysteriousness has led one recent critic to characterize it as 'an exhibition of pure poetry', or possibly an 'ironic response' to other poems, but in any case as having only a literary referent (Buxton, pp. 55, 52), and the Arden editor to call it 'slight' (Prince, p. xlii). The poem's 'characters', such as they are, are usually viewed as chiefly allegorical, and its progression certainly tells no unfolding story. Yet Bock argues that its movement reflects the fundamental story of human growth from narcissism and dependence to interdependence and love, and that the poem deals with the feelings relating to the great processes of individuation and death.

Bock suggestively gives an account of a strange *trompe-l'oeil*-like structural aspect of the poem that involves 'overlapping frames' violating the distinct identities of its named sections. His essay then considers the central paradox of the Phoenix and Turtle in 'dual unity', in being one yet not merging their separate identities. This is connected with the dual unity discovered by Freudian theory in the initial human mother–child relationship. This dual unity of infancy involves an ambiguity of subject and object, and of internal and external, within the symbiotic matrix of dependence. The dynamics of this earliest relationship are compared with unusual features of Shakespeare's poem, for example the femininity of the Phoenix and the mirroring of the Turtle in the Phoenix's eyes. A similarity is noted between the 'locked' dual unity portrayed in the poem and failures in psychic growth implied within *Hamlet* (these failures are closely examined in this collection by M. D. Faber). Links are explored with a number of traditions in poetry, art and mythology. These investigations, supported by an insightful close attention to the poetic text, substantiate Bock's view of the poem as much more psychologically realistic than is allowed by conventional allegorical readings that he discusses. I believe he establishes that his less mystical, less cosmic reading of the poem is best suited to account for its challenging tone, mood and language. Finally he suggests that Shakespeare deliberately chose to address in this poem the 'paradox of ideal love out of the depths of his personal experience' when he began 'his great tragic period'.

M. D. Faber's essay on *Hamlet* treats similar phantasy material, as I have said, and also, like Philip Bock's essay, uses an anthropological as well as a psychological framework for the consideration of family relations. These two essays are similar too in their close observation of text and symbol and their attention to the quality and texture of emotional language. Yet Faber writes of the play as play (and of the play-within-the-play as play), and Bock writes of the poem as poem. This similarity within difference illustrates how appreciation of such matters as object relations may illuminate our understanding of literature without in any sense reducing or forcing it into a mould. As Bock suggests, Freudian theory does not explain away the work of art, yet may 'deepen our understanding' of it. This is 'exactly analogous with the way in which clinical psychoanalysis (contrary to much mistaken prejudice) properly seeks to understand patients as unique entities, not as entities to be classified or shaped by a predetermined scheme.

Faber significantly extends Freud's and Ernest Jones's classical interpretations of *Hamlet* by using the post-Freudian appreciation that unconscious phantasy can wield exceptional power over adult life due to earlier oral as well as later oedipal influences, and that the Oedipus complex itself may partake of powerful primitive oral impulses as well as of the later phallic ones. This allows Faber to understand in new ways Hamlet's dilemma, the problems in his family and society, his behaviour in relationships, and the structure and symbolism of the entire play.

Lyn Stephens brings Freudian, Jungian and Kleinian concepts to bear on that most troubling Shakespeare comedy, *The Merchant of Venice*. At the same time she brings to bear on the play cultural, historical and theological knowledge, exposing problems and paradoxes that were current in Shakespeare's time and are far from being resolved today. All of this is in the service of her sympathetic and lively account of the psychodynamic patterns and forces driving the suffering, yearning and often psychically trapped inhabitants of Shakespeare's Venice. Her 'character criticism' is of the sort I have suggested possible, not centrifugal but centripetal, aimed toward the play's most intimate concerns.

Stephens also supplies a glossary of terms clearly explaining a number of psychoanalytic concepts which are not at all easy to summarize. This, together with her use of these concepts in her essay, yields perspectives that help us grasp their complex qualities.

Angela Sheppard's essay on *Troilus and Cressida* has a single focus, penetrating the enigma of Cressida's behaviour. Her approach is to analyse her own reactions to Cressida's character and actions. These contrast strongly with reactions expressed both by the male characters in the play and by many critics of it. She brings to bear knowledge of the psychodynamic issues involved in a woman's development to maturity, and knowledge concerning typically mistaken reactions to such development. Her interpretation makes it possible to see new and stimulating possibilities in the play. Its status as a 'problem play' is often discussed in terms of the cynicism and world-weariness that seem to overwhelm in it a whole range of contending notions of value. The valorous men at war and men in love seem in it puppets of hollow codes such as 'honour', or of implacable and futile instincts, while other Greek and Trojan men are merely self-serving. In contrast, Sheppard's new reading of Cressida allows us to see the chief woman character in the play as courageously struggling in very difficult circumstances for the autonomy to be a moral agent, and to see her as a model for creativity in a less than ideal world.

Ruth Nevo's essay is the only one in this collection readily available elsewhere. I have been fortunate to be able to include it both because it illuminates a fascinating and often underrated play, and because in doing this it contains a most lively treatment of very important procedural issues. These involve the question of how a Shakespeare critic may approach a work which is mimetic only up to a limited degree. *Pericles* is a play in which a combination of formality of narration, self-conscious archaism of plot, often shallow characterizations, incredible happenings, weird repetitions, seemingly unjustified sufferings, unmotivated behaviours, pure magic, and magic purity, might seem to more than justify a judgement as dismissive as Ben Jonson's contemporary gibe: 'a mouldy tale'. Yet, as Nevo points out, this play was exceptionally popular. And that may have been for good reason, for she finds *Pericles* 'precisely because it is closer to primary process, more anomalous, "crude", absurd, strange, a representation of elemental and universal fantasy of great power'.

To prove this Ruth Nevo demonstrates within the play's purposively fragmentary framework, its impossibilities, splittings, anomalies and 'nagging questions', a 'degree of unity bordering on the obsessive'. She achieves not only this, but moreover enables for us an entry into what she describes (using André Green's words) as 'an affective matrix in which the spectator sees himself involved and feels himself not only solicited but welcomed, as if the spectacle were intended for him'. I believe the availability of a sense that there is meaning which we can enter into, not only grasp intellectually, produces the pleasure we derive from the lifelikeness of Shakespeare's creations. This sense comes not particularly from verisimilitude (which is in part deliberately curtailed in *Pericles*), but rather from resonances of that 'elemental and universal fantasy of great power'. Nevo locates this fantasy in the play's family relations. By exposing and resolving enigmas she shows how densely and ambivalently familial emotional turbulence, 'the pendulum swing of desire and dread', permeates the play.

Finally she finds a note of 'unresolved indeterminacy' after all the returns, recognitions and rebalancing at the end of *Pericles*. I certainly agree this note is struck, yet do not think that it undermines the play as a representation of a maturing process. Rather it shows the cyclical nature of such processes, their endless returns. In growth we find movement toward life and toward death at the same time. A play such as *Pericles* thus may, as she concludes, put us 'in touch with the familiar ghosts – the desires and terrors – that habitually haunt our minds'.

One way of avoiding such deeply troubling contact is to deny the power of theatre (or life) to confront us with autonomous subjects, and thus with the desires and terrors of object relationships. This can be done by taking dramatic characters – or even our own – as radically unreal, as texts, as 'the speech assigned to names we conventionally reify and imagine as persons' (Berger, 1985b, p. 228). This I refuse to do when discussing *The Tempest*. This play's non-naturalistic characters and actions may well invite sub- or supra-personal interpretations, allegorical analyses or analyses of 'discourses', but I consider the play's representations as indicating centrally painful growing points of social and familial relationships. The main schools of criticism give this play wholly optimistic or wholly pessimistic outlooks, but I believe there is more truth in a psychodynamic perspective that finds in it intense hatred, violence and struggle intrinsically combined with agencies capable of allowing each man to become 'his own'.

Finally Christine Levey provides a bibliography covering ten years of psychoanalytic and psychological Shakespeare studies in English. This follows on from the bibliography published over a decade ago by David Willbern (1978). Levey describes her work in her own introduction, so I will add only that I fully expect others to find her work as valuable as I have.

I must add two editor's comments. As this collection is derived from authors in four different countries and as many professions, an impulse to make it entirely uniform might best be honoured in the breech. Various writers used several editions of Shakespeare, with the consequence of differing lineation, and sometimes none. Some use of terms also may be confusing; in particular both 'phantasy' and 'fantasy' appear in these essays. The individual authors and their contexts will best explain this, but a brief explanation of 'phantasy' by Juliet Mitchell may be helpful. This begins, 'The "ph" spelling is used to indicate the process is unconscious', and goes on to explain that Klein's phantasy 'emanates from within and imagines what is without; it offers an unconscious commentary on instinctual life and links feelings to objects and creates a new amalgam: the world of imagination' (1986, pp. 22–3). That world is the world we hope to explore.

B. J. Sokol

NOTES

1. This is not to say that all such work is uninteresting. See for instance Marjorie Garber (1987) and John Padel (1981). Padel's work is continued in two later articles (1985, 1989).

2. Stage representation forces recognition of Shakespeare's multiple ironies which Frattaroli says are typically ignored in readings based on theories of 'semantic autonomy' (p. 423, note). Full awareness of other communicative potentials of dramatic construction, such as rhythm, scenic counterpoint, or locally heightened tension, also typically falls victim when critics remove theatre texts from theatre-oriented readings. I am amazed by contrary claims such as that of Harry Berger Jr that 'theatrical limits' render invisible Shakespearian 'structural irony' which is available only to 'text-centered' and not to 'stage-centered' readings, because actual or imagined individual characterizations must inhibit our potential for imagining the existential 'fact and true cause' of suffering, the social- or familial-functional configuration, or the intra- or supra-personal possibilities implicit in a dramatic text (1985a, pp. 213, 212, 227–8). Such notions desperately underestimate the subtler possibilities of theatrical presentation, assuming a one-dimensional allegorism or one-dimensional naturalism the modern theatre almost never descends to. If our sensibilities cannot feel, our intuitions cannot sense, and our structural/linguistic abilities cannot subliminally perceive *in a performance* all that Berger suggests is available only from reading – if this is not possible even when we are aided by theatrical genius providing apt music, costume, spectacle, tone of voice, movement, gesture, and perhaps lighting – I wonder how we can ever detect such things in living language, no less language only read. Berger's admitted support of the '*anti*theatrical' (1985b, p. 213) seems to me a modern Puritanism

preferring 'pure' text to spectacle-plus-text for fear of dimming imaginary inner lights; I react to the claimed superiority of a 'text-centered reading' of a Shakespeare drama over a theatrical one rather as I reacted when a young German once told me that Shakespeare's writings are really much improved when translated into his finer language.

3. Unconscious models for such damage and an ensuing redemption or exclusion are found in the Winnicottian concept of the *use* of objects versus their *annihilation* (1971, pp. 101–11), concepts undoubtedly very familiar to Jonathan Miller's original audience. Some similar aspects of *King Lear* are treated *passim* in his book *Subsequent Performances* (1986).

1 *KING LEAR* IN REHEARSAL: A TALK

JONATHAN MILLER

I find it quite hard to talk about a play which is actually in rehearsal, although that is the subject of this talk. When you are in the middle of it, it is very hard to see the wood for the trees. I will try and describe both the wood and the trees, but I will describe the wood first of all.

I think the great problem with *King Lear* is that it is a play which in production in the recent past – for I suppose the best part of a hundred years – has been bedevilled by certain ideas of the cosmic. It has been inclined traditionally toward a Druidical representation partly because of that damned storm that takes place in it. Because of the iconography of that storm, in which you see a figure with a long white beard ranting at the clouds and the thunder, there is a feeling that the play is about large cosmic archetypal issues. But it has always been my sense while doing the play, and this is the fourth time I've done it, that the cosmic is really the least important aspect of it. That doesn't mean that its themes are not large and eternal, that they are not themes which repeat themselves constantly, or that they aren't in fact deeply preoccupying themes, but I don't think that the play has anything to do with storms at all. The storm is rather as it were a ground bass against which entirely human actions occur.

It's also a play which people have been misled into thinking takes place in a sort of timeless antiquity, particularly a pre-Christian

All Shakespeare citations are from *King Lear*, Kenneth Muir, ed., The Arden Shakespeare, London: Methuen, 1955.

antiquity. People have been misled by its references to the gods, as opposed to God, and by what seems to be its conspicuous abstention from references to Christianity. But I believe at least one of the themes that has got to be brought out and developed in production cannot be understood unless you set the play in a period which is recognizably Christian.

In fact, although it makes no explicit references to the Christian religion or to God, and indeed it expresses a sort of quasi-atheistic nihilism by the time that it reaches its conclusion, *King Lear* is a play which I think is largely unintelligible unless you take into account certain Christian themes that would have been current and salient at the time when Shakespeare was growing up. We must remember that Shakespeare as a child, like anyone else in Elizabethan England, was a compulsory church-goer – not a *compulsive* one, but a compulsory church-goer. He was compelled to go to church as everyone was on Sundays. The reading of texts – of the Gospels and other passages from the Bible – was so repetitive, so unremitting, that their images and tenets recur as a central motif in almost all of Shakespeare's plays. They come to the surface perhaps more conspicuously in *King Lear* than in any other play.

One central notion of *King Lear* which cannot be understood beyond the context of Christianity, and beyond the context of sixteenth-century Christianity, is the notion that it is impossible to enter the Kingdom of Heaven unless you have actually gone through the experience of poverty. I think that a central metaphor of the play is the metaphor of trying to get a camel through the eye of a needle, representing the idea that until you have lost everything there is complete impossibility of gain. One of the words central in the play, as William Empson emphasizes, is the word 'fool', to which I will return presently. But I think that the word 'nothing' is the most central word, from which everything in the play develops. Lear has to learn in the course of the play the falsity of 'Nothing will come of nothing', as he says when Cordelia refuses to give him a protestation of her love. He has to undergo a rough tuition to learn, as so many of the other characters do, that it is only in the process of losing everything and gaining *nothing* that you actually are in a state to achieve everything. Nothingness and nullity are the centre of the play.

All sorts of losses are presented in the play: a loss of kingdom; a voluntary divesting of authority, power and privilege; an involuntary divesting of subjects' love and the love of children; ultimately an involuntary divesting of sense, sensibility and sanity. The play shows that it is only in the process of divesting yourself of all these things – of shelter, of clothing, of warmth, of love, even of sense and of intelligence – that you can actually build yourself anew. This process of complete reduction calls to mind the notion of liminality that Victor Turner develops at length in his various books (1957, 1969, 1974). It is only by the process of undertaking the role of the 'liminal' – the person who falls between the cracks by divesting himself of all category and of authority – that you actually can restore your humanity and can develop a genuine sense of *Gemeinschaft* as opposed to the formal structures of *Gesellschaft*.

Lear undergoes his losses without knowing that this is going to happen. He attempts to divest himself of authority and power while wickedly retaining all the privileges that go with kingship. He then enters a curious path which starts from a voluntary act of abnegation but leads on to a slippery slope where he has no control over the further things that are stripped from him by virtue of the fact that he abdicates.

The issue of Lear's abdication brings me to another reason why it is impossible to set the play outside the period in which it was written. *King Lear* is a play which resists transposition either backwards into the notional antiquity where it is so often set, or forwards into a more modern period because you have to take note in it of a constitutional and political theme which is central to the seventeenth century. That theme involves notions of kingship and sovereignty which give blasphemous connotations to abdication. In 1605 Europe was still shaking from the experience of the abdication of the Emperor Charles the Fifth, fifty years earlier. This abdication was regarded by the literate population as something blasphemous as a usurpation: not only was it seen as blasphemous to usurp a crowned and anointed King; it was seen as blasphemous for a crowned and anointed King to pre-empt the decisions of God and voluntarily to give up the office which was assigned to him by virtue of being crowned and anointed. One still sees traces of this in the reluctance of the present Queen to give up the throne in favour of her ageing son. The reason for this is not that she is obstinately enjoying the privileges of power, which are extremely dubious, I would have thought, at this particular moment in history. I think she still retains some sort of belief that it is not within the gift of the officer to resign what in fact is given to the officer by virtue of the fact that she or he has been incorporated into the immortal corporation of monarchy by the act of being crowned and anointed.

I would like to remind you of a medieval theory of kingship which was still current in the seventeenth century, of an idea dealt with by Ernst Kantorowicz in *The King's Two Bodies* (1957). That great work on medieval constitutional theory suggests that the King hath in him two bodies, a body politic and a body mortal. The body mortal was that part which died with the death of the officer, but the body politic was the immortal corporation of sovereignty into which he was incorporated by virtue of being anointed. By being anointed he was incorporated into an immortal pedigree of monarchs which had descended from the first act of anointing, which was of course the anointing of David by the priest Samuel. For the Middle Ages and for the Renaissance there was a fundamental theory that once the officer was incorporated into this immortal office of sovereign it lay with him or with her until in fact his or her mortal life had been brought to an end by a decision other than his or hers. It was not within the sovereign's gift to resign, it was not within his gift to abdicate, just as it was not within the gift of perhaps a morally better-qualified monarch – such as for example Bolingbroke in *Richard II* – to usurp a frivolous monarch like Richard. In other words there was some notion of the office being more important than the officer. Even though the officer could be either a villain or a ninny, as soon as he was incorporated into that immortal corporation of sovereignty he was there for life.

This thought is expressed clearly in two images. One is found in the royal tombs at St. Denis outside Paris, where you see the double effigies of the King. You see the King in his regalia, kneeling with his eyes wide open, wearing his crown, carrying the sceptre – the figure which represents the immortal corporation of sovereignty, while in a balustraded canopy underneath lies the naked body of the mortal officer. This is often taken to be a *momento mori* to remind the proud and the mighty that they must return to the state of the worm-eaten and the mortal. But it is not really a *momento mori*; it is much more an emblematic representation of the constitutional theory that once an officer had been incorporated into this corporation of sovereignty he had a divine power and a divine sanction. A similar image is to be found also in the famous practice of the royal touch. The royal touch was thought to be a sacred power which was invested not in the person of the sovereign, but in his person as crowned monarch. He could exercise that power and touch for the 'king's evil' (a tuberculous gland in the neck), could touch and heal this illness not by virtue of any particular shining characteristic that he had as an individual but by virtue of the power that was invested in the office that he was now a representation of after the act of anointing and crowning. It is almost as if the regalia were endowed with the power to heal rather than the officer himself. You could see this ritual of the royal touch enacted year after year in the long line of French kings from the Capetian monarchs right the way through the Valois monarchs and the Bourbon monarchs. It was connected with the office of the King and, whether the officer was a villain or a ninny, his touch healed. He did not heal by virtue of his personal charisma, because he might have none at all; he healed by virtue of the charisma which was attached to the office. It was not within his gift to withdraw himself from that office until he had died. At that moment, then, when 'the King is dead, long live the King', instantly the role was assigned to the successor who continued the unbroken line of this immortal corporation.

So that when Lear undertakes almost frivolously to lay down the burden and 'crawl toward death', as he says in the first act, there should be in his court a sense that something exceptional has happened. This is not simply a casual incident in which a monarch has said, 'right, I feel my time has come to hand it on'; it's not a resignation of a secular office as it would be if the president of a business said, 'I am getting too old to do this properly.' There is no way you can get too old to do it properly as a King. You only get too old to do it properly when you are dead. So at the moment when Lear actually tells the court his intention to 'Unburdened crawl toward death', it should produce a *frisson* because all the court know that in fact he should be, when crawling toward death, still with the regalia on his head at that moment. The power would still be invested in him, even though crawling toward death, because the power of majesty and the power of monarchy are undiminished and uninfluenced by the diminishing power of the officer.

Lear then compounds that particular sin or blasphemy by doing something amiss which has no place in constitutional theory, but has a place in psychological theory. That is that he offers to divide his kingdom in terms of the avowals of love which will be given to him by each of his three daughters in turn. It is this act that in rehearsal makes you realise that you have to present King Lear at the outset of the play as partly mad already, not as someone who goes mad. He must be presented as someone who is already on the edge of some sort of mental disorder, in a state of depression, or some condition which makes him do something which, once again, is not within the gift of human beings. Just as it is not within the gift of a monarch to renounce his office, so it is not within the gift of any mortal to ask other mortals how much they love him or her. Still less can avowals of love be purchased, and still less can they be obtained by offering gifts in return for which you will get a certificate from your own children of how much they love you. One becomes aware at a very early stage in the play that something very eccentric and anomalous is going on with the King. His decision at the outset can scarcely look like a decision, but must look like a sudden capricious outburst which should startle the court and indeed even startle the two elder daughters.

Too often, I think, in rehearsal and in production, the elder daughters give their 'glib and oily' speeches automatically, implying that they immediately have at their disposal the eloquence which will satisfy Lear. But his demand has to come as a surprise to them as much as it outrages and comes as a surprise to the younger daughter who fails to give the avowal which Lear demands. Too often Goneril and Regan leap into their speeches as if in fact they had already-prepared manifestos, which means that they have anticipated what he is going to ask of them. But the demand on them should come as a total surprise, so that when the daughters actually start their flattery they must be seen as beginning to formulate it, asking themselves, 'how can I express this in a way which will convince this mad, eccentric father of mine that I do indeed love him?' So I believe in rehearsal it is necessary to work towards some pregnant pause as the elder daughters seem to formulate their speeches. It is very interesting that in the first line of Goneril's speech, when 'our eldest-born' speaks first, she actually anticipates in some way the thought Cordelia later expresses in saying, 'I cannot heave/ My heart into my mouth.' Goneril is often condemned for being a glib daughter, but this is contradicted by her first line: 'Sir, I love you more than words can wield the matter.' In other words, she starts by saying that it is in fact difficult to utter such an avowal, that the demand is in fact as awkward for her as it later turns out for Cordelia. Cordelia actually follows through by refusing to meet the demand, but nevertheless Goneril announces that such an avowal is difficult for her and is not actually readily formulable. So she should pause in saying: 'I love you . . . more than . . . words can wield the matter.' There must be pauses within the speech so that we see she finds flattery hard, although not as hard as does Cordelia, who actually withholds it. It must seem difficult for Regan too, for otherwise, as I say, you will presuppose that they both anticipate exactly what is going to happen, which makes the outcome of the play decided before the start.

This brings me to another issue which I think again often bedevils the play in production. That is, because we are so familiar with the play, and actors and actresses are so familiar with it, and because the outcome is ultimately so atrocious, there is a temptation to make these two wicked daughters who do such ultimately wicked things start out as wicked. If they start out as monsters, as they are perhaps most spectacularly in the Riemann opera version [*Lear*, 1978], as satanic punk monsters who cannot wait to humiliate and destroy their father, you might as well merely summarize the rest of the play and then say, 'it turned out pretty badly as well.'

The reason why evil in the play takes time to develop is that we must be able to witness something which in fact is more than ever apparent to us now in this part of the twentieth century, and that is the strange imperceptibility of the individual steps towards an atrocious outcome. Actually for each of those daughters, and for each of those sons-in-law, it should become hard for them to say, looking backwards over the course of the action, at what point they started to do something which was so unacceptable and so outrageous that it actually culminates in the gouging of an old man's eyes and the locking of doors to a demented father. It shouldn't be apparent at the outset that this is what is going to happen merely because we, who have read the play, know that's how it turns out. Too often when the theatre takes up this play it actually writes the end into the beginning, so that it seems to be already wound up like a piece of clockwork with an absolutely inevitable conclusion built into the first scene. So it becomes interesting in rehearsal to minimize as far as you possibly can the atrociousness, the wickedness, the expedience, of these daughters, and to make them reasonable. We have to make them seem so reasonable that when we come to that wonderful scene before Gloucester's castle (II, iv) – after the stocking of Kent, when Regan and Goneril arrive and both try to persuade Lear that he does not in fact need a retinue of the size that he has – their position should be so ordinary that much of the audience should feel: 'My God, I've done exactly that to my parents in the recent past; I hope that this half is not going to be too long, I must get on the phone and see if Dad and Mum are all right.'

In other words, I believe it is the responsibility of producer and actors alike in doing *King Lear* to actually induce deep senses of uneasiness and misgiving in the audience *vis-à-vis* their own parents. They should not be able to distance themselves and say, 'well, that's what monsters do, we are unlike that.' There should be a banality of evil in this particular case just as there was in the case of the Nazis. It should be very hard for us to identify any particular point during the plot when we could say, 'that is when it happened, that's when the thing became irreversibly atrocious.' These steps should be minuscule and imperceptible, both for the protagonists and I think for the audience, so that they begin to feel merely a cumulative sense of a tragic outcome, rather than knowing at any particular moment that the predetermined outcome is now on its way.

In this particular production that I am working on I have tried to
stress this by casting the children, for the first time, as grown-ups.
Perhaps this is due to the fact I've been rehearsing the play on and
off over the last twenty-five years, and have grown that much older
in the time myself. When I first directed the play at Nottingham
many years ago, I cast young daughters and young sons, a young
Edmund and a young Edgar. Now I find myself quite inevitably,
without actually consciously thinking of it, casting daughters in
their fifties and sons in their fifties as well. This is partly because I
have been struck by the curious discrepancy in the age of both
parents and their children, which didn't strike me earlier. Why is it
that this man who is meant to be more than eighty so often has
children of no more than twenty? Why is there this sixty-year
difference between father and children? Might it not be more
reasonable to assume that both sets of children, sons on the part of
Gloucester and daughters on the part of Lear, are in fact the same
age as I the producer, and have actually gone through experiences
comparable to the ones that I have had with my parents and that
people of my age have had with their parents, and perhaps also have
had with their children of their own?

As soon as you start to play the children at that age suddenly the
production starts to take on a different shape. I found certain lines
which previously remained almost inaudible suddenly start to shine
with a strange salience which had remained unnoticeable to me
before. For instance in the little letter that Edmund forges to
persuade his father Gloucester that his brother is in fact a villain,
there are things which until now simply remained inaudible to me.
Edmund says in the letter:

> This policy and reverence of age makes the world bitter to the best of
> our times; keeps our fortunes from us till our oldness cannot relish them.
> I begin to find an idle and fond bondage in the oppression of aged
> tyranny . . .
>
> (I,ii,47–51)

Now the fact is that this is a villain trying to present a letter which
will convince his father that villainy is afoot. It's a very peculiar
choice of motive that he actually writes into that letter; he writes
of the sense of dissatisfaction which is felt by children who in fact

are growing old themselves, old enough to feel that even if they
come by their patrimony they are on the edge of being too old to
enjoy it, so that they are experiencing a 'fond bondage in the
oppression of aged tyranny'. If you start to develop groups of
children who in fact are old enough to feel that they cannot enjoy
their full independence, cannot enjoy full self-determination until
these ageing parents are out of the way, the play suddenly becomes
much more interesting than it would be if these are merely Satanic
youngsters who are destroying venerable old creatures.

So the casting of older children in this production has made a
difference not simply by virtue of the fact that people in the
audience of a particular age will recognize something common to
us all at that age, but also because it makes it possible to avoid what
I think is an impossible obligation to represent metaphysical
wickedness, wickedness which is transcendental. You remember
when Hannah Arendt wrote about Eichmann, she was puzzled by
the fact that in witnessing him it was very hard to understand how
someone who looked as ordinary, as commonplace, as that, could
have done something as monstrous as he did. The thing is that we
want the monstrous to be visibly monstrous. We want those who
perpetrate the outrages to look Satanic in some way so that we can
as it were confidently identify them before they do it. But it is in the
nature of human life that the atrocious creeps upon us impercep-
tibly, so that we cannot identify the moment when the process
becomes irreversibly atrocious. Once you play these children as
older, merely impatient, merely looking for what they believe is
their due, you actually start to relieve yourself of the false necessity
of presenting them as outrageously sadistic creatures.

This consideration of the children brings me to another issue which
is related to the Christian theme. One recognizes around these
grown children a range of relationships, motives and ideas which
are very similar to the ones which ordinary people here and now
still experience, and indeed hate themselves for, and would like to
conceal and not to acknowledge. But there are also other aspects
of the children which are I think emblematic of certain great
Christian issues which I mentioned at the beginning. Without
wishing to say explicitly that Edgar is Christ and Edmund is Lucifer,

I think there are undoubtedly resonances to that effect. For instance, when Edgar gives an account of the whole course of his action to his brother at the end – when Edmund lies dying, and Edgar is describing the death of their father Gloucester – he says, 'I asked his blessing, and from first to last/ Told him our pilgrimage' (V,iii,195–6). I think that the choice of the word 'pilgrimage' is very significant. The view that Edgar presents of himself, and that we have of Edgar, is only intelligible if you see it contrasted with a certain view of Edmund. This contrast lives in the light of the relationship, I think, between Christ and Lucifer. Again, I am not saying that Edgar is to be seen as Christ or that Edmund is to be seen as Lucifer, but nevertheless there are metaphorical affinities between these two pairs. The course of action that Edgar undergoes in the play, his pilgrimage, or ministry, culminates in an emblematic fight at the last day with Edmund. A challenger must come forth, if you remember, 'by the third sound of the trumpet', and indeed Edgar 'appears/ Upon this call o' th' trumpet' (V,iii,112, 119). When Edgar answers the third trumpet, and throws down his brother Edmund, Shakespeare requires us to see some sort of metaphorical representation of the final struggle between Christ and Lucifer.

The way in which Edgar humiliates himself, becoming a Bedlam beggar, a wanderer in anonymity on the heath, and undergoes mockery, disdain and humiliation, only to return as this great soldier of Christ at the end, is I think unintelligible outside the mesh of Christian iconography. In contrast, Edmund is to be seen in some respects as a representation of a Miltonic Lucifer. Shakespeare represents in Edmund the pride of a rootless intelligence, an intelligence that is unrelated to life and to family affinity. Edmund is prompted entirely by expediency and commodity, like the bastard in Shakespeare's *King John*. He is prompted by nothing other than pure ratiocinative self-interest, whereas Edgar is prompted throughout his ministry by the process of love, by the urge to reconciliation with his father, and above all by forgiveness. When you think for example how easy it could be for him to exult in his father's misfortune, having gone through his terrible experience as a result of his father's failure to recognize that he is in fact the loving son, you begin to see the extraordinary act of generosity on the part of Edgar.

This act I think is a transcendental one, and a prescription for a Christian type of love and forgiveness. Also I think it has relationships to the healing of the blind man in the Gospels. Edgar heals Gloucester of his blindness by actually making him go through that absurd self-mocking ordeal of the fall over the imaginary cliff. It is only when Gloucester 'falls' over the cliff and goes through the experience of total despair that he actually recovers the sight of which he has been deprived at the hands of Cornwall. Now if he does indeed heal a blind man, but restores to him not physical sight but moral sight, we see in the action of Edgar once again the exercise of a Christian ministry which is concluded and brought dramatically to its end when Edgar and Edmund encounter one another in a great emblematic battle.

This is rather like the great apocalyptic battles which are mentioned again and again in Norman Cohn's book *The Pursuit of the Millennium* (1957). In these there will be a final struggle in the East when Lucifer and Christ will meet one another, and justice and the Last Judgment will in fact prevail. I think this is what we are being invited to consider in *King Lear*. Of course in the context of a pre-Christian, neolithic antiquity this falls apart; it simply has no meaning at all. It has to be rooted in something which inspires a Christian recognition on the part of the audience.

We also see in Gloucester and again in Lear the process of Christian renunciation. Lear starts by a spurious act of renunciation. He renounces nothing because he will keep everything. He will keep his hundred knights; he will keep all the respect due to a king; he is divesting himself only of the burdens of kingship, only of the duties. What he has to go through is the experience of being divested – as opposed to divesting himself actively – of being divested of everything. And so also does Gloucester, who, by his gullibility and by his failure to recognize the virtue in his son Edgar, must himself be robbed of everything before he gains anything at all.

In fact all in *King Lear* have to go through the experience of being reduced to nothing before there can be any gain. I believe the central metaphor of that diminution and reduction to nothing is contained in that wonderful moment on the cliff when Edgar describes the appearance of things from the top. This is often merely regarded as a prelude to a farcical piece of drama in which someone simply falls over a non-existent cliff, or as an opportunity for Shakespeare to word-paint a wonderful picture of what it looks like from the top of Dover cliff. But something much deeper is going on in that Shakespeare is giving us in one image two versions of nullity and diminution, while at the same time he is giving us perhaps the finest representation in literature of Renaissance perspective. We see the gradual reduction of the appearance of things as they recede from the gaze down to the tiny fishermen that walk like mice upon the beach: 'half way down/ Hangs one that gathers sampire, dreadful trade!' (IV,vi,14–15) As we see these objects diminishing in size we actually are beginning to see in that a representation of shrinkage, of annihilation, and of progress towards nothingness. But at the same time, by choosing a vantage point at the top of a cliff in order to achieve that, Shakespeare provides another metaphorical resonance. That is the idea that from various kinds of great height all things look small, and never more than from the great height of social authority, of majesty, from the height which you enjoy by virtue of occupying office. We and Gloucester are being encouraged to consider what is like to look down not merely from a cliff, but also what it is like to look down from a social cliff, at the people below who in fact look like nothing more than mice from that height, and with whom it is therefore impossible to sympathize. You feel how difficult it is to sympathize with things that look like mice when in fact you feel the size that you are and they look the size that they appear. Therefore Gloucester, even if only imaginatively and notionally, has to tumble amongst them in order to identify with their genuine humanity. Edgar correspondingly has to play two roles. First he has to play the role of a commentator on the top of the cliff. Then, when Gloucester falls down over the notional cliff, he has to play the role of one of the imaginary fishermen who previously were mice-like. He has to comfort the fallen victim and present him with the sympathy which Gloucester was unable to extend to the fishermen when viewing them from the great height of social authority.

I think I may have said this in public once before, and if any of you have heard it forgive me for repeating myself, but I believe that is very like what happens in *The Third Man* when Harry Lime takes

Hollie Martins to the top of the enormous ferris wheel in the Viennese Prater Park. You remember that in order to justify his actions in dealing in diluted penicillin, Harry Lime pulls open the sliding door of the carriage and says, 'Would it really matter to you, old man, if one of the dots down there stopped moving? A thousand dollars each one, tax free, old man – would it really matter?' And indeed from that height, as those dots move stochastically below on the pavement, it's quite hard even for you as a cinema spectator not to say, 'well, perhaps it doesn't really matter, if they are nothing more than dots after all.' Hollie Martins himself tumbles amongst them, or is made to tumble amongst them, when Calloway the Security Officer takes him into the hospital where he sees full-sized children dying of meningitis. It is at that moment, if you remember, that Martins decides to turn in his friend because he would be doing the greater evil by allowing him to continue his actions.

I believe that what we are seeing in that imaginary fall over the cliff in *King Lear* is something closely analogous to that. This brings up the way in which you actually stage it. I believe it is terribly important that when you stage that moment of the description, Edgar himself must be seen to close his eyes, in order to abstain from what is visible so that he can concentrate upon what is in front of his mind's eye. So we should at that moment dramatically confront two blind people, one who is permanently blinded by Cornwall's sadism, and the other someone who, as it were, is voluntarily abstaining from sight in order to be able to concentrate on something which he is imagining. There should be a paradox when Edgar says, 'How fearful/ And dizzy 'tis to cast one's eyes so low!' (IV,vi,11–12), because he cannot, and does not, actually do this. He must stand there and give an imaginary account so that we see two differently blinded people standing side by side, one giving a commentary on something which is not in front of his physical eyes but which is in front of his mind's eye, broadcasting it into the head of someone who will never have eyes at all, but nevertheless retains the capacity to conjure visions before his mind's eye which is still intact. The moment then when Edgar says 'I'll look no more' (IV, vi, 22) actually, paradoxically, should be the moment when he opens his eyes.

'I'll look no more' signals the moment when Edgar starts to look because he is actually saying, I will look no more at what I'm imagining. That moment seems to me to be the still centre of the play with respect to the trajectory of Edgar's and of Gloucester's pilgrimage. We are seeing two people who are going through the experience of loss and reduction, because not only is Edgar acting as a spiritual physician for his father, but also because he himself is undergoing a spiritual discovery.

I feel that in the representation of Edgar not only should we have in mind a Christian image, but also some sort of vision of figures similar to the holy fools in Dostoevsky. Edgar should present a Prince Mishkin-like figure who almost seeks the role which is forced upon him by misfortune. Indeed he shows a curiously rhapsodic eagerness when he anticipates how he is going to play poor Tom. Immediately after Kent falls asleep in the stocks, suddenly Edgar appears and simply announces that he is in flight. It might seem he is merely putting on a 'base' disguise for protection. But the way in which he chooses the disguise that he will assume makes it look as if he has sought all his life this particular form of self-humiliation, for he shows a rhapsodic, ecstatic excitement when he anticipates the role that he is about to undertake. He says:

> No port is free; no place,
> That guard, and most unusual vigilance,
> Does not attend my taking. Whiles I may 'scape,
> I will preserve myself;

> (II,iii,3–6)

Up to that point it seems that this is merely expedient. But he goes on:

> and am bethought
> To take the basest and most poorest shape
> That ever penury, in contempt of man,
> Brought near to beast.

> (6–9)

And it then becomes a scherzo of excitement:

>   my face I'll grime with filth,
>   Blanket my loins, elf all my hairs in knots,
>   And with presented nakedness outface
>   The winds and persecutions of the sky.
>   The country gives me proof and precedent
>   Of Bedlam beggars, who, with roaring voices,
>   Strike in their numb'd and mortified bare arms
>   Pins, wooden pricks, nails, sprigs of rosemary;
>   And with this horrible object, from low farms,
>   Poor pelting villages, sheep-cotes, and mills,
>   Sometime with lunatic bans, sometime with prayers,
>   Enforce their charity.
>
>   (9–20)

The excitement now culminates:

>   Poor Turlygod! poor Tom!
>   That's something yet: Edgar I nothing am.
>
>   (20–21)

In the process of discovering what it will be like to be the most humiliated and basest thing in nature, he discovers the intense and euphoric excitement of suddenly annihilating his previous identity as Edgar. He as it were launches himself out into this act of self-discovery which he then reiterates, if you remember, in the scene on the heath immediately after the storm, after the blinding of Gloucester, when we actually hear him exulting in his nothingness. He says here, immediately after the blinding:

>   Yet better thus, and known to be contemn'd,
>   Than still contemn'd and flatter'd, to be worst.
>   The lowest and most dejected thing of Fortune,
>   Stands still in esperance, lives not in fear;
>   The lamentable change is from the best;
>   The worst returns to laughter.
>
>   (IV,i,1–6)

This is as if to say that only in the state of liminality, only in the state of nothingness where your own identity is completely obliterated, is there the chance of joy. Bertrand Russell once said in one of his essays, 'only if you recognize that the world is horrible, horrible, horrible, can you begin to enjoy yourself'. I believe that in fact Edgar

makes this wonderful act of self-discovery, that in the process of
paring yourself down to the minimum where you have nothing, not
even what our basest beggars have, where you actually have
reduced yourself below the level where you need anything, can you
actually be safe from the ordeals of existence. But then of course
he discovers that when you think you are at the worst you are likely
to be surprised. In saying, 'The wretch that thou hast blown unto
the worst/ Owes nothing to thy blasts', Edgar says in effect, 'here I
am at the lowest level, and I can actually have euphoric enjoyment
of being nothing'. Then suddenly his new-blinded father appears
on the horizon and he says:

> But that thy strange mutations make us hate thee,
> Life would not yield to age . . .
> O gods! Who is't can say 'I am at the worst'?
> I am worse than e'er I was . . .
> And worse I may be yet; The worst is not
> So long as we can say 'This is the worst'.
>
> (IV,i,11–12, 25–8)

In other words, he says that there is no possibility of escaping from
the worst while you are still able to formulate that you are at the
worst.

Nevertheless there is this movement towards some moral
asymptote at which you gradually approximate to zero but never
actually reach it. Always you can be defeated by the practical jokes
the world can inflict upon you which can make it worse than your
worst anticipation. Even so, Edgar undergoes a strange euphoric
self-discovery in finding that in the process of ridding yourself of
everything you actually have the possibility of being in some
respects invulnerable. This ridding is of course what all the
characters in the play, certainly Gloucester and Lear, actually
undergo. Although they don't see it that way and are not
regenerated by it, the daughters also discover that they are stripped
of everything. All that Goneril can find in this is the fact that she has
a 'hateful life'; she actually uses that phrase. What we see in the
play, and it is almost too self-evident to insist upon, is an elaborate
symphonic development upon the notion of nothingness and
stripping, of reduction to some sort of hypothetical zero which in

fact is never reachable because there is always the possibility that the world will do something worse to you than what you have actually anticipated.

This happens to poor Lear himself at the moment when he has been reduced to nothing and is just about to be restored to his daughter. Then he loses his daughter and ultimately he must die, and one feels that Shakespeare actually punishes him for what he does at the beginning of the play. It is in fact a pessimistic ending because you do not get in Lear a recovery, a reconciliation, or a discovery. Or if there is one, it is never a discovery which enables him to say 'I did wrong'. He believes that he behaved wrongly to Cordelia but at no point does he ever seem to acknowledge how wrongly he behaved to all his daughters, and how wrongly he behaved to his society. He has glimpses of this and he occasionally glances at the fact that he has taken too little note of it, that pomp should take physic and that he should encourage himself to feel what wretches feel. But all his advances in this direction are tentative, and never complete themselves in the way they do with Gloucester, and with Edgar. So there is this marvellous death of Gloucester which is so unlike the death of Lear; we are told Gloucester's heart 'burst smilingly'. There is no sense in which Lear's heart bursts smilingly. It bursts tragically and to no good purpose. He has learned nothing; he has picked up fragments of wisdom but has not achieved a comprehensive moral vision in the way that Gloucester has, and certainly in the way that Edgar has.

Let me say something briefly about interpreting the fool because that is something that I have always remained fairly constant about in rehearsal. Once again there is an aberration which traditionally bedevils the play, and that is the capricious capering youngster who is so often cast as the fool. People have been misled I believe by the word 'boy'. Because Shakespeare makes Lear refer to him as 'boy' he is often played as a young falsetto creature who crouches and clutches the calves of Lear and, rather nervously gnome-like, presents strange/wise formulae. But I believe that the things which the fool says are so wry, so ripe in the sense of 'ripeness is all', that they are inconceivable in the mouth of such a creature. I believe that we have been misled for years by the wrong connotation of 'boy', and that in *Lear* it means no more than '*garçon*' does to a waiter, or no more than 'boy' does when a Southern Colonel addresses his black body servant. The 'boy' fool is simply someone who is politically junior to Lear, or socially junior, and nothing more than that.

Indeed I believe that the moral of the play becomes much more clearly recognizable if in fact you make Lear and his fool two creatures who are nearly indistinguishable, two old boys. One of them has grown fond and foolish in his old age, and one has grown wiser and more mature with age, but they both must otherwise be absolutely on a par with one another. I was prompted to do this in the first production I did of *Lear* by reference to Louis XIV's body servant Bontemps, who was the only man in the court who was allowed to call Louis, 'Louis'. He had grown up with the monarch from the age of twelve, had always stayed with him, had grown old with him, and knew him inside out. I believe that if the fool is presented as an old man who is exactly the same age as Lear, who has grown up with him, every single one of his otherwise gnomic, runic formulae becomes understandable. He is like an ageing coachman who utters wisdom which would be incomprehensible in the mouth of an adolescent. If we put the fool's country wisdom in the mouth of an old man who has known Lear as long as he has been monarch and probably longer, suddenly we find an intelligible relationship. What you see is simply two people who differ from one another merely by virtue of the office that they have been assigned; one has been assigned the role of monarch, one has been assigned the role of numskull, of nothingness, of someone who in fact means nothing. But by meaning nothing the fool can say everything. Therefore he is in a position to have a reciprocal relationship with his master which actually allows him to be his conscience, and so allows him to say the things which go some way toward restoring Lear's sanity.

It isn't until Lear undergoes the restorative process of becoming completely insane that the fool can disappear. People often ask, 'why does the fool vanish at the close as he does?' and the traditional tedious answer, which is a purely scholastic one, says that 'the fool vanishes because he is actually played by the same person as Cordelia, and so when Cordelia comes back . . .', and so forth. That is a boring piece of Mermaid Theatre mythology which simply doesn't help one to rehearse the play at all. Merely knowing that the two roles might have once been played by the same person could lead you into the disastrous choice of following suit, which I think leads to nonsensical outcomes. It is much more interesting to ask psychologically, rather than as it were historically, 'why does that fool disappear at the point that he does?' He disappears at the point when Lear takes full leave of his senses, after the joint-stool scene in the Farmhouse (III,vi). At the end of that scene Kent says to the fool, 'Thou must not stay behind', and the next time we see Lear he has incorporated into himself all the wisdom that the fool has had. Apart from those wonderful passages of completely demented discourse where he hallucinates brown bills and a mouse which he pursues with a piece of toasted cheese, everything Lear says afterwards is sane, and wise, and almost indistinguishable from the sorts of thing which the fool had been saying in the previous act. So the fool no longer has to be a ventriloqual presence who stalks King Lear through the action; he is now incorporated into a Lear who, through the process of fully taking leave of his senses, is beginning to take possession of them again.

The fool has become incorporated into Lear in that moment of divine insanity on the cliff when he comes up with the wisest political insights which are in the play. All the wonderful things which he says then are folly:

> *Lear*   What! art mad? A man may see how this world goes with no eyes. Look with thine ears: see how yond justice rails upon yond simple thief. Hark, in thine ear: change places, and, handy-dandy, which is the justice, which is the thief? Thou hast seen a farmer's dog bark at a beggar?
> *Gloucester*   Ay, Sir.
> *Lear*   And the creature run from the cur? There thou might'st behold
> The great image of Authority:
> A dog's obey'd in office.
> Thou rascal beadle, hold thy bloody hand!
> Why dost thou lash that whore? Strip thy own back;
> Thou hotly lusts to use her in that kind

For which thou whipp'st her. The usurer hangs the cozener.
Through tatter'd clothes great vices do appear . . .

(IV,vi,151–66)

These remarks are levelheaded and sane, but they only acquire that
sanity by virtue of the fact that Lear has acquired the wise folly
which Erasmus praised in his *The Praise of Folly*. So we see that
the fool has vanished because he is actually present now in Lear,
and is present there as a sane person. And so we see the restoration
of reason through the loss of sense.

This is a much more interesting reason for the fool's disappear-
ance than expedience. It leads to the question of interpreting one
of Lear's final lines: 'And my poor fool is hang'd!' All this week I
have had a long and interminable argument with Eric Porter about
what that line means. I believe it refers to Cordelia, and that Lear
says 'And my poor fool is hang'd!' not because she once was played
by the actor who played the fool but because his term 'fool' is an
endearment. Eric Porter doesn't think that. He actually wants Lear
to say that line because he is tying up a loose end and letting the
audience know that his fool has been in fact hanged. I actually think
that Lear's 'my poor fool' is a reference simply to the dead body of
Cordelia which is in front of him, not that he sees her
metaphorically as his fool but that it is simply a phrase of great
pathos when he confronts the body of his young daughter.

Which brings me to one final point about Cordelia. I have
mentioned all the other daughters and haven't talked about Cordelia
at all, about how we actually rehearse her and present her. I in fact
have cast someone who is very young to play Cordelia, so in this
production there is a wide separation between the two elder
daughters and the younger one. It is as if she really is an
afterthought, someone who was produced from even another wife,
for whom Lear has a rather peculiar and distinct feeling, and who
is virtually unknown to the other daughters. If you play the other
daughters as fifty, so they have gone away and lived elsewhere and
hardly know this child, they will have a natural sense of resentment
about the larger part of the kingdom being given to someone whom
they don't know at all, who is in fact a step-sister.

There isn't much more I can simply say now because, as I say, it is extremely hard to describe rehearsal when you are actually in the middle of it. I can only do what I have tried to do, which is to sketch some of what I believe to be the salient themes of the play.

2 'NEITHER TWO NOR ONE': DUAL UNITY IN *THE PHOENIX AND TURTLE*

PHILIP K. BOCK

Written at about the same time as *Hamlet*, Shakespeare's brief poem, *The Phoenix and Turtle*, bears little superficial resemblance to his longest play. Yet condensed into its 67 lines one finds a number of dynamic elements that may have been displaced from the author's awareness while he was writing the tragedy. *The Phoenix and Turtle* depicts a paradoxical dual unity that, I shall argue, can best be understood as representing the early 'normal symbiosis' between mother and child. This developmental phase is nostalgically commèmorated (it has been lost), and it is represented as 'chaste' (devoid of genital sexuality and its attendant anxieties). The poem thus mediates contradictions (found clearly in *Hamlet*) between reality and appearance and between good and bad mother images, though at the great cost of dissolving the ego and negating procreation.

The main focus of this paper is on the text of the poem and its developmental resonances, but a larger cultural problem is also addressed. This has to do with the responses of audiences since Elizabethan times to the treatment of dual unity in the poem. Unlike *Hamlet* which is probably Shakespeare's best known work, *The Phoenix and Turtle* has suffered a virtual cultural repression, neglected by critics and anthologists, at times even denied a place in the canon. To understand this treatment we must first grasp what the poem is saying about the process of individuation and death.

All Shakespeare citations are from *The Riverside Shakespeare*, G. Blakemore Evans, ed., Boston, MA: Houghton Mifflin, 1974.[1]

I believe that Shakespeare has managed to represent the dynamics of early (pre-oedipal) experience, especially our unconscious desire to merge with the maternal imago. This representation is so threatening that we will systematically misread the poem until we are prepared to wrestle with its deep ambiguity. Western civilization has denied the paradoxical nature of the experience out of which the human capacity for culture develops; but we now suspect that the separation of mother from child is what first constitutes the opposition of culture to nature, and that the 'transitional object' (Winnicott, 1971), created in the widening space between mother and child, is the first genuine artefact.

Shakespeare used the formal resources of Elizabethan verse together with the multivocal avian symbols of his tradition to embody his (and our) nostalgia for a lost unity. His vision, I believe, has validity across cultures: the 'dead birds' of the poem's final line are exactly analogous to the *Dead Birds* that, in Robert Marshall's classic ethnographic film, symbolize human mortality to the Dani People of New Guinea. Let us now examine the crucial text.

THE PHOENIX AND TURTLE

Let the bird of loudest lay,
On the sole Arabian tree,
Herald sad and trumpet be,
To whose sound chaste wings obey.

But thou shriking harbinger,
Foul precurrer of the fiend,
Augur of the fever's end,
To this troop come thou not near.

From this session interdict
Every fowl of tyrant wing,
Save the eagle, feath'red king;
Keep the obsequy so strict.

Let the priest in surplice white,
That defunctive music can,
Be the death-divining swan,
Lest the requiem lack his right.

And thou treble-dated crow,
That thy sable gender mak'st
With the breath thou giv'st and tak'st,
'Mongst our mourners shalt thou go.

Here the anthem doth commence:
Love and Constancy is dead,
Phoenix and the Turtle fled
In a mutual flame from hence.

So they loved as love in twain
Had the essence but in one,
Two distincts, division none:
Number there in love was slain.

Hearts remote, yet not asunder;
Distance and no space was seen
'Twixt this Turtle and his queen:
But in them it were a wonder.

So between them love did shine,
That the Turtle saw his right
Flaming in the Phoenix' sight;
Either was the other's mine.

Property was thus appalled,
That the self was not the same;
Single nature's double name
Neither two nor one was called.

Reason, in itself confounded,
Saw division grow together,
To themselves yet either neither,
Simple were so well compounded:

That it cried, 'How true a twain
Seemeth this concordant one!
Love hath reason, Reason none,
If what parts, can so remain.'

Whereupon it made this threne
To the Phoenix and the Dove,
Co-supremes and stars of love,
As chorus to their tragic scene.

THRENOS

Beauty, Truth, and Rarity,
Grace in all simplicity,
Here enclos'd, in cinders lie.

Death is now the Phoenix' nest,
And the Turtle's loyal breast
To eternity doth rest.

Leaving no posterity,
'Twas not their infirmity,
It was married chastity.

Truth may seem, but cannot be,
Beauty brag, but 'tis not she,
Truth and Beauty buried be.

To this urn let those repair
That are either true or fair;
For these dead birds sigh a prayer.

THE STRUCTURE OF THE POEM

The Phoenix and Turtle falls into three apparently clear sections: the opening five stanzas that I shall call the invocation, an eight stanza anthem and a closing threnody of five stanzas that is attributed to 'Reason'. The general tone of the poem is nostalgic: someone is looking back on unique events that cannot recur. As William Matchett (1965) notes, the diction is legalistic and the syntax highly compressed; there is also a high incidence of scholastic and logical terminology (Alvarez, 1955). The avian symbols employed are conventional with one crucial exception: in Shakespeare's poem, the Phoenix seems finally dead, never to be reborn, though an alternative reading of even this point seems to be possible (Wilson Knight, 1955; Axton, 1977).

All of the birds mentioned have traditional connotations: the screech owl foretells death; the eagle is King of the birds and must therefore be invited to the ceremony although other 'fowl of tyrant wing' (birds of prey) are excluded. The 'death-divining' white swan and the long-lived black crow are named as priest and mourner, respectively. The Phoenix is unique and beautiful, while the Turtle (-dove) represents constancy in love (cf. *Troilus and Cressida*, III, ii, 178, a work of the same period). Nevertheless, the invocation is quite indirect. The identity of the narrator is uncertain. The 'bird of loudest lay' who is to call the others to assemble is not further identified, and the owl is not directly named; rather, a 'shriking harbinger' is cautioned to 'come not near'. Order is imposed by the narrator so that the 'obsequy' will be 'strict', with all due ceremony observed (unlike the 'maimed' rites of Polonius and Ophelia in *Hamlet*).

The anthem begins in stanza six and only then do we learn the identity of the dead birds. The cause of their immolation is not given; instead, we move to a description of their unique relationship:

> Hearts remote, yet not assunder;
> Distance and no space was seen
> 'Twixt this Turtle and his queen.

The opposition between unity and duality was overcome in their love: 'Number there in love was slain' for 'Either was the other's mine'. Reason itself is 'confounded' by the perfect union of this 'twain' and declares that

> Love hath reason, Reason none,
> If what parts, can so remain.

The threnody follows and we are informed that, hereafter, 'Truth may seem, but cannot be' for 'Truth and Beauty buried be' with the ashes of the two rare birds. They left 'no posterity', but this was not due to any 'infirmity', rather, 'It was married chastity'. Their burial urn is presented as a shrine for latter-day lovers who are urged to 'sigh a prayer' for the departed.

Although the sections of the poem appear to be clearly marked, a curious *embedding* actually takes place. The lines, 'Here the anthem doth commence' and 'Whereupon it made this threne' belong neither to the anthem (which they seem to begin and end, respectively) nor to the other sections. Throughout the poem, categorical boundaries are established only to be immediately violated. Birds of 'tyrant wing' (predators) are forbidden to attend the ritual, but the royal eagle is made an exception. The owl is excluded because of its association with death, yet the 'death-divining' swan is invited to serve as priest. The crow, a scavenger, is admitted among the mourners due to its black color, with an allusion to the folk belief that crows conceived orally. No simple criterion is allowed to stand: both structural and conceptual category boundaries are deliberately obliterated. Even the rhyme scheme (*abba*) involves embedding.

These 'overlapping frames' give additional depth to the poem – a literary technique that Robert M. Adams (1953), borrowing from the visual arts, called *trompe-l'oeil*. In *The Phoenix and Turtle* there is a similar deepening of perspective as we move from the invocation to the threnody, and beyond.

The anthem, like many Metaphysical lyrics, dwells upon a paradox, using figures drawn from diverse fields of knowledge including law, logic and mathematics. In John Donne's (1965) poem 'The Canonization' (written after 1602), the dual unity of a much more sensual love is celebrated in a series of similes. Curiously, Donne refers to three of the birds that appear in Shakespeare's poem:

> Call us what you will, we're made such by love;
> Call her one, me another fly,
> We're tapers too, and at our own cost die,
> And we in us find the Eagle and the Dove;
> The Phoenix riddle hath more wit
> By us; we two, being one, are it,
> So, to one neutral thing both sexes fit.
> We die and rise the same, and prove
> Mysterious by this love. (19–27)

Here, too, the lovers' ashes are consigned to 'a well-wrought urn' (33), and others are urged to invoke the 'pattern' of their ideal love – a love that also dies in flames and that is 'Mysterious' (i.e., beyond reason).

THE PARADOX OF 'DUAL UNITY'

The Phoenix and Turtle were one, yet they did not merge their separate identities: 'Two distincts, division none', and yet 'between them love did shine'. This paradox appalls 'Property' and confounds 'Reason':

> Single nature's double name
> Neither two nor one was called.

Alvarez (1955) is certainly right to see here a systematic attack on Reason, using her own logical devices; however, I choose to follow Joel Fineman (1977, pp. 409–10) who sees in this and other instances of dual unity a 'delicate paradox at the center of Shakespeare's erotic imagination', a theme that he traces through several 'branching pairs of siblings' in the plays.

From the perspective of modern Freudian theories of psychic development, the anthem may be interpreted as a veiled account of early childhood experience (see Faber, 1985, p. 71). During the second through fifth months of life, the child is gradually differentiated out ـ of the symbiotic matrix of the maternal environment and begins the transition to individual ego organization. As summarized by Mahler, Pine and Bergman (1975), the 'normal symbiotic phase' constitutes

> a vague dual unity that forms the primal soil from which all subsequent human relationships form . . . Vestiges of this phase remain with us throughout the entire life cycle . . . Here the world becomes increasingly cathected, especially in the person of the mother, but as one dual unity with the not yet clearly demarcated, bordered-off, and experienced self. (1975, p. 48)

D. W. Winnicott (1971) has emphasized that human individuation is a paradoxical process, for an initial 'perfect' adaptation of the mother to her infant's needs must 'fail' so that the new self can be born. Mothering must be 'good enough' to ensure the child's survival; but if it is too good it may prevent the 'psychological birth' of the child, creating an overwhelming nostalgia for dual unity. Particularly important in the early months is the *mirroring* by the mother of the child's face and experience (Lacan, 1968; Robson, 1967). I detect this type of reflection in the ninth stanza:

> So between them love did shine,
> That the Turtle saw his right
> Flaming in the Phoenix' sight;
> Either was the other's mine.

That is, the Turtle sees his own self mirrored in the eyes of the Phoenix. But this exceptionally intense, 'flaming', mutual gaze is also dangerous, for as Otto Fenichel wrote, 'In the unconscious, to look at an object may mean . . . to devour the object looked at, to grow like it [or] to force it to grow like oneself' (1937, p. 9).

In most Renaissance works, the unique phoenix is depicted as genderless or as vaguely masculine. Shakespeare's rare bird is female, but this is also the case throughout Robert Chester's compilation, *Love's Martyr* (see Grosart, 1878), where the poem first appeared. Shakespeare may simply have adopted the convention of the larger work in which the dove is male and the phoenix is the turtle's 'queen' (Grosart, 1878). In twelve other places in Shakespeare the gender of the bird is unstated, reference being made primarily to its beauty, rarity, long life or resurrection, while in two plays the phoenix is merely the emblem of a house or of a ship. Two passages, however, clearly indicate that Shakespeare's phoenix can be female. The phrase 'her blood' in Sonnet 19 refers to a phoenix, and in *Henry VIII*, Cranmer prophesies the spiritual rebirth of Princess Elizabeth, 'the maiden phoenix', as Queen (V,iv,40). Political interpretations of *The Phoenix and Turtle* (Grosart, 1878; Matchett, 1965; and Axton, 1977) will be discussed below.

The Phoenix of our poem is, I feel, more maternal than 'maiden'. She relates to her constant lover through an intense mutual gaze that dissolves boundaries. G. Wilson Knight called the poem a 'celebration of a mystical love-union beyond sex' (1955, p. 199), and there is something quite *magical* about this perfect relationship. In a totally different context, Hans Loewald wrote of 'the original oneness, most obvious in the mother–infant dual unity, which shines through or is sensed as remaining the innermost core in later family relations . . . an intimate unity that is anterior to what is commonly called sexuality' (1980, p. 396). This is the magical innocence that pervades the great Medieval paintings of Virgin and Child. But Loewald suggests that our vision 'tends to be blurred by a nostalgic longing for such a state', and he reminds us that this relationship 'may be experienced by the child . . . as a *threatening, overpowering force*' (1980, p. 19, emphasis added; cf. Holland, 1975, pp. 35–8). (As a first surviving son, Shakespeare may well have experienced maternal over-protection during the eighteen months before his younger brother was born.)

The developing child must move away from the 'vague dual unity' of normal symbiosis to construct an ego that will embody the reality principle and deal reasonably with the external world. Oedipal struggles follow and build upon this achievement. The Phoenix and Turtle, however, seem locked into a static dual unity. Reason (an ego function) is unable to resolve the paradox: 'How true a twain,/ Seemeth this concordant one,' it cries. In admiration of this irrational state, Reason creates the *Threnos* in which those who are 'either true or fair' are invited to pray at the shrine of ideal Truth and Beauty; for with the death of our protagonists,

> Truth may seem but cannot be,
> Beauty brag, but 'tis not she,
> Truth and Beauty buried be.

CONNECTIONS WITH *HAMLET*

The echo in the penultimate stanza (quoted just above) of Hamlet's repeated references to 'seeming' versus 'being' first stimulated me to investigate the relationship between the poem and the play. Contradictions between reality and appearance are, of course, widespread in Shakespeare's plays, and it is possible that these works are no more closely related than any two works from the same pen; however, careful examination reveals some striking parallels.

Let us begin with the birds referred to in the poem. The owl is explicitly mentioned only once in *Hamlet*, when the mad Ophelia says, 'the owl was a baker's daughter' (IV, v, 42). King Claudius calls

this a 'conceit' on her dead father, although later in the same scene
Ophelia refers to her father as 'my dove' (168). Some critics have
suggested that Ophelia's words allude to a legend in which a baker's
daughter was turned into an owl when she refused to give bread to
Jesus. Perhaps we may use this information to interpret the second
stanza of our poem. The owl would then symbolize the 'bad mother'
who withholds nourishment and comfort from her child, and who
is therefore excluded from the memorial service. On the other
hand, the idealized female Phoenix of the poem would represent
the 'good mother'. The eagle could then be interpreted as a negative
father image: although feared as a 'tyrant', he cannot be excluded
from the domestic scene any more than Claudius can be excluded
from the Danish court.

The eleventh stanza of our poem is marked by an extra syllable
in each line. Here the central paradox is restated in slightly different
terms:

> Reason in itself confounded,
> Saw division grow together,
> To themselves yet either neither,
> Simple were so well compounded.

Reason is unable to comprehend the dual unity in which simple
elements are 'compounded' yet retain their essential identity. (Note
the enactment of the paradox in the singular subject and plural verb
of the last line. The plural subject and singular verb of line 22 was
pointed out to me by Andrea Good.) Likewise, 'Property' was
'appalled,/ That the self was not the same'. The words 'confound'
and 'appall' appear together in only two other places in
Shakespeare's works. The earliest is in *Venus and Adonis* (line
882). The goddess (whose emblem is the dove) is startled by the
sudden yelping of hounds which 'Appalls her senses and her spirit
confounds'. This line follows a passage in which Venus is likened
to a doe with 'swelling dugs' who hurries to nurse her fawn – clearly
a 'good mother'.

The only other co-occurrence of these terms is in Act II of
Hamlet. The first Player has just given the Prince a 'taste' of his
quality – a passionate speech about the death of Priam and the grief
of Hecuba, during which he seems to weep. Left alone, Hamlet

reflects on the irony that this actor, 'in a fiction', could express such deep emotions while he, with far truer motives, can do (and perhaps can feel) nothing. What if the Player had a genuine 'cue for passion'? He might then weep and scream in ways that would

> Make mad the guilty, and appall the free,
> Confound the ignorant, and amaze indeed
> The very faculties of eyes and ears.
>
> (II,ii,564-6)

I read this passage as an ironic reflection on how strong emotions can be represented on the stage and the effects of such 'playing' on different parts of an audience. (Cf. Adams 1953, p. 240, on this scene.) It leads logically to Hamlet's decision to *use* the players to test the conscience of the King (i.e., to 'Make mad the guilty'), although the scheme ultimately falls on its inventor's head.

The words 'confound' and 'appall', then, appear in both poems and the play in contexts that involve conflict between appearance and reality. The maternal concern of Venus for her reluctant young lover corresponds to the relationship of the Phoenix to the Turtle and also to Gertrude's attitude toward Hamlet. Indeed, Gertrude later compares her son to a dove (V, i, 286)! I shall argue below that the Phoenix, though not named, is also present in *Hamlet*. Now, however, let us consider one other pair of words.

In the second stanza of *The Phoenix and Turtle*, the owl is referred to as a 'harbinger' and a 'precurrer' of death. As noted by F. T. Prince (1960, p. 176, n.6), a similar pair of words occurs in the very first scene of *Hamlet* when Horatio describes the spiritual and astronomical omens that foretold the murder of Julius Caesar, adding:

> And even the like precurse of fear'd events,
> As harbingers preceding still the fates
> And prologue to the omen coming on,
> Have heaven and earth together demonstrated
> Unto our climatures and countrymen.
>
> (I,i,121-5)

The Ghost enters immediately, enhancing the *trompe-l'oeil* effect, for Horatio's words refer both to Caesar and to the play, *Julius*

Caesar, which Shakespeare's audience may have seen the previous year on the same stage, perhaps with the same actors. Also, 'our countrymen' are both Danes and Englishmen, for Horatio's mention of a Roman lunar eclipse is usually taken as an allusion to the celestial events of 1598, when one solar and two lunar eclipses were visible in England. At some level of symbolism, the Phoenix and Turtle may also be the sun and moon, with their mutual annihilation representing an eclipse, for there is ample evidence to link the Phoenix with the sun god, Hyperion, and thus with Hamlet.

SYMBOLISM OF THE PHOENIX

In Egyptian religion the phoenix (*bennu*) was associated with the sun gods, especially with Osiris when he was represented as the morning star. This glorious bird (probably a heron), spent the night in a sacred tree near the temple of the sun. Its morning flight from its nest in a high palm or sycamore through which shone the rays of the rising sun may be the source of legends about its periodic rebirth from the ashes of a fiery death (Muller, 1918). Herodotus recorded parts of the legend, including the association of the phoenix with the temple at Heliopolis.

I agree with William Matchett (1965, p. 19) that not every element of the phoenix legend need be used to interpret Shakespeare's poem; however, it is far from self-evident just which parts of the legend *are* relevant. For example, the Chinese phoenix (*fêng-huang*) is one of four spiritual animals, the others being the unicorn, the tortoise and the dragon. It appears to belong to a sign system that is entirely different from that of Shakespeare's animals. However, when one reads that it too is associated with the sun, that other birds 'assemble to pay it homage', and that 'when it goes away the country is visited with calamities' (Ferguson, 1928, p. 99), one hesitates to dismiss this information.

Shakespeare's knowledge of the phoenix myth was most likely derived from Ovid's *Metamorphoses*. Neither in the original nor in Arthur Golding's translation of 1567 (Rouse, 1904) is there any mention of the flames in which the bird expires, but this element could have been known to him from other sources. (Dryden added the flames to Ovid's poem in his translation a century later.) The Latin version, which Shakespeare certainly knew, stresses the *filial piety of the phoenix* in transporting its genitor's ashes to the temple of the sun. In Miller's literal rendering, after he has built his nest of spices, the old phoenix 'ends his life amidst the odours. And from his father's body . . . a little phoenix springs.' When he is strong enough, the new phoenix 'bears his own cradle and his father's tomb through the thin air, until, having reached the city of the Sun, he lays the nest down before the sacred doors of the Sun's temple' (*ante fores sacras Hyperionis aede reponit*) (Miller, 1916, pp. 392–3).

In Golding's translation we find only a reference to *Phebus* (Book XV, 447); however, I believe the word 'Hyperion' in the original Latin is highly significant.[2] The name of the Titan links the phoenix legend with Hamlet's idealization of his dead father, for on two occasions the Prince compares his father to Hyperion (I, ii, 140; III, iv, 56). There is a double irony in this identification, for in the myth, Hyperion married his sister, Theia, and passed his authority over the sun to his son, Helios. In the play it is Claudius who marries his 'sometime sister', Gertrude, while Hamlet is frustrated in his hope for succession.

A few lines later in Book XV of *Metamorphoses* we come to the story of Egeria, a queen who mourned continually for her dead husband. Her tears of grief were finally pitied by Diana (= Artemis = Phoebus' sister) who 'made of her body a cool spring and of her slender limbs unfailing streams' (Miller, 1916, p. 393). The contrast with Gertrude's hasty remarriage is striking; however, Shakespeare chose to use the more familiar figure of weeping Niobe, applying the image of dissolving flesh to Hamlet himself (I, ii, 129). Ovid stresses the purity of the phoenix, and Golding's translation mentions the bird's 'unsullied' beak and claws. Perhaps Hamlet's flesh was too 'sullied' by ambivalence to perform adequate mourning rites for his father. There are other hints in the *Metamorphoses* about the possible symbolic meanings of birds mentioned in *The Phoenix and Turtle*, but these would take us too far afield.[3]

INTERPRETATION

Some critics connect the assembly of birds in *The Phoenix and Turtle* with the literary convention of the 'parlement of fowls', dating back at least to Chaucer, but I believe that we must seek a more dynamic interpretation. There is something dreamlike about the assembly. It has, for me, the quality of a screen memory representing and concealing the primal scene. If I let myself freely associate to the remembered poem, I find the following sequence: a phallic image of the 'sole Arabian tree', a loud cry (in the night), a silent approach to the 'tragic scene' in which a loving pair are witnessed in the frightening dual unity of coitus, confounding Reason and threatening the observing self by reactivating early memories of pleasure and danger. Reason (ego organization) now reasserts itself by denying what has been seen and insisting on 'married chastity' (or perhaps oral conception, as in the crow). It punishes the parents by wishing for their death, but makes restitution by idealization, projection of the parental imagos into 'eternity', and perhaps by a regressive fusion with the lost maternal object. If these associations seem more oedipal than symbiotic, we should recall Loewald's observation that the oedipal stage contains 'in its very core features of primary identification and symbiosis' (1980, p. 399; cf. Hamilton, 1969).

Let us review the poem once again. Although it uses the same vocabulary as the Sonnets that deal with dual unity (e.g., Sonnet 36), it does not have the *texture* of a Sonnet (cf. Wheeler, 1972, on Sonnets 88–96). Murray Schwartz (personal communication) has suggested that there is something highly depersonalized and austere about *The Phoenix and Turtle*. In the opening stanzas, a narrator issues commands, positioning other actors and assigning roles for the ritual to follow. The care with which this is done indicates that something of great importance is taking place and that the ritual can be dangerous if not properly conducted. At the very least, it provokes anxiety-laden memories.

Rosalie Colie wrote that 'paradox demands of its framers both total control over expression and thought, and the appearance of effortless manipulation of expression and thought' (1966, p. 34).

The anthem section, however, is far from effortless; *obsessive* would be a better word. The mourners turn the paradox this way and that, as if to reassure themselves that dual unity is possible. Colie is correct that 'Love gives the illusion of solving, for a time at least, the fundamental metaphysical problem of the one and the many' (1966, p. 96), but the perfect love of the Phoenix and Turtle is too fantastical to produce this illusion. For me, at least, Anthony and Cleopatra are better examples of dual unity, as are the lovers in many of Donne's poems (see Faber, 1985; Donne, 1965). In *The Phoenix and Turtle*, Reason acknowledges and accepts the paradox, but does not resolve it. Indeed, the final response of Reason to dual unity is not logical but *aesthetic*: 'Whereupon it made this threne'.

The threnody (in tercets, each with a single rhyme) is more serene than the anthem and it employs an even higher level of abstraction. We have moved from the strong commands of the invocation through the repeated paradoxes of the anthem to a soft sigh of resignation. I envision the assembled mourners circling an urn in which the merged ashes of Phoenix and Turtle rest, solemnly chanting the first four stanzas of the *Threnos*. But the last stanza (like the disputed final lines of Keats's 'Ode on a Grecian Urn') seems to me to be in a different voice:

> To this urn let those repair,
> That are either true or fair,
> For these dead birds, sigh a prayer.

Who speaks these lines? As part of the threnody they should be chanted by the chorus of birds; however, I suspect that they are spoken by the voice of Reason (heard briefly before in stanza 12). Another possibility is that the narrator who began the poem, 'Let the bird of loudest lay', concludes it with a parallel command: 'To this urn let those repair . . .' In either case, the *trompe-l'oeil* technique places the threnody within yet another frame. As Adams observed, 'Shakespeare violates the aesthetic frame by calling attention to it in order to . . . create the effects of depth and distance' (1953, p. 242). We move back from the dream, or the memory, or the memory of the dream, into nostalgia for a dual unity that will never again be ours.

CONCLUSIONS

Can we have it both ways? Can *The Phoenix and Turtle* represent the symbiotic dual unity of mother and child during the early months of life and also express much later oedipal conflicts? And does this poem help us to understand Hamlet's 'awful dilemma'? I believe so.

We have Loewald's (1980, pp. 398–9) authority for recognizing the symbiotic core of the oedipal situation; he also summarizes the traditional psychoanalytic view of Hamlet as a play in which 'incestuous oedipal fantasies' dominate sexual life in adulthood. The oedipal situation is a drama of frustrated succession, and the Prince is trapped in a no-win position. Following Freud, Ernest Jones (1949) argued forcefully that Hamlet's unconscious identification with his uncle would not allow him to act out the revenge that was his duty. Behind this conflict, I suggest, lies an earlier, ambivalent identification with his mother: a desire to return to her womb coupled with an intense fear of personal annihilation (cf. Fineman, 1977). The only 'resolution' of this paradox that Shakespeare could then envision was the death of both parties.

Hamlet's ambivalence toward Ophelia involves the problems of reality and appearance, expressed in terms of truth and beauty ('Are you honest? . . . Are you fair?'). He fears the power that beauty has to corrupt honesty, and he concludes that truth and beauty can coexist only in a nunnery ('married chastity') or in death (III,i,101ff.; I am indebted to Marian Bock for this suggestion). But since their love was perfectly true and chaste, why must the Phoenix and Turtle die?

A number of scholars answer this question by denying that the phoenix is really dead. Grosart argued that all the poems in *Love's Martyr*, including Shakespeare's, constitute an elaborate political allegory in which 'the "Phoenix" was Elizabeth and the "Turtle Dove" Essex' (1878, p. xliv). Despite the forced reading that this imposes on many lines (and the embarrassing fact that Essex was dead and the Queen still alive in 1601 when Chester's book appeared), Matchett (1965) reluctantly concludes that Grosart may have been correct.

Marie Axton has also given qualified support to an allegorical interpretation. In her fascinating study of theological and legal doctrines related to the succession, she finds that 'the love between the Turtle and his Queen is described in language used by lawyers and poets for their phenomenon of the king's two bodies' (Axton, 1977, p. 128), and she concludes that 'The urn which encloses the cinders of Beautie, Truth and Raritie is, of course, the Phoenix . . . If the miracle occurs the birds who burned in mutual flame *are* the true and fair who come to the urn; there is never a moment when there is not a fire or a Phoenix' (1977, p. 129).

I cannot accept Axton's mystical interpretation. *Love's Martyr* contains political allegory, but I doubt that this helps us to understand Shakespeare's contribution. *The Phoenix and Turtle* is too brief (and too ambiguous) to make a final decision possible, but I believe that Shakespeare took the occasion of Chester's volume to write about the paradox of ideal love out of the depths of his personal experience, using several images that preoccupied him at the beginning of his great tragic period.

To summarize, I have not argued that Freudian theory explains the creation of this or any other work of art; but I do believe that consideration of early developmental experience can deepen our understanding of *The Phoenix and Turtle* and can illuminate its relationship to *Hamlet*. Similar echoes of dual unity are found in some of the other plays, but it is above all in Prince Hamlet that we sense, despite all his intelligence and wit, what Winnicott (1971, p. 83) called 'a crippled capacity to be'. More intensely than most people, Hamlet both longed and feared to lose his self. He yearned for the ideal; but perfect love, truth or beauty exist only within the mind. Thus, Shakespeare's urn – the final repository of Truth and Beauty – is one with Donne's 'well-wrought urn', with Keats's Grecian urn, and even with a certain plain gray jar upon a hill in Tennessee.[4]

Notes

1. This edition differs from the original text of *The Phoenix and Turtle* only in its modernized spellings and in the word 'queen' which is capitalized in Robert Chester's book, *Love's Martyr* (Grosart, 1878).

When the words 'phoenix' and 'turtle' are capitalized in this paper they refer to the birds in Shakespeare's poem only.

2. In his notes on the source of *The Tempest*, Robert Langbaum comments that Shakespeare 'paraphrases a speech of the witch, Medea, in Ovid's *Metamorphoses* – using Arthur Golding's translation (1567), which he apparently checked against the Latin original' (Langbaum 1964, p. 126). Shakespeare seems to have used a similar procedure in relation to the phoenix legend.

3. Bruno Bettelheim (1976, p. 213) reminds us that the owl, raven and dove visit the sleeping Princess in the Brothers Grimm version of 'Snow White'; in that context, he interprets them as symbols of wisdom and maturity. See also Bock (1984, pp. 89–93). Shakespeare may have been aware of *The Phoenix Nest* (1953), a memorial to Sir Philip Sidney, who died in 1586, but I doubt that there is any connection between this work and his poem.

4. See Wallace Stevens, 'Anecdote of the Jar'. For an unusual interpretation of *Othello* see Kirsch, who comments on the 'child-like wonder' in Othello's character and his investment of Desdemona with 'that sense of symbiotic exaltation which is the remembrance of childhood' (1978, p. 731). Barron (1960, p. 268) views Macbeth and Lady Macbeth as resembling 'a mother and son who have failed to achieve separate identities' (1960, p. 268). He argues that they are unable to procreate because they are too closely merged, and refers to the same theme in *The Phoenix and Turtle*. Felperin (1964) suggests that Keats's ode was directly influenced by Shakespeare's poem.

3 *HAMLET* AND THE INNER WORLD OF OBJECTS

M. D. FABER

1

The following discussion is grounded in specific theoretical and critical propositions which should be stated clearly at the outset. I believe that Western tragedy, whether it receives narrative or dramatic expression, invariably presents us with characters who undergo a traumatic reactivation of infantile feelings. Tragedy's inner chaos, tragedy's inner disruption expressed through the character of the hero, is always a chaos, is always a disruption grounded in reactivation. What is reactivated? Basically, the unconscious ego, the repressed introjections of very early experience during which a splitting of the maternal image takes place. The hero discovers himself in a situation that reactivates the bad maternal object, which is but another way of saying that the hero confronts within himself a constellation of repressed desires; the introject is an expression of the forbidden aim.

The splitting of the maternal object is prompted by maternal ambivalence; I regard it as a primitive defensive manoeuvre whose intensity will vary in proportion to the ambivalence expressed toward the subject. Where the mother harbours truly annihilative inclinations the splitting will be radical. Where the mother's

Unless otherwise indicated, all Shakespeare quotations are from *The Complete Works*, Stanley Wells and Gary Taylor, eds, Oxford: Clarendon Press, 1986. Those marked Q2 are taken from the Second Quarto text (1604–5).

ambivalence is minimal the splitting will be minimal. In most instances splitting results from the mother's confusional behaviour, rejecting at times, accepting at others. This can be particularly destructive. The ubiquity of maternal ambivalence is grounded in a patriarchal social organization, a social organization which all of Western literature reflects. The male child is both the mother's phallus and an exemplification of her inferiority. The male child is something to cherish and seduce on the one hand, and to abuse and destroy on the other. To be raised at the hands of an ambivalent Western mother is to undergo a confusing, damaging experience which creates in the male child – who is at the level of artistic expression captured in the character of the Western tragic hero – a primal anxiety over loss, mutilation, abandonment, betrayal (catastrophic death complex), and a deep, regressive predilection that is ultimately oral in nature but that can receive expression at the genital level as well: incestuous inclination results from early trauma. What all of this means is that Western tragic heroes will be vulnerable to female influences or to the power of women who are able to reawaken through their behaviour the anxiety of the early period, anxiety that is invariably bound up with the split-off bad object which, in turn, is expressive of forbidden aims. The deepest urge of the Western tragic hero is to resolve the mystery of maternal ambivalence, and the quest to resolve that mystery is often given disguised expression in Western literary works, such as *Oedipus Rex, Hamlet, Othello, Werther, Pierre, The Sound and the Fury*, and countless others. The male Western belief, often given literary expression, that woman is a mystery, is also rooted in maternal ambivalence.

Because the Western hero experiences an emotional crisis bound up with the reactivation of early affect, and because this affect is integrally associated with maternal power, and because the Western literary work *invariably* brings about such reactivation through the hero's involvement with a female (actual mother or mother-substitute) who confuses and betrays (either in actuality or through loss), the Western tragedy achieves its conflict, its artistic tension, through a partial regression to matriarchy. The hero moves toward the female realm, is absorbed into the dreaded maternal environment, exemplifies the motive power of woman and the danger inherent in her subjection. It is artistically and culturally significant, then, that the hero is always destroyed by patriarchal forces, by male forces which represent a hierarchical order that is ultimately patriarchal in nature. Such destruction is enacted either from within by the suicidal hero who obliterates himself in deference to the introjected father (super-ego) and in remorse for his oral, incestuous defection to the mother, or from without by the representatives of the patriarchy, such as Macduff who is, as we all know, not of woman born. In his life, the Western tragic hero is the transgressor who threatens the patriarchy. In his death, he is the scapegoat who re-establishes and reaffirms that patriarchy. The conflict of Western tragedy is ultimately the conflict between male and female control. Its heroes are overwhelmingly male and its secret, enigmatic, confusional influences are overwhelmingly female because the culture is patriarchal. This macrocosmic model expresses the conflict within the Western home, the Western family, the microcosmic unit in which the Western hero is bred.

My argument here is based upon phenomenological as well as analytic grounds. The literary work is the artist's elaboration through fantasy of the reality factors that stand behind his development as a person and drive him to seek a positive, enlarging solution to his own human dilemma through his own imaginative work. The characters he creates – the vulnerable hero who undergoes reactivation, the enigmatic female who seduces, betrays, and thereby catalyses reactivation – behave upon the stage or upon the page in such a way as to call to our minds the kind of early experience that would perforce stand behind the 'present' character. In a word, the text allows us to complete the picture in our heads.

Having set forth these critical and theoretical propositions, I would move on to Shakespeare's play.

2

What must be stressed immediately is Hamlet's idealized view of the marriage of his father and mother, an idealized view which we confront very early in the action. I will cite the relevant lines, and I will return to them later in another and related context. The hero cries out upon the 'wicked speed' with which Gertrude has hastened to the 'incestuous sheets' of Claudius (I,ii,156-7), remembering that his father was so 'loving' to his mother that he would not allow the 'winds of heaven' to 'visit her face too roughly' and mother so enamoured of father that 'she would hang on him/ As if increase of appetite had grown/ By what it fed on' (142-5). Hamlet dwells here upon the 'excellence' of father, his likeness to 'Hyperion', god of the sun, and upon Claudius' baseness, his likeness to an ugly lecherous goat, a 'satyr'. I must also emphasize that Hamlet's idealized version of the marriage is not confined to this passage; on the contrary, it is the general rule. The fact of the mother's overhasty marriage to the satyr, the fact of the Ghost's curious conduct toward Hamlet in I,v when he not only questions Hamlet's love but promises not to describe horrors and then goes on to describe them, fail to alter Hamlet's attitude. Harry Guntrip gets at the root of the trouble when he talks of the need to

> distinguish between an earlier pathological Oedipus complex and a later healthy oedipal phase of development. In the latter, a boy needs a mother he can fall in love with and a father who will be a friendly rival. This promotes growth. In the earlier pathological complex mother and father have become unreal idealized good and bad internal objects. The primary emotional attitude to the parents is the same, though in fact that to the mother is fundamental. (1968, p. 45)

Guntrip goes on to describe the way in which the bad object abides in the unconscious as a 'fifth column' with the potential of undoing the equilibrium precariously grounded in the good object. The entire personality is, in this way, split.

The divisiveness in Hamlet's character, the disintegration which gradually overtakes him as the play moves on toward its tragic conclusion, is rooted fundamentally in his unwillingness to re-examine his origins, to rethink the idealized version of the parents, to admit their imperfection. It is his inability to connect his altered view of the mother with his altered view of himself, and in turn to integrate this with the alteration in his idealized view of the marriage, that prevents him from achieving a workable personality that can function as it is asked to function in the here-and-now of the action. Hamlet has oriented himself toward mother and father as a 'good boy' and only as a 'good boy', in the very deepest sense of the term.

One may appreciate here the similarity in the basic situations in *Hamlet* and *Oedipus Rex* and the plays' different formal expression of similar emotional predicaments. In *Oedipus* powerful anxiety is engendered in the relationship between seduction and mutilation at the end of the drama, and this results in the hero's self-castrative, self-mutilating conduct. In *Hamlet* the same threat lies behind the anxiety that has been defended against through the development of the 'good boy' personality, the personality that idealizes the parents and the parental relationship. When the possibility of preserving the image of a good mother breaks down, Hamlet finds himself in a false position. He can no longer maintain the illusion about the mother, and this releases repressed early aims toward her, as witnessed by his preoccupation with her sexual behaviour. At the same time, Hamlet cannot entirely give up either the good son's idealized version of the marriage, or the good son's personality, because this would release forbidden aims and cause unbearable anxiety. Although it is very difficult for him to preserve the good object in the face of the bad reactivated one, he must exist in this double-bind. What is the upshot? The hero is in an emotional situation that ultimately causes him to sharpen the split between the good and bad maternal objects. Because he cannot integrate these objects for the reasons just outlined, and because his personality is bound up with these objects, is in a sense a function of them, he is in a divisive condition, morally confused, and dwelling upon self-destruction as a way out.

There is significant reinforcement of this emotional dilemma when Hamlet encounters the Ghost. The good Father–Ghost alludes to the good marriage; he speaks of his dignified, holy love for Gertrude and buttresses thereby the 'good boy' personality of the hero. Indeed, the Ghost functions as a powerful super-ego figure here, reminding Hamlet to treat his mother honourably, to be a dutiful son. The 'good boy' personality is to remain, for father says so; Hamlet is not to change but to do what a good boy would be expected to do. At the same time, however, the Ghost presents Hamlet with a picture of the lustful bad object, the adulterous mate of the satyr preying upon 'garbage'. Thus the hero is permitted to witness the primal scene, and of course he experiences in the process of doing so further reactivation of the infantile complex. Best of all, the Ghost, having allowed Hamlet to gaze upon the unthinkable, proceeds to insist that he murder the rival dispassionately, in an untainted fashion, as God's minister. No wonder Hamlet talks of his 'distracted globe' here, and behaves oddly upon rejoining his companions. The world of internal objects in which he has come to exist is making it very difficult for him to distinguish what is from what is not. And the mysteriousness, at the deepest level, is integrally bound up with the transformation of the maternal figure. For even if Claudius has 'won to his shameful lust' Gertrude's 'will', lust, according to the Ghost, is not a true expression of her nature: it is only 'linked' to a 'radiant angel' (I,v,45–55). In this single image, splitting the maternal figure, and in the Ghost's inclination to preserve both sides of the split, the resulting double-bind in which Hamlet discovers himself is epitomized.

For the distanced audience, of course, there is irony in the Ghost's behaviour and in Hamlet's interaction with it, irony rooted in the Ghost's manipulativeness. We apprehend that the real father behind the Ghost was not the perfect father Hamlet must in his defensive system preserve. We obtain insight into the elder Hamlet's personality, into his tendency to deceive himself, to persist in idealizing his wife, in treating her as faultless. We suspect, in fact, that the Ghost's internal method of punishing Gertrude for her 'fall' is to remain very kind and very decent, to adopt the attitude of victim. All of this helps us to grasp why Gertrude may have gone to Claudius in the first place, for to live with an imperfect human who must at all costs maintain perfection, and expect his partner to maintain it too, can be intolerable. But Hamlet, who does not share the audience's distanced perspective, cannot detect the falseness in the Ghost's behaviour. Rather, he comes away from his encounter with the Ghost in worse emotional shape than he was when he underwent the initial reactivation bound up with the father's death and the mother's remarriage.

The reactivation of the hero's unconscious aims entails, as one component, the desire to take the object in, to incorporate the object and thereby to overcome separation; at the same time it entails, as another component, the desire to be taken in *by* the object, to be devoured *by* the object and thus to achieve symbiotic union. As Roy Schafer writes:

> The subject takes his chances with the external world. He leaves himself vulnerable to the independent activity of the external object – to its abandoning, rejecting, punishing, demanding, traumatizing influences, and to its stimulating and gratifying influences too. The subject cannot attempt to control his external objects with absolute confidence of success. Through internalization, he seeks, among other things, to minimize his vulnerability to objects and to maximize his control of them. (1968, p. 235)

Thus Hamlet feels not only the aggressive and sensuous aims connected with the surfacing of the bad object; he feels in addition the 'corruption' that attends *the desire to take the bad object in*, to have it inside of him. And we have here another dimension of his double-bind, of the hopelessness of his moral position. 'Something is rotten in the state of Denmark' (I, iv, 67) calls to mind not only what Hamlet has come to spy in his own personality. 'Something' is also 'rotten' in terms of what Hamlet wants to make a part of himself even after he has discovered his objectionable aims. The blight, the inner corruption, the inward-working disease is of a nature to feed on that which has caused the corruption in the first place, to take in *again* that which has initiated the emotional and moral crisis. The hero's self-revulsion is partly rooted in his awareness of wanting what disgusts him.

However, as I have just said, Hamlet also wants to be taken in *by* the object. In the unconscious, the fantasy of incorporation is always bound up with the problem of union, union that can be accomplished either actively or passively. Hamlet's wish to be devoured, to be incorporated into the mother's body, appears again and again during the course of the action. Indeed, this wish is finally expressed, as we shall see, in the hero's desire for death.

3

The nunnery scene effectively illustrates the points we are making. Here, Hamlet's viciousness toward Ophelia reaches a climax. His attacks upon her take the shape of an orally aggressive onslaught with strikingly sarcastic overtones which reveal his aggressive and incorporative aims. According to Joseph Slap:

> Patients who are liable to depressive moods growing out of experiences of rejection often use sarcasm to express their anger toward those who have hurt them . . . [Sarcasm] represents an oral aggressive attack either on the frustrating object who withholds narcissistic supplies or on an envied rival who appears orally satiated . . . The sarcastic attack is an attempt to punish the disappointing object . . . or is aimed at making the envied rival feel deprived of the good object . . . In the unconscious this attack takes the form of a cannibalistic onslaught . . . The sarcastic person is still needy, involved, and dependent on his objects . . . Persons with problems of oral deprivation are most apt to use sarcasm. (1966)

Again, it is the split of the female object, and specifically the maternal object, that is on Hamlet's mind during the course of his abuse of Ophelia, and this is substantiated not only by his direct references to this split but by his dwelling upon the impossibility of seeing into the inner world so as to discover repressed materials. Hamlet refers to the transformation of woman in his key utterances; he tells Ophelia not to allow her beauty to have commerce with her honesty because 'the power of beauty will sooner transform honesty from what it is to a bawd than the force of honesty can translate beauty into his likeness' (III,i,113–15). In this way Hamlet focuses for us the opposed images of woman as 'honest' and of woman as 'bawd' that comprise the split in his experience of the maternal presence. 'Get thee to a nunnery', or 'To a nunnery, go' he cries again and again in a richly sarcastic pun which also focuses for us in a flash the nature of the split that makes him 'mad'. For the 'nunnery' is, on the one hand, a place to which woman proceeds in order to remain pure, virginal, unstained, in order to obviate the expression of the other self that harbours objectionable desires and prompts the release of objectionable aims in the male; on the other hand, 'nunnery' signifies, as Hamlet sarcastically employs this word, the brothel, the place in which dwell incarnate versions of the repressed bad object of the inner world. Hamlet dwells in this scene upon woman's 'painting', upon her tendency to *transform* herself from one thing into another, to hide the truth about herself, to remain a secret, an enigma, to intentionally mislead. This complaint is, of course, related to the problem Hamlet expresses tacitly when he stares into Ophelia's face as she sews in her chamber (II,i,76–101). In the nunnery scene (III,i) Hamlet also dwells upon the matter of Ophelia actually becoming a mother, bearing children, and he tells her to go to a nunnery so that she will not bear children who will, perforce, grow up to be 'sinners'. The point is, Hamlet *sees Ophelia as mother* in the nunnery scene and thus implicitly connects her to his own mother, which deepens the incorporative significance of his sarcastic language.

But there are further reasons for Hamlet's vicious treatment of Ophelia in this scene, reasons that are more deeply rooted in the action of the play, the now of the play, and that go beyond Ophelia's rejection of Hamlet's 'tenders/ Of his affection' (I,iii,99–100). Ophelia enacts in this scene a version of the very betrayal – the betrayal by Gertrude of Claudius – that stands directly behind the reactivation of Hamlet's repressed impulses. Just as Jocasta betrays Oedipus both before the action of the play commences and within the actual play, and just as the behaviour of Oedipus in the play is importantly bound up with this repetition of the betrayal, so does Gertrude betray Hamlet both before the action of the play commences, and, in Hamlet's mind, through the function of the mother-substitute, in the now of the play. Hamlet's behaviour is importantly bound up with this repetition of the initial betrayal. When Hamlet asks Ophelia, 'Where's your father?' (III,i,132), and she lies 'At home, my lord', he then cries out against women and marriages. He shouts, 'I say we will have no more marriages. Those that are married already – all but one – shall live' (III,i,150–1), with obvious menace. We recognize not only that Hamlet is aware of those who are watching him from behind the arras,[1] but also that he experiences here, at the unconscious level, another defection of the mother to the very person who supplanted his father and catalysed his mother's 'fall'.

What also becomes clear is that Hamlet's talk of frightening dreams in his 'To be, or not to be' soliloquy (III,i,67) and the presence of Polonius and Claudius behind the arras in the nunnery scene proper are analytically related in a significant way. That is, the arras serves as a *screen* (in the sense of dream screen) lending reinforcement to the renewed reactivation of the basic conflict that Hamlet experiences in Ophelia's presence when she actually betrays him and goes over to the rival. Behind the arras are concealed 'the fathers', those who stand against the hero, those who represent the defection of the mother and who possess the fallen object in actuality. Everything, then, conspires to create in this scene a mirrored version of the reactivating experiences that occurred in the pre-play action and gave shape to Hamlet's conduct from the play's inception.

Two additional significances should be mentioned here, both of which apply broadly to issues arising from the play as a whole. First is the manner in which this scene demonstrates how ongoing events serve as receptacles for the projection of the hero's underlying conflicts, how everything is coloured by the hero's overinvolvement with the maternal object and with the problem of identity that has arisen within him as a result of her sudden transformation. Again, and this is directly related to the point just made, the nunnery scene reminds us of the play's tendency to repeat on numerous occasions versions of the events that reactivated Hamlet's repressed desires, and thus to reinforce the double-bind that he grapples with from the start. This principle of reinforcement will be explored in detail later. Here it will suffice to point out in a preliminary way a couple of striking instances, such as the re-enactment of the murder during the performance of the 'Mousetrap', and the embrace of the Player King and Player Queen, representing the primal scene, and to mention the over-all significance of Claudius seeking Hamlet's death: the super-ego forces that threaten the hero as a result of his incorporative desires are reinforced in the play by the figure of the father–King (Claudius) actually striving to destroy him. These considerations help us to understand not only Hamlet's aggressive language but the way in which that language is related to his apparent madness. The first thing Ophelia cries when the 'nunnery' outburst has concluded and he exits is that Hamlet's mind is 'o'erthrown'. The point is, those who are 'mad' tend to spy in the world around them versions of their own intrapsychic predicaments, although rarely without a degree of complicity within the environment. All too often the world in which the individual exists does reinforce wounding incidents, does confirm the 'mad' person's inner expectations. Much of the critical controversy that swirls about *Hamlet* is centered precisely here, in the tension that lies between Hamlet's tendency to 'spy' the worst, to project his sickness into everything and everyone around him, and the tendency of Denmark to re-engender in its rottenness the betrayal, the murderousness, and the forbidden sensuousness that wound the hero.

4

Hamlet's fascination with the players, his gravitation toward them, his interest in watching them perform, derives from the fact that the actor's basic function and basic strength lie in his ability to bring forth objects, to transform himself into someone else, to change 'reality' by discovering presences within himself and then giving those presences life by bringing them up and out in actual performance. To say that actors identify with characters or parts as if they go out to them and take their shape is to miss the point of this 'mystery' or craft. The actor takes *in* the part or the character and then brings forth from within himself a *version* of the character that is bound up with an inner object to which the newly internalized character more or less corresponds. Acting consists in the recreating of character out of inner objects that allow the actor to make the crucial identification in the first place. Thus the actor possesses a range of objects from which he can derive his power to identify – which is another way of saying that his inner world is not 'fixed' in terms of the objects that comprise it. It is a flexible world, capable of change and alteration to more or less fit or correspond to that which enters it in the form of a character or part. For 'part' is a kind of 'part object' which the actor 'completes' with his own objects as internalization occurs. Little effort is required to appreciate how all of this relates to Hamlet's struggle, a struggle that is integrally bound up with the bringing forth of objects, with the discovery of a 'new' inner world, with the problems of transformation of character and flexibility of identity, Hamlet's own as well as others'.

What must be noted in particular is this: because the actors can reflect in a harmless, acceptable, even amusing way the processes that have wrought such havoc in Hamlet, because they confirm again and again, at the drop of a hat as it were, the existence of an inner world of objects, because they can bring forth from within themselves creatures who have an unseen 'existence' and with whom we can identify, they provide Hamlet with an opportunity to 'peer' into his own inner world, the endogenous world that ultimately comprises his identity, his self. The actors provide Hamlet with an opportunity to test reality, particularly his own inner reality, for it is this that he is confused about as a result of the double-bind in which he exists. Hamlet takes advantage of this opportunity *at once* through a request for a brief performance on the part of an actor, a performance in which he himself briefly participates, for he too can bring forth objects. The request holds real significance for us in terms of Hamlet's development in the play.

Hamlet's first demand of the players is that one of them recite a speech that involves the murder of Priam, the good father, and concludes with the intensive mourning of the Queen, Hecuba, who is a version of the good, loyal mother–wife, who can scarcely tolerate the impact of the husband's death (II,ii,471–524). Hamlet's interest in this aspect of the speech is intense. When Polonius interrupts the recitation just as the Hecuba passage is about to be uttered, Hamlet says, 'Prithee, say on . . . Say on. Come to Hecuba' (503–4). Thus the actors are able to bring up from within themselves presences which Hamlet then takes in, or internalizes, and which correspond to his good objects, the noble father slain and the loyal mother mourning. To say that Hamlet wants to see the oedipal crime enacted is to miss the point. What the hero needs here is reinforcement of his good objects; he asks the players to bring forth good objects and he starts them on their way himself, which attests to the viability of that part of his personality. Hamlet wants to see these objects, to look at them in all their fullness, to make sure they exist (which is another way of saying, to test his capacity to identify with them). He wants to make sure of this because he is losing touch with them, because he is drifting in ambivalence and confusion toward the bad objects that have risen within him, as witnessed by his melancholy and by his use of sarcasm.

Again, Hamlet asks the players not only to bring forth the good parental objects but to do this in a way that undoes the behaviour

that brought forth the bad ones. Priam is slain by an outsider who
has no libidinal designs on the Queen; the Queen mourns genuinely
for the dead husband–father; she is not the sort to defect to another;
it was really a good, clean marriage. Hamlet, in his mind, stares upon
these idealized creatures; they do exist, they are there. In other
words, *I* am what my conscience takes me for, *I* am the potential
good revenger, *I* please the Ghost. However, having 'peered at' the
good objects, and having brought forth feelings corresponding to
them – in a word, having reassured himself about their existence –
Hamlet can only feel guilt, self-revulsion, and confusion for not
having fulfilled the command to revenge his father's murder, for
not having acceded to the Ghost's request. The hero is unable to
understand his own behaviour. It is in the context of the players'
first performance and Hamlet's increased confusion and guilt that
we grasp fully the meaning of the lines in which the hero hits upon
the Mousetrap as a means of dealing with the double-bind that
tortures him. Conjuring up the *good* object has not solved anything;
it has only made things worse. Why not, then, examine the reality
of the *bad* object; why not conjure it up?

I will consider the Mousetrap in the context of the stage business
that surrounds it in an effort to appreciate both the manner in which
its performance draws forth Hamlet's most vicious sarcasm and the
manner in which the little play constitutes in itself a method of oral
aggression. The First Folio stage direction immediately preceding
the entrance of the King and Queen into the hall where the
Mousetrap is to be performed – '*Enter King, Queen, Polonius,
Ophelia, Rosencrantz, Guildenstern, and other Lords attendant,
with his guard carrying torches. Danish March. Sound a
Flourish.*' – has the effect of confronting Hamlet once again with
the splendid married couple, with the satisfied man and wife. Once
again, as we might anticipate, he reacts to the confrontation by
taking up not the direct, blunt kind of sarcasm he shows Ophelia
but the snide, ironic variety he displays earlier in the action. 'How
fares our cousin Hamlet?' asks the King. The Prince replies (notice
how he seizes on the word 'fares' and couches his retort in
transparently oral terms), 'Excellent, i'faith, of the chameleon's
dish. I eat the air, promise-cramm'd. You cannot feed capons so'
(III,ii,90–1). Thus Hamlet, his 'antic disposition' allowing him to

play with words in a psychoanalytically interesting fashion, alludes to his diet of nothing, as well as to his hopes of future satisfaction ('air' 'promise-cramm'd'), in the presence of the well-fed, satiated Claudius. The rival is envied indeed.

Yet Hamlet also has plenty of comments in reserve for the frustrating object. Lounging at Ophelia's feet, and within earshot of Gertrude and the King, his response to the girl's observation that he is merry is: 'O God, your only jig-maker. What should a man do but be merry? For look you how cheerfully my mother looks, and my father died within's two hours' (III,ii,119-21). Thus it is his mother's appearance, her cheerfulness, her satisfied air that continues to gall him, to remind him of his lack of narcissistic supplies. And when Ophelia reminds him that his father has been dead for 'twice two months', the Prince replies viciously (both Claudius and Gertrude are within earshot):

> So long? Nay then, let the devil wear black, for I'll have a suit of sables. O heavens, die two months ago and not forgotten yet! Then there's hope a great man's memory may outlive his life half a year. But, by'r lady, he must build churches then, or else shall a suffer not thinking on . . .
>
> (III,ii,123-8)

Once more, then, Hamlet's experience of betrayal, of deprivation, prompts him to cry out at his mother's remarriage, to jab at her, and to attempt to cheapen her in the envied rival's eyes.

Nor can Hamlet's raucous, sensual, 'dirty' treatment of Ophelia be overlooked here, the exchanges in which he talks of lying between a maid's legs, in which he hints of 'country matters', of sexual contact. All of this takes place, of course, upon the verge of the dumb show in which the players evoke the events that catalysed the emergence of the bad object. Moreover, all of this sexual banter takes place in the presence of Gertrude and Claudius, and within earshot; it is an additional 'play' Hamlet stages for their benefit. Indeed, Gertrude has nothing to do on stage at this point but to note the bawdy exchanges between Hamlet and Ophelia, exchanges which are, from Hamlet's point of view, directed toward her 'education'. Hamlet is being 'dirty' in front of mother, and to mother's substitute. He is telling mother in an oblique, insidious way that she is a whore, that she has made her son into a satyr, that her behaviour is causing a breakdown of morals all around her, that the court has become a brothel, indeed a theatre where men seduce girls in the audience. That Claudius is meant to 'get the message' is clear enough too, for he is the chief of this court, and he is married to Gertrude who once again, through Hamlet's sarcasm, is being cheapened in his eyes. Nor does Polonius escape; he must sit by helplessly while his daughter is put through these paces, and ironically, he deserves it, since he instigates her rejection of Hamlet and, more, since he suspects the worst about her himself. In this way, Hamlet gets at everyone through his performance, which reminds us once again of the broad metaphoric significance of acting in the play: all are actors here in that all are concealing something; thus all are prone, because they are concealing something, to act-out. The objects of the concealed, unseen world may surface at any moment, as they do shortly in this very scene.

In one sense, however, the entire Mousetrap, the entire play-within-the-play, can be regarded as an oral aggressive attack, as an attempt on Hamlet's part to put Claudius and Gertrude through an excruciating visual and auditory experience. Designing it carefully, he pens the viciously barbed allusions to their marriage, thereby creating an effective means of torture. Hamlet, sadistically delighting in watching the King and Queen listen to the accusations, has the Player Queen say to the dying Player King when the latter suggests that she marry a second time:

> O, confound the rest!
> Such love must needs be treason in my breast.
> In second husband let me be accurst;
> None wed the second but who killed the first.

> (III,ii,168–71)

At that point Hamlet passionately breathes, 'Wormwood, worm-wood'. Some forty lines later, feeling a desire to peer at his victims and see how the torture is affecting them, Hamlet, playing innocent, asks Gertrude, 'Madam, how like you this play?' The Queen replies lamely, 'The lady doth protest too much, methinks' (Q2). 'O, but she'll keep her word,' says Hamlet mercilessly (218–20). And when the King demands whether or not there is an 'offence' in the argument, Hamlet announces sarcastically, 'Your Majesty, and we that have free souls, it touches us not. Let the galled jade wince, our withers are unwrung' (229–31). Thus does the Prince reveal his urge to 'gall' his rival and to see his mother 'wince'. It is only when Claudius, unable to endure the torture any longer, bolts out of the hall crying 'Away!' that Hamlet's engine of torture grinds to a halt. What has that engine accomplished? Only the venting of the hero's aggression. His attempt to cope with the double-bind in which he struggles by bringing forth, externalizing, and thereby mastering the bad object is no more efficacious than his attempt to resolve his dilemma by bringing forth and re-identifying himself with the good object.

5

Of the many feelings that surge through Hamlet at the conclusion of the Mousetrap the feeling – newly aroused – of having been betrayed by the mother is perhaps the strongest. Note, in support of this, that Hamlet's first private revelation – and I mean by that the first thought he reveals when alone upon the stage following the performance of the play-within-the-play – involves the temptation to murder the Queen, to commit matricide. Parallels with Sophocles are striking. Oedipus is in a matricidal mood upon ascertaining the 'truth' and in such a mood proceeds to his mother's chamber. Hamlet, who has also ascertained what he takes to be the truth, stalks toward his mother's closet hoping that the 'soul of Nero' – a matricide – will not 'enter this firm bosom'. Oedipus, upon the threshold of Jocasta's chamber, asks those in attendance there to 'give him a sword'. Hamlet aligns himself with Oedipus and differentiates himself as well when he says, thinking on what he will do to Gertrude momentarily, 'I will speak daggers to her, but use none.' The point is, Hamlet reminds us here of his tendency to stab the betrayer orally, to rely upon his mouth as a means of aggression, as a means of acting destructively from within the double-bind.

   It is in this context that we must view Hamlet's impulsive stabbing of whomever is behind the arras (in III,iv). He does not really know what he is doing when he lunges toward the screen, and his question, 'Is it the king?' – which comes *after* he has stabbed – contains a magical wish for relief. Again, the arras serves in this scene a function similar to that which it serves in the nunnery scene; it is a kind of dream screen that reveals the preconscious and unconscious dimension of the action.

By the time he reaches his mother's chamber, Hamlet has come to realize – and the realization makes him desperate – that he cannot change himself, that he cannot integrate the antithetical aims bound up with his split maternal objects and reinforced by super-ego pressures connected with the Ghost's declarations and with the investment in his former identity as 'good son'. Yet he must do something now; his passivity has not usurped him to the point where he would simply lie down and allow Claudius to precipitate the consummation. Nor can he just exist quietly within the double-bind, for the feelings that divide him will inevitably express themselves in some sort of acting-out which will, in turn, create new situations which must be coped with in their own right. What, then, does Hamlet do? Relying upon magic, magic connected with the actors and their ability to bring forth objects from the inner world, and relying also upon his awareness of the ability of those around him to change, to bring forth new identity – particularly Gertrude's ability to do this – Hamlet attempts to resolve his dilemma by restoring the past, specifically by changing Gertrude back into the good object. Hamlet, in III,iv, tells his mother how she should act; in effect, he demands that she act in such a way as to stop within him the ever-recurring reactivation of aims connected with the bad internalization. She must not sleep with Claudius: ' . . . go not to my uncle's bed./ *Assume* a virtue if you have it not' (III,iv,160, italics added). She must not continually create the primal scene in his mind, for at the genital level this is what keeps charging him with unacceptable aims, aims that threaten the loss of his identity and transform the just revenge into the actualization of impulses he is not even supposed to have. If he is to control himself – and Hamlet is very nearly out of control at this point – he must control Gertrude. This he can do by getting her to control herself, which, at the level of magical thinking, is equivalent to changing her back into the good object.

Hamlet, after his explosive outburst toward the pathetic creature concealed behind the arras, begins to work upon Gertrude, accusing her of being 'bad' in the same utterance in which he ironically calls her 'good-mother' (III,iv,27), thus focusing for us the split with which we are most concerned. 'What have I done?' asks the Queen. Hamlet replies:

> Such an act
> That blurs the grace and blush of modesty,
> Calls virtue hypocrite, takes off the rose
> From the fair forehead of an innocent love,
> And sets a blister there, makes marriage vows
> As false as dicer's oaths – O, such a deed
> As from the body of contraction plucks
> The very soul, and sweet religion makes
> A rhapsody of words. Heaven's face doth glow,
> Yea this solidity and compound mass
> With tristful visage, as against the doom,
> Is thought-sick at the act.
>
> (III,iv,39–50)

If we listen to this speech with Reik's proverbial third ear, and if we view it in the total context of our discussion, we recognize that Hamlet is accusing his mother of *betraying him*, of betraying his expectations of her behaviour, his conceptualization of the good marriage and of those who comprised it. Psychodynamically inherent in these accusations is a further one which is never made explicit: Hamlet, regressively and defensively, is accusing Gertrude of awakening his forbidden urges, the repressed wishes bound up with the repressed version of the mother. The hero then goes on to present his mother with a split version of the father, with the good paternal object, portrait and all, and the bad paternal figure who represents the negative or unacceptable side of his own personality. Needless to say, were she to incline toward the values represented by the portrait of the good father – such inclination expressing itself in sexual continence – she would move that much closer to restoring her role of good mother and thus resolving, albeit in an artificial way, the son's emotional dilemma. Curiously, after having presented the paternal portraits, Hamlet proceeds to deny the reality of the mother's sexual passion, as if the magical attempt

to transform her back into the good object, to deny her 'badness' –
and by extension his – knows no bounds. Gertrude's 'blood' is
'tame', it is 'humble', it can 'wait upon the judgement'. And what
judgement, he asks, would cause her to choose the bad paternal
figure? 'What devil was't,' he asks, 'that thus hath cozened you at
hoodman-blind?' The bad mother, then, is aligned with the devil,
with hell, with blackness, and the good mother with 'virtue', with
whiteness, cleanliness, heaven. Even Gertrude echoes the symbolic
system when she says:

> O Hamlet, speak no more.
> Thou turn'st my eyes into my very soul,
> And there I see such black and grained spots
> As will not leave their tint.

(III,iv,78–81)

But Hamlet, heated up, his mind working fast, and focusing in
fantasy upon the primal scene, betrays the obsessive aspect of his
mentation and runs on with:

> Nay, but to live
> In the rank sweat of an enseamed bed,
> Stewed in corruption, honeying and making love
> Over the nasty sty . . .
>   A murderer and a villain,
> A slave . . .
> A king of shreds and patches . . .

(81–93)

It is at this point that the Ghost enters, intervening between mother
and son.

The intervention of the Ghost attests, of course, to Hamlet's
failure, to the enormous emotional distance that lies between him
and his goal, to the continued existence of the paralyzing
double-bind. Most of all, however, this intervention reminds us that
Hamlet's deepest intention in this scene is, as I have suggested, to
resolve the double-bind and through that resolution to discover an
emotional path that might actively lead to Claudius' destruction. In
other words, the Ghost in this scene is pressing for a solution to the
hero's emotional dilemma, which means, of course, pressing for
the accomplishment of the revenge. The Ghost is saying to Hamlet,

in effect, 'you are losing sight of your aim; stop torturing your mother; stop dwelling upon the bad object's behaviour with Claudius; stop your tripping around the primal scene, and return to the business of transforming Gertrude back into the good object' – for this solution, while magical and probably fated to fail, is still a kind of solution and will to some extent satisfy the super-ego. What I am suggesting, then, is that the Ghost is an aspect of Hamlet's mind, an hallucination stemming from a conscience that is unwilling to allow Hamlet to indulge himself further in the primal scene of betrayal and in the aggression that arises therefrom. All of this ultimately attests, of course, to the power of the bad object over the hero.

Back on the track, Hamlet proceeds in his effort to change his mother back into the good object. He tells her to confess her faults to Heaven, that is, to gravitate toward the Good Father, the Good Father–God who is an extension of the Good Husband; he tells her not to sleep with Claudius, to break her bad libidinal habits. His words here point up in a most striking way the splitting of the maternal object that runs through the scene as a whole:

> My pulse as yours doth temperately keep time,
> And makes as healthful music. It is not madness
> That I have uttered. Bring me to the test,
> And I the matter will reword, which madness
> Would gambol from. Mother, for love of grace,
> Lay not that flattering unction to your soul,
> That not your trespass by my madness speaks.
> It will but skin and film the ulcerous place
> Whilst rank corruption, mining all within,
> Infects unseen. Confess yourself to Heaven;
> Repent what's past, avoid what is to come,
> And do not spread the compost o'er the weeds
> To make them ranker. Forgive me this my virtue,
> For in the fatness of these pursy times
> Virtue itself of vice must pardon beg,
> Yea, curb and woo for leave to do him good.

(III,iv,131–46)

Gertrude's response to this also points up the splitting, and Hamlet's comment upon her line brings his motivation – that is, the transformation of the object – unforgettably into the open.

'O Hamlet,' says the Queen, 'thou hast cleft my heart in twain', to which the Prince replies:

> O, throw away the worser part of it,
> And live the purer with the other half!
> Good night – but go not to my uncle's bed.
> Assume a virtue . . .

(148–51)

What we must concentrate upon now is the manner in which Hamlet's latest solution manifests itself in subsequent scenes, the manner in which it does provide him with respite from the constant reinforcing of aims connected with the bad object, and finally, the manner in which the ensuing action demonstrates the *limitation* of that solution, its unsatisfactory nature as a genuine method of coping with underlying stress. While Hamlet's transformation of the mother allows him to muddle through to the revenge, while it does quiet the obsessional side of his personality, it does not allow him to achieve a genuine resolution of deep, long-standing conflict.

6

Let us notice, to begin with, that after the closet scene in which he stabs Gertrude with words, finally convincing her to give over sexual contact with Claudius, Hamlet completely ceases to be sarcastic toward his mother. In fact, he does not direct toward her one single additional sarcastic remark during the remainder of the play. This does not mean, of course, that his deepest conflicts are no longer operative. They are, for Hamlet is still sarcastic, still preoccupied with death, still suffering the agony of loss and betrayal that catalysed the release of his infantile aims. He is still as bound to the mother as he ever was, but he succeeds, with Gertrude's aid, in controlling his aims to a much greater degree than he controlled them prior to the closet scene.

These developments in Hamlet are vividly expressed in the scene in which Claudius tells Hamlet he is to be sent immediately to England. I said a moment ago that the hero ceases suddenly to be sarcastic toward his mother, but that he is still prone to be sarcastic toward others, something which attests to the persistence of his deep oral cravings, to the mood that has characterized his conduct all along. Not surprisingly, it is toward Claudius that Hamlet now directs his sarcastic thrusts, as in the scene we are now considering; for while the frustrating object is no longer on Hamlet's mind in the way that she once was, the envied rival is quite as intolerable as ever. Notice, for example, this oral-aggressive exchange between the Prince and the King: 'Now Hamlet, where's Polonius?' 'At supper', replies the Prince. 'At supper! Where?' demands the King, to whom Hamlet responds in his most sarcastic fashion:

> Not where he eats but where a is eaten. A certain convocation of politic worms are e'en at him. Your worm is your only emperor for diet. We fat all creatures else to fat us, and we fat ourselves for maggots. Your fat king and your lean beggar is but variable service, two dishes, but to one table.
>
> (IV,iii,17–24)

How much does Hamlet disclose here! The King, of course, is the 'fat' one, the satiated one, the commander of narcissistic supplies, and it is Hamlet who is the 'lean beggar', the deprived one, the empty one, the one whose hostile behaviour is a kind of begging for the return of the frustrating object. It is also of interest to note here the manner in which Hamlet dwells upon death's incorporative power. Polonius, dead, does not eat, he is eaten; death is a devourer, a thing which absorbs one, takes one back into the earth. Hamlet, looking for narcissistic supplies throughout the play and finding himself frustrated, fantasies death as a magical solution to such frustration. His imagery, in other words, highlights the close emotional connection between the desire to incorporate (sarcasm, cannibalism) and the desire to be incorporated, to be made one with the feeding body. Those who are alive must *eat*, or strive to; those who are dead are eaten and, as Hamlet feels it, *fed to*.

Nor can we overlook here the disgusting side of Hamlet's fantasy, the ugly, raw quality of the imagery, for this too points up the hero's deep ambivalence toward death, something which emerges with startling clarity, as we shall see, in the graveyard scene. More important to my present argument, however, is Hamlet's next exchange with the King, an exchange in which a number of crucial fantasies are made open to us. In response to Hamlet's speech about Polonius being 'at supper', Claudius remarks, 'Alas, alas!' as though the hero were mad and his speeches senseless. Hamlet at this juncture declares, 'A man may fish with the worm that hath eat of a king, and eat of the fish that hath fed of that worm.' Asks Claudius, 'What dost thou mean by this?' Replies Hamlet, 'Nothing but to show you how a king may go a progress through the guts of a beggar.' Recalling who is the 'beggar' in these exchanges and who the king, we recognize that Hamlet is entertaining a fantasy of incorporation involving Claudius, indeed, a fantasy of taking Claudius in, of having him inside of himself. How can this be? Why should the hero be entertaining – at the unconscious level, of course – such a fantasy? To get at this we must remember that Hamlet has magically transformed Gertrude back into the good object, that he has suddenly ceased to be sarcastic toward her, and that he is now directing his frustration and anger toward the rival exclusively. In a very real way, then, Claudius has come to represent to Hamlet all of his thwarted oral aims, his betrayal at the mother's hands, and, paradoxically, the possible gratification of his deepest needs. Hamlet would have Claudius inside of him because, as Hamlet sees it, Claudius possesses Gertrude. Locating the bad object in the King and identifying with the King not simply at the genital level, as the orthodox analytic criticism maintains, but at the *oral and anal levels* as well (the whole business of Polonius and the worms has excretory overtones and is anally aggressive), Hamlet would dissolve ego boundaries and merge with the rival. To suggest that Hamlet feels tainted because he too wants to sleep with Gertrude is to suggest too little. The 'corruption', the 'rottenness' goes deeper than that; it has, in fact, seeped into the hero's very bowels to the point where he would incorporate the rival, devour the rival, cannibalize the rival in order to get at the mother whom the rival possesses. Claudius and Gertrude are one now, and this is indeed what Hamlet himself tells us a moment later:

King Hamlet . . .
  prepare thyself.
  . . . everything is bent
For England.

Ham.   For England?
King   Ay, Hamlet.
Ham.   Good.
King   So is it, if thou knew'st our purposes.
Ham.   I see a cherub that sees then. But, come,
for England! *Farewell, dear mother.*
King   *Thy loving father, Hamlet.*
Ham.   *My mother.* Father and mother is man and wife, man and
wife is one flesh, and so, *my mother.*

                                        (IV,iii,39–54, italics added)

It is as if the Prince has come to see in Claudius alone the very be-all
and end-all of his misery.

7

To soften the egotistical character of the central fantasy, namely the
longing to merge with the enigmatic betrayer, this play employs
two basic, formal devices and they are, first, the displacement of
the central quest to the problem of the father's slayer; and second,
the displacement of the multilevel longing for the mother's body to
the longing for death. In examining the graveyard scene (V,i) we
should notice, first, that it is replete with oral and olfactory imagery
of a particular kind, of a kind that recalls the oral and anal imagery
of the scene at which we have just glanced in which Hamlet tells
Claudius he is his mother. Everywhere we are confronted with
strong smells, with decaying corpses, worm's meat, gnawed
carcasses, the very bones of the dead. Death as devourer, death as
ingester, death as a kind of dumb feeder with an unstoppable
mouth – this particular conception of death is very much on
Hamlet's mind here. No one else in this scene is both attracted and
repelled by the 'realities' of death, by the conception of death as
ugly devourer; only Hamlet reacts to this notion in a revealing,
ambivalent fashion. The Gravedigger goes about his business in, as
Hamlet calls it, an 'absolute', matter-of-fact way; there is nothing
curious or frightening to him about the yard and its rotting corpses.
As for Horatio, he spies significances, external ones perhaps, but
remains as collected as ever. Here is death; it is a fact; it smells bad;

that is that. 'Prithee, Horatio, tell me one thing,' says Hamlet. 'What's that my lord?' 'Dost thou think Alexander looked o' this fashion i' the earth?' 'E'en so', is Horatio's laconic reply (V,i,190–5). The point is, Hamlet in this scene views the world of the dead, as well as the world of the fleshly living, in the light of his newly discovered inner world of objects, objects which attest to aims and needs that make him – as well as others – corrupt, rotten, stinking. The hero *projects* the discovery of his own repressed nature into all men, the entire world. In this way, people become worm's meat, little more, and the world itself a painted illusion. Death is everywhere, in every one, every rotten one; just breathe deeply and you have your evidence.

But it is when Hamlet becomes specific, when he begins to associate freely with specific images in mind, that the essential nature of his deepest conflicts is revealed. Note, for example, that as he associates over Yorick's skull Hamlet's thoughts turn to his childhood. This is, of course, perfectly natural, for Yorick was alive when the hero was a small boy. Hamlet connects the skull of the clown with the activities of that 'innocent' time. However, his mind having been turned in that direction, and his 'gorge' beginning to 'rise' – a striking oral image – the hero quite suddenly and quite arbitrarily begins to associate Yorick's skull with the 'chamber', presumably the bedchamber, of an unnamed 'lady' and launches into a bitterly sarcastic attack on that lady's 'painting'. This is an attack which calls explicitly to mind the nunnery scene in which Ophelia is reproached for 'painting', in which the central action is Hamlet sarcastically castigating Ophelia for having betrayed him, in which Ophelia obviously functions as a version of the mother. Here are the relevant lines from the graveyard scene; notice how the associations run on to reveal the unconscious shape of the action:

> Alas! poor Yorick. I knew him, Horatio – a fellow of infinite jest, of most excellent fancy. He hath borne me on his back a thousand times; and now, how abhorred in my imagination it is! My gorge rises at it. Here hung those lips that I have kissed I know not how oft. Where be your gibes now, your gambols, your songs, your flashes of merriment that were wont to set the table on a roar? Not one now, to mock your own grinning? Quite chop-fallen? Now get you to my lady's chamber and tell

her, let her paint an inch thick, to this favour she must come. Make her
laugh at that.

                                                        (V,i,180–90)

Thus it is *the mother, the mother as betrayer*, the mother who, like
Gertrude, appears to be one thing but really is another, that is on
Hamlet's mind here, and it is the skull of Yorick that drives the hero
back to the time of childhood, the time associated with dependency
upon the maternal figure.

Having discovered Yorick's skull and associated to it, Hamlet
goes on to dwell not only upon the transforming power of death,
but its power to transform us basely: 'To what base uses we may
return, Horatio! Why may not imagination trace the noble dust of
Alexander till he find it stopping a bunghole?' ''Twere to consider
too curiously to consider so,' replies Horatio; but Hamlet's mind
runs on:

> No, faith, not a jot; but to follow him thither with modesty enough and
> likelihood to lead it, as thus: Alexander died, Alexander was buried,
> Alexander returneth into dust; the dust is earth; of earth we make loam;
> and why of that loam, whereto he was converted, might they not stop
> a beer-barrel?
> Imperious Caesar, dead and turn'd to clay,
> Might stop a hole to keep the wind away.
> O, that that earth which kept the world in awe
> Should patch a wall t' expel the winter's flaw.

                                                        (V,i,198–211)

Clearly, the notion of Alexander stopping a hole, the notion of his
transformation into a thing that plugs a barrel, follows naturally
upon the passage in which 'my lady's chamber' is at the centre of
Hamlet's mentation. The maternal figure is still the hero's chief
unconscious preoccupation. What Hamlet fantasies here reveals in
a flash the essence of his ambivalence: his attraction to, and his
terror of, death. The imaginary fate of Alexander projectively
measures his own fate: Hamlet's aim has been, and is, to prevent
narcissistic supplies from flowing elsewhere, to prevent his
nourishment, conceived in primal, oral terms as liquid, from
reaching the rival, and he has, as we have seen, regarded death,
with its incorporative powers, as a method of assuring oral

gratification, or, conversely, preventing oral frustration. Now Alexander's dust ultimately fills a hole in a barrel; it keeps the liquid in; it prevents the loss of liquid supplies; at the same time, to stop the barrel is not simply Alexander's destiny, it is also his degradation. Let us explore this very carefully.

Hamlet is preoccupied here with death as a transformer; the transformative powers of death, at the deepest unconscious level, bear upon the problem of Hamlet's identity which, in turn, is integrally bound up with his aims toward the reactivated object. What this means, of course, is that death for Hamlet harbours a loss of identity, a loss of identity concretely imaged in death's transforming power over the remains of Alexander. That this loss of identity is directly connected with mother is clear when we recall that Hamlet's mind has already turned toward mother at the sight of Yorick's skull. In this way, death, the transformer, transforms us into a thing *incorporated into the mother's body*. In death we are eaten, devoured, absorbed and, finally, changed into an object that plugs the hole of the 'barrel' whence issue narcissistic supplies, an object that fuses defensively with the life-sustaining maternal figure. Because this is Hamlet's deepest regressive aim, because its fulfilment means loss of identity, and because death provides that fulfilment, death equals loss of identity. From this perspective we understand fully Hamlet's powerful ambivalence toward death. On the one hand, he desires it as a way to the lost object, as a way to reunion, symbiosis, the quelling of infantile frustrations. On the other hand, his desire to regress is a degrading desire, one that he is ashamed of, that argues corruption, a disgusting longing for the painted lady, the forfended object, the mother's parts. In the graveyard scene, Hamlet's rottenness, his sense of corruption, is objectified in the rottenness of death, just as his ambivalent longing for Gertrude is concretized in his images of worm's meat, the barrel, transformation and re-absorption into earth. What this suggests about Hamlet's overall development at this point in the play is clear enough. In spite of his transformation of the maternal object, in spite of his magical attempt to go back to an earlier time, he is still bound to the mother in a regressive, crippling way. He is still unable to overcome the effects of the reactivation he has experienced. For all its rottenness, for all its terrors, death appears increasingly to be the only solution.

8

From the powerful dependency which persists in Hamlet during the dramatic moments that follow the closet scene one would suspect that Gertrude, long before her 'fall', in fact, within the time of Yorick's tenure, was the kind of mother who would be apt to breed dependency in her boy, to confuse him with contradictory cues – an over-solicitous, seductive mother encouraging closeness and, at the same time, because of the son's arousal, discouraging the full expression of his nature. The maternal introject is to a significant extent a version of the mother's impulses that find their counterpart in the aims of the dependent child. And interestingly enough, the play provides us with three or four striking clues to the nature of Gertrude's mothering.

The first of the clues to which I am referring occurs in the scene at which we are now looking, when Hamlet leaps into Ophelia's grave crying, 'This is I,/ Hamlet the Dane.' He continue, twenty lines later, for Laertes' benefit:

> 'Swounds, show me what thou'lt do.
> Woot weep, woot fight, woot fast, woot tear thyself,
> Woot drink up eisel, eat a crocodile?
> I'll do't. Dost thou come here to whine,
> To outface me with leaping in her grave?
> Be buried quick with her, and so will I.
> And if thou prate of mountains, let them throw
> Millions of acres on us, till our ground,
> Singeing his pate against the burning zone,
> Make Ossa like a wart. Nay, an thou'lt mouth,
> I'll rant as well as thou.

At this point Gertrude (Q2) observes:

> This is mere madness,
> And thus a while the fit will work on him.
> Anon, as patient as the female dove

When that her golden couplets are disclosed,
His silence will sit drooping.

(V,i,272–86)

These vivid, remarkable figures reveal the woman's natural or automatic way of thinking about her boy. An exaggerated maternal image comes first to her mind as she describes metaphorically Hamlet's mood. We are made to see a mother-bird sitting upon her precious eggs until they break and the helpless, dependent little chicks emerge. Thus does Gertrude characterize what is going on inside her son, revealing, in this way, her persistent tendency to treat him as a dependent, a tendency that reveals by implication the nature of her mothering during the early time, the time of Yorick, the time to which Hamlet wants, regressively and ambivalently, to return.

Nor can we overlook in this regard the manner in which Gertrude offers her son her 'napkin' so that he may wipe his brow during his swordfight (V,ii). We must imagine the action as it transpires upon the stage, mother hovering, just like the mother bird, over her 'fat' boy who is 'scant of breath' and needing her assistance. Such actions call immediately to mind, and lend a deeper significance to, Claudius' earlier response to Laertes' question, why did you not kill Hamlet outright for his crimes? Claudius, it will be remembered, announces that Gertrude 'lives almost by [Hamlet's] looks' (IV,vii,12), that she cannot do without him, that she is, in other words, dependent upon *him*, which takes us back, of course, to the closet scene where Gertrude's change of behaviour depends upon Hamlet's assertion of will, just as his change depends upon *her* assertion of will.

We are now in a position to differentiate the betraying, confusional mother of *Hamlet* from the betraying, confusional mother of *Oedipus Rex*. The kind of damage rendered by Jocasta involves a deeper ambivalence, an ambivalence comprised in large part of maternal hostility and destructiveness and catalysing in Oedipus a violent, catastrophic sense of annihilation, an ambivalence that calls to mind the image of the terrible Sphinx. Gertrude's confusional, crippling quality is more closely associated with seduction and over-protection, with the mother who encourages dependence and symbiotic union, thus creating in the child aims that cannot be gratified and anxieties that are attendant upon those aims.

9

Shortly before the denouement we encounter Hamlet and Horatio conversing in such a way as to bring the audience to an understanding of the precise emotional and moral condition in which the hero finds himself. Especially noticeable here (V,ii) is the ambivalence in Hamlet's attitude, an ambivalence that underlies the external calmness he makes such an effort to achieve. Still caught in the double-bind which took shape during the scene upon the platform (I,iv), still talking about the 'king' who killed his 'King' (that is, the idealized father – Hyperion) and who 'whored' his 'mother' (that is, the reactivated bad object), Hamlet discloses how close to the surface is the material he strove to re-repress during the closet scene and to keep under control thereafter. Hamlet asks Horatio – and it is pathetic to hear it again at this late stage in the play – if he has good cause to kill the King. Nor does he fail to mention here his lost kingship, something of which we have not heard before. Claudius, Hamlet tells us, 'Popped in between th'election and my hopes' (V,ii,66), as if the partial working through, or resolution, of the deeper issues against Claudius has allowed this practical or secondary issue to surface. Referring to the evil Claudius has done in terms that recall the inner world and its power to dictate the shape of outward events through reactivation of introjects, Hamlet asks,

>   is't not perfect conscience
> To quit him with this arm? And is't not to be damned
> To let this canker of our nature come
> In further evil?

>   (68–71)

Hamlet, of course, maintains his balance in the presence of Osric, when the latter brings word of the proposed fencing match. But the underlying damage is there; the disease of dependency, of loss, of betrayal is there. The sense of impending doom, the need to relinquish an identity long adhered to, all of this is there. Resigning himself to 'fate', putting himself in the hands of the higher powers, feeling negated in his being by his inability to act, Hamlet chooses to resolve his hopeless dilemma by *reacting* to events, by doing what he must do in the face of what must happen. In order to control himself, in order to achieve a certain self-mastery, the hero must withdraw from active participation in the world, for activity only activates the insoluble double-bind.

In this way, the price Hamlet pays for his calm, for his resignation, is a terrible one, one that involves a regressive style of being, and, as he himself recognizes, a hopeless, diseased drifting toward total annihilation in death. 'You will lose this wager, my lord,' says Horatio. 'I shall win at the odds,' replies Hamlet (V,ii,155–7). And then, deeply isolated and needing to express his despair to someone, Hamlet continues, 'But thou wouldst not think how ill all's here about my heart' (Q2). Horatio, immediately sensing that something is wrong and that something dreadful may happen, reacts 'normally' by telling Hamlet to guard his life: 'If your mind dislike anything, obey it' (163). But Hamlet, seizing upon the opportunity to lose his life, passively surrendering to the part of himself that longs to be dead, responds with, 'Not a whit', and later goes on to command, 'But let be. Horatio, I am dead . . .' (290).

The final scene of the play is pervaded by *drinking*, by toasts, by the conspicuous elevation and quaffing of wine; indeed, drinking becomes one of the central metaphors of the scene as a whole and a key to the underlying dynamics of the hero's behaviour. For example, seconds before the actual sword play begins, Claudius commands (and this is, of course, a part of his murderous plan):

> Set me the stoups of wine upon that table . . .
> The King shall drink to Hamlet's better breath,
> And in the cup a *union* shall he throw
> Richer than that which four successive kings
> In Denmark's crown have worn.
>
> (V,ii,214–21, italics added)

That Hamlet connects Claudius' *drinking* with the *union* of Claudius and Gertrude is clear from utterances made in the dramatic context. When he tells Gertrude to forego the King's bed he refers with disgust to Claudius' 'reechy kisses' (III,iv,168). When he stands over the praying Claudius and ponders a better time to kill him he again connects the bed and the wine: 'When he is drunk asleep . . . / Or in the incestuous pleasure of his bed' (III,iii,90). Shortly after the conclusion of the Mousetrap, the subject of which is, in part, the union of uncle and mother, Hamlet is told that the King is 'marvelous distempered'; immediately he asks, 'With drink, sir?' (III,ii,288–9). The point is, Hamlet's disgust with Claudius has an explicitly oral side to it. His fantasy of the union of Claudius and Gertrude is one in which the rival takes possession of the mother during the process of satiating himself. In this way, Claudius' drinking becomes to Hamlet a reminder of his loss of the mother to the rival, a reminder of his loss of narcissistic supplies integrally associated with the requirements of the oral stage. In the final scene Hamlet not only confronts the splendid married couple, the kind of confrontation that provoked so much of his sarcastic aggressiveness during the play's second scene and during the Mousetrap, but also confronts, through the wine, the multi-level union of Claudius and Gertrude.

The most striking reinforcement of the hero's psychic disruption occurs when Gertrude really dies, her death transpiring ironically as she ingests the poisoned wine, the wine that contains the 'union'. Not only must Hamlet be reminded of his lack of oral gratification by the sight of the cup in the hand of the king, he must suffer the actual loss of the mother from whom such gratification issues. Which brings us to the thesis of this section: the actual wounds that Hamlet suffers in this scene, the wounds inflicted by the poison that fills the cup and that tips the sword, are metaphoric representations of his inner wounds, the wounds that have predicated the shape of the tragedy. But they are *dynamic metaphors* operating at the level of the *action* in that they really do re-open the psychic wounds which the hero has striven to close through his transformation of the maternal object and through his passive drifting toward death. Think, for example, of the manner in which Hamlet receives his death wound: he is hit when he is not expecting it by Laertes who passes at him while he is resting. He is killed, in other words, through an act of treachery, an act which, by its very nature, betrays the code of honour, the code bound up with the paternal ideal, with the image of the Good Father and the influence of the super-ego. That this act of betrayal culminates in the poisoning of Hamlet, in a death that works from within in an unseen way, is too obvious a metaphorical expression to require lengthy exposition. Hamlet's whole life has been poisoned or blighted from within where dwelt the bad object, the object about which swirled the hero's repressed inclinations, the forbidden aims that ultimately catalysed, as the poison here catalyses, his destruction. The 'mole of nature,' referred to by Hamlet on the platform (Q2,I,iv) while Claudius swilled down his draughts of Rhenish wine, has worked out its destiny.

But it is Hamlet's last action that ties together the variegated strands of his basic, underlying conflict, that expresses unforgettably the nature of his torment. I am referring, of course, to the moment when he pries open Claudius' mouth and pours down Claudius' throat the wine that contains the 'union', the poison-filled pearl dropped into the cup shortly after the inception of the fencing match. 'Is thy union here?' cries the hero in his last sarcastic outburst against the King. Let us notice that Hamlet has *already* given Claudius his death wound with Laertes' poisoned sword. Thus the action with the wine, the wine that contains the 'union', is an entirely gratuitous action, one that expresses the depth of the frustration and the nature of the frustration which Hamlet has been experiencing all along. Thinking upon this gesture, upon Hamlet's question 'Is thy union here?', and thinking too upon the oral, incorporative conception of death which Hamlet has presented to us in previous scenes, it seems to me metaphorically fitting that Fortinbras, who is the play's thrusting, genital, outgoing version of the son, should remark as he stands over the bodies of all these dependent people during the final moments of the tragedy, 'O proud Death,/ What feast is toward in thine eternal cell . . . ?'

Freud was right to link *Hamlet* and *Oedipus Rex* during the course of his monumental discoveries. What we realize now, however, is that Freud's preoccupation with the Oedipus complex and with the problem of incestuous attachment prevented him from recognizing the crucial link between, and the central concern of, these masterpieces. What *Oedipus Rex* and *Hamlet* have in common at the deepest level is the problem of maternal betrayal, the quest for the mothering figure, the attempt to resolve the mystery of maternal ambivalence, and a specific vulnerability in the hero where the reactivation of early object relations is concerned. Hamlet and Oedipus are both incestuous, patricidal figures. But their incestuous, patricidal inclinations *result* from the kind of mother–child interaction which they have experienced. The unconscious inner world of the hero is stirred to life in the now of the action. That is what produces tragedy, at least as we know it in the Western world.

NOTE

1. The actress Claire Bloom informed me, in conversation, that she always played Ophelia so as to indicate to the audience Ophelia's recognition of Hamlet's knowledge that Claudius and Polonius are concealed behind the arras. 'Of course he knows they are there; and she knows that he knows; I have never imagined it otherwise.' That Hamlet is aware of the listeners is sometimes debated in the criticism; I side, obviously, with Miss Bloom.

4   'A Wilderness of Monkeys': A Psychodynamic Study of *The Merchant of Venice*

LYN STEPHENS

The Merchant of Venice seems a simple enough play: it appears to tell us that mercy ought to outweigh revenge and that the spirit of the law is better than the letter. But on closer investigation it is neither simple nor does it come to such presentable conclusions. There is a surprising savagery and ruthlessness in *The Comicall History of the Merchant of Venice*, as the Quarto half-title describes it. My first experience of seeing the play left me troubled and puzzled. I felt cheated and robbed at the end of the production and could not tell why. Now I think I know.

Bassanio says:

> So may the outward shows be least themselves:
> The world is still deceived with ornament.
> In law, what plea so tainted and corrupt
> But, being seasoned with a gracious voice,
> Obscures the show of evil. In religion,
> What damned error but some sober brow
> Will bless it and approve it with a text,
> Hiding the grossness with fair ornament?
> There is no vice so simple but assumes
> Some mark of virtue on his outward parts.
>
> (III,ii,73–82)

All Shakespeare citations are from *The Merchant of Venice*, M. M. Mahood, ed., The New Cambridge Shakespeare, Cambridge: Cambridge University Press, 1987.

This is the central theme of the play, I have come to think. This signals that Portia's plea may fall into the category of the tainted and corrupt, for almost every other action in the play is an outward show. We are directed inwards towards the intra-psychic realities, and not to the ornament of the apparent.

ANTONIO: THE TAINTED WETHER OF THE FLOCK

Melancholic Antonio haunts the play through omission and lack: he is set against Shylock who shrieks through it by commission and possession. Antonio begins the play, and in many productions is the last to leave the stage, still alone and lonely, rescued but untransformed. Attempts to feel sympathy for him never really work; our resentment of his passivity, rooted in his failure to be changed by his experiences and in response to the other characters, blocks compassion.

Some see Antonio as an unfinished character (see for example, Mahood, pp. 24, 39). I do not think this is so. Antonio is perfectly portrayed as what he is: sadistic and manipulative; latently homosexual; unable to inhabit potent manhood and be a father; and without the courage to have his anima* enlivened by a woman, never having progressed beyond the anal stage*. Antonio denies this to himself and to the world by a fastidious concern for the multivalent 'gentle', the antithesis of Jewish, of trading and coarseness.

He does not know the source of his melancholy and quite rightly says:

> It wearies me, you say it wearies you:
> But how I caught it, found it, or came by it,
> What stuff 'tis made of, whereof it is born,
> I am to learn.

(I,i,2–5)

---

* For these and other terms marked with an asterisk, see Glossary at the end of this chapter.

But he does not. I think the reason for his melancholy is to be found in his unconscious maternal phantasies about Bassanio and about the function both Bassanio and Shylock have in his internal world. Tragically, these phantasies also prevent Portia, or any other woman, from rescuing him. Only Portia and Shylock do not collude with his narcissistic* self-assessment; Shylock alone speaks and acts openly against him, while Portia castrates him.

Antonio provides Bassanio with money for his youthful pursuits, consciously believing himself a father-figure. Were he really in this role it would make sense for him to delight in Bassanio's coming quest, and for there to be a shared understanding of the sexual nature of the venture. We might expect Antonio to experience envy at Bassanio's youth and at his chances of getting Portia to bed, and expect also a degree of shared pleasure in the expected conquest. But all of this is absent.

Instead, we have a picture of a wounded man, although others cannot see the point of entry of the injury. He says, in his narcissism:

> I hold the world but as the world, Gratiano,
> A stage where every man must play a part,
> And mine a sad one.
>
> (I,i,77–9)

The dying fall in the half-line presents him as an implacable victim, match for an implacable enemy. Bassanio is about to desert him for Portia, and Antonio is faced with every *mother's* crisis when her son prepares to leave her for 'another woman'. It is not just that Bassanio betrays Antonio in the homosexual mode, but also that he repudiates him as the mother he, in his phantasy, is attempting to be. It is true that Antonio provides Bassanio with means to follow the life of a rich young gentleman, much as a father would provide for his son. But throughout the play there is the theme of the inability to distinguish between life and livelihood, and Antonio is as much a victim of this delusion as Shylock. He, like Shylock, conflates money with living, and when Antonio gives Bassanio money, in phantasy he gives him life, as mothers do. But this life-giving is in the anal mode where faeces, children and money are interchangeable, hence the confusion and misidentification of one for the other.

Antonio's life is built on denial*. One of Shylock's reasons for hating him is that

> . . . in low simplicity
> He lends out money gratis, and brings down
> The rate of usance here with us in Venice.

(I,iii,35-7)

To lend money for nothing may well be commendable, and it is enjoined by both the Testaments, but in the society in which Antonio lives and by the dynamics of the profession he has chosen, not to take interest on a loan is to deny how he makes the very money which he uses to make those loans. He is a merchant. Merchants make their money through venture and risk, and by charging more money for their goods than they paid for them. It is a system where profit, a legitimatized form of usury, cannot be ignored. Mercantilism is economic protectionism; its psychic version is defence.[1]

Another example of Antonio's denial may also be seen in the way the bond with Shylock becomes forfeit. He says to Salarino:

> My ventures are not in one bottom trusted,
> Nor to one place; nor is my whole estate
> Upon the fortune of this present year.

(I,i,42-4)

Were this true, then the calling in of the bond would present him with no problems of repayment, but if it is an overestimation of his means (which we would expect from Antonio) it is denial and a loss of the reality of the Rialto. Further, none of the other merchants, nor the Duke himself, offer Antonio three thousand ducats before the bond is called. It is tempting to see this collective failure as carrying in dramatic form Antonio's fellow merchants' destructive rivalry, but there is no textual (or psychodynamic) support for this view. Instead, I think Antonio himself is at the root of their helpless inability to rescue him. He is unable to join with the men who are the merchants because he has no notion of relatedness, an 'us'. In part this is because his narcissism is so entrenched, but more importantly because he may not use the benign form of projective identification*, the aim of which is communication and empathy, for fear of his own envy. So Antonio is isolated from the Duke by his own pathology. His fellow merchants do not so much abandon him as present a tableau of Antonio's inability to be projectively identified with them.

When Bassanio leaves on his quest for Portia, 'the golden fleece', the parting between Bassanio and Antonio is described by Salarino and Solanio in the same scene as Shylock's loss of Jessica is reported. Perhaps we are pointed to the similarities in so seemingly different events. Both men lose people whom they perceive through the template of their own phantasies, and, although they experience loss, they experience it in the fraudulent mode which their phantasies dictate. Antonio shows his trademark, depressed blackmail, when he says to Bassanio:

> Slubber not business for my sake, Bassanio,
> But stay the very riping of the time; which
> And for the Jew's bond which he hath of me,
> Let it not enter in your mind of love.
> Be merry, and employ your chiefest thoughts
> To courtship and the fair ostents of love
> As shall conveniently become you there.
>
> (II,viii,40–46)

If Antonio's intention were really to speed Bassanio on his quest, unencumbered by worry about the bond, why mention it at all? He does so, in my view, because the bond is not only a bond between Antonio and Shylock; for Antonio it is the usurious bond between Bassanio and himself made manifest.

Thus in the letter he sends to Bassanio, which arrives at the high point of Belmont's joy, Antonio sounds like a mother who will give all for her son:

> Sweet Bassanio, my ships have all miscarried, my creditors grow cruel, my estate is very low; my bond to the Jew is forfeit, and since, in paying it, it is impossible I should live, all debts are cleared between you and I if I might but see you at my death. Notwithstanding, use your pleasure; if your love do not persuade you to come, let not my letter.
>
> (III,ii,314–19)

But then he calls in the forfeiture of *his* bond and Bassanio is impaled on Antonio's narcissism when he adds:

> Grieve not that I am fall'n to this for you . . .
> Say how I loved you, speak me fair in death,
> And when the tale is told, bid her be the judge[2]
> Whether Bassanio had not once a love.
> Repent but you that you shall lose your friend
> And he repents not that he pays your debt.
>
> (IV,i,262, 271–5)

Here he poses a double-bind: he appears to say, 'I love you, and this cancels all debts between us', yet he leaves Bassanio with a burden which is genuinely insupportable. To refuse to help means to leave Antonio to an unjust fate and to count as nothing the bond between him and Bassanio, but to accede is to appear to honour the relationship as it exists in Antonio's phantasy. If Bassanio were to do that, Portia realises, this would entirely jeopardise her union with him, and she fights against that with all the power and cunning at her disposal.[3]

Antonio may have made the offer of his life as a reparative act*; it fails because it does not repair, but harms. Hence it is hostile and destructive in intention. Had he been able to say, as in the final couplet of Sonnet 30,

> But if the while I think on thee (dear friend)
> All losses are restored, and sorrows end,

then perhaps he would have been able to make good the damage he had intended and caused thus far. But it is not within Antonio to inhabit this non-narcissistic stance.

Antonio has some sense of reality, but uses it only to bolster up a feeling of hopelessness which he desires. He therefore says:

> The Duke cannot deny the course of law;
> For the commodity that strangers have
> With us in Venice, if it be denied,
> Will much impeach the justice of the state,
> Since that the trade and profit of the city
> Consisteth of all nations.
>
> (III,iii,26–31)

In the trial scene when asked whether he will confess to the bond, Antonio says, 'I do', echoing the marriage service. It binds him to Shylock, albeit in the mode of destruction and death. Antonio would be deeply disappointed if Shylock forgave the bond, for he would have no place to stand, having no ability to receive, and therefore none to show gratitude. Notice his use of projection* in this speech: all the images of implacability apply to Antonio and not primarily to Shylock.

> I pray you think you question with the Jew.
> You may as well go stand upon the beach
> And bid the main flood bate his usual height:
> You may as well use question with the wolf
> Why he has made the ewe bleat for the lamb;
> You may as well forbid the mountain pines
> To wag their high tops and make no noise
> When they are fretten with the gusts of heaven;
> You may as well do anything most hard
> As seek to soften that – than which what's harder? –
> His Jewish heart. Therefore I do beseech you
> Make no moe offers, use no further means,
> But with all brief and plain conveniency
> Let me have judgment, and the Jew his will.
>
> (IV,i,70–83)

Death is welcome to Antonio. He may see it as a judgment for some unspecified sin, a sense of a deep perversion of the rightful place of things within himself. If Antonio is activated by the mother archetype*, then it is out of control and hysterical. It does not enable him to be properly maternal towards Bassanio, because it is unrealized or unenlivened. When Antonio says,

> I am a tainted wether of the flock,
> Meetest for death; the weakest kind of fruit
> Drops earliest to the ground, and so let me . . .
>
> (IV,i,114–16)

he is prepared to preserve his inner *status quo* at the expense, even, of his own death. When he is delivered from the bond, Antonio is not freed to rethink his other bond with Bassanio. He persists in his hatred of the marriage union between Bassanio and Portia by putting so much pressure on Bassanio that he gives away the ring his wife has so recently placed on his finger. He cannot allow Portia into the realm of love, instead making her exist in the realm of law, of which he has so recently been shown the limitations.

It would seem that Antonio is able to be generous to Shylock in defeat. But if we look carefully at the terms of the judgment, I think a different story emerges. Portia's judgment is in three parts: first, half of Shylock's goods now belong to Antonio; second, half are to go to the State; and third, Shylock's life is in the hands of the Duke. The Duke will not take the option of executing Shylock (he does not need to, Shylock is already destroyed), but does give half his goods to Antonio and accepts on the State's behalf the other half, with the hint that it may be ameliorated into a fine if Shylock is humble enough. Antonio is asked by Portia, 'What mercy can you render him, Antonio?' (IV,i,374) and Antonio places the *cost* of being merciful on the State. He requires the State 'To quit the fine for one half of his goods' (IV,i,377) and then asks to have what amounts to an interest-free loan of the half of Shylock's substance to which he is entitled by Portia's judgment. He says:

> I am content, so he will let me have
> The other half in use, to render it
> Upon his death unto the gentleman
> That lately stole his daughter.

(IV,i,378–81)

'Use' here may mean to hold in trust or for Antonio to have benefit of usufruct, but whichever reading of it we take, there is a sinister echo of usury and of emotional prestidigitation. The logic appears impeccable, dominated as it is by Antonio's anima, for Antonio has projected out of himself the domain in which mercy may be operative; it is projected into the State. Instead of it being a function of his inner world, he defends against its absence by retaining the phantasy that he is being merciful within, and we are left with a sense of being cheated, but not quite seeing how it was done. This trickery also defends Antonio against his own greed, which we see earlier in his fastidious objection to lending money for profit. It is a kind of moral reaction formation*.

The two further provisions Antonio makes are similarly bogus. It looks as though he limits Shylock's opportunity for posthumous revenge by way of a will cutting out Lorenzo and Jessica, but what has Shylock left to leave anyone? What motive has Shylock for working as a merchant any more? If all his wealth is for another, it is not within his pathology to build up wealth for them. Antonio's 'provisions' deprive Shylock of control over his future and the distribution of his goods on his death.

The other condition is that Shylock become a Christian. Ignoring the difficulties raised by how conversion is ensured by compulsion (this was within the customs of the time, as in the treatment of Marrano Jews), the more interesting issue is what it is that Antonio intends by this requirement. Is it an inclusive act, showing concern for Shylock's soul, wishing him to be within the Christian communion? (see Hobson, 1972) Nowhere in the play do we see Antonio perform any act which acknowledges the existence or worth of anyone other than himself. Antonio's concern is for vengeance, and in making it a condition that Shylock become a Christian he both robs Shylock of his faith and Shylock's God of his child. Such is Antonio's envy of motherhood. In the same way, we have seen the only attempt the gentile world makes to include Shylock (the dinner party) turned against him as a monstrous parody because it is made the occasion for the theft of Shylock's fortune and the flight of his daughter.

In Antonio's 'judgment' what looks like a caring concern for Jessica and Lorenzo, putative objects of Shylock's continuing hatred, is really an attempt by Antonio to provide himself with a family. He knows no other way of getting one but to buy it. He has failed to secure Bassanio as a son, and now he looks like a father, making a will (with someone else's money) in order to provide for his children after his death. Antonio sees money as supplies and provisions. This is not in the father-mode but in the mother-mode, resting as it does on phantasies of nurture through his own body. Thus Antonio says:

> I once did lend my body for his wealth,
> Which but for him who had your husband's ring
> Had quite miscarried. I dare be bound again,

My soul[4] upon the forfeit, that your lord
Will never more break faith advisedly.

(V,i,249-53)

In Antonio's 'I once did lend my body . . .' we hear the tones of a
mother over her child. I think this is supported by his use of
'miscarried'.

When the 'winners' of the trial return to Belmont, Portia is
introduced to Antonio, who is the man 'To whom I am so infinitely
bound' (V,i,135). She hears what Bassanio says, and yet changes the
'infinitely' to 'much', saying of him to Bassanio, 'You should in all
sense be much bound to him/ For as I hear he was much bound
for you' (V,i,136-7). Play between Nerissa, Gratiano, Portia and
Bassanio about the rings ensues, and in rebuking Bassanio Portia's
words are also aimed at Antonio:

What man is there so much unreasonable,
If you had pleased to have defended it
With any terms of zeal, wanted the modesty
To urge the thing held as a ceremony?

(V,i,203-6)

Antonio's response is typically narcissistic: 'I am th'unhappy
subject of these quarrels' (V,i,238). Antonio proves he does not
understand what is and has been happening by trying to underwrite
Bassanio's promise of faithfulness hereafter with 'I dare be bound
again'. Portia takes her opportunity. She gives Antonio the ring to
hold, and says, 'Then you shall be his surety. Give him this,/ And
bid him keep it better than the other' (V,i,254-5). In this way
Antonio is made a priest officiating at Portia's marriage who
receives the ring only to give it away to the man who will be making
a bond with 'this woman'. Thus he is castrated and presents no
further threat to Portia's and Bassanio's marriage. Portia's action
with the ring makes her, not Antonio, into the 'best man'. Indeed,
I argue later that she is, by far, the best 'man' in the play.

At the beginning of the play Antonio is shown as a man of wealth,
and yet he is also shown as not having enough to meet Bassanio's
needs. At the end he has acquired half of Shylock's wealth (who, in
a sense, does have enough), and his ships have been restored to
him, and yet he still does not *possess* enough. He is unloved

(because he cannot receive love) and impotent (because he cannot receive empowering). Antonio is not rescued, as a son usually is, from over-identification with his mother by a counter-identification with his father. Antonio needs what he appears to be to Bassanio – a father. Among the men in *The Merchant of Venice*, where may Antonio find a father? The obvious person is the Duke, father of the State, but he is both ineffectual and remote. For a while it looks as though Shylock may stand for one, but he is outside and thus not allowed to occupy the place of a father, and he has already repudiated his role as father (to Jessica). It may also be that Antonio is so deeply entrenched in his 'mother' role that Shylock cannot see him as anything other. Certainly Shylock treats him as a mother by his sadistic attempt to cut off Antonio's breast. And Antonio has no chance of developing a relationship with a woman because his identification with women is too strong, and the opportunity to distance himself and to differentiate himself from that identification has not arisen.

In many productions, Antonio is left alone on the stage at the end, just as, in his isolation, he is the sole figure on it at the beginning. I think this pictures the grief always felt to be present in Antonio. His attempt to turn his grief into a grace is a painfully powerful perversion of being receptive, the mark of the feminine.

PORTIA: 'SWEET MADAM'?

We are introduced to Portia in the same terms as we are to Antonio. Both reveal their melancholy in proximal texts with strong parallels, so we are led to assume that there is an important connection between the two of them. Portia says to Nerissa: 'By my troth, Nerissa, my little body is aweary of this great world' (I,ii,1). Nerissa makes her reply against a background of Aristotelian thought. Her aim is to give Portia a different perspective on her problem, to argue that her fortune (not wealth) lies in balance rather than amount. Nerissa says:

> . . . and yet for aught I see, they are as sick that surfeit with too much as they that starve with nothing. It is no mean happiness, therefore, to be

seated in the mean – superfluity comes sooner by white hairs, but
competency lives longer.

(I,ii,4–8)

Unexpectedly, Nerissa replies in terms of *competency*, which
means a capacity to deal with a matter. It derives from two root
words: to strive, and to do so together. It is therefore not far from
the issue of mastery, the degree of skill and ability required to
achieve an end regarded as desirable, yet which is not omnipotent
power. The women in *The Merchant of Venice* struggle, together,
for a way to be properly potent and then to hold a position neither
omnipotent nor impotent. Portia says, rather, 'But the full sum
of me/ Is sum of something' (III,ii,157–8), describing herself
realistically to Bassanio after he has made the correct choice of
casket. But most often for women to be active and potent in
Shakespeare's world requires disguise. This does not rest on stage
convention either alone or centrally, but rather, I think, Shakespeare is being as deeply critical of his own society, albeit in a veiled
way, as he is openly hostile to the values it holds in being
anti-semitic, seeking revenge and keeping slaves.

The potent women must act within and not separately from the
world of men. This kind of play with reality and appearance is made
necessary by the system within which they are forced to operate,
and it affects the quality of the solutions they are able to achieve.
Thus the disarming of Shylock's revenge and envy rests on a
quibble, and is not a real resolution.

In Act V, that most difficult of Shakespearian acts to stage with
any sense of coherence with the rest of the play, the women show
how competency may be achieved. Previously they have had to
resort to the masculine protest*, now they attempt reconciliation
in their true form. It is given to Gratiano to speak the last words of
the play, and perhaps he has learned something from his
adventures, and has realized a different kind of respect: 'I'll fear no
other thing/ So sore as keeping safe Nerissa's ring' (V,i,306–7). It is
not just that he will not expect Nerissa to be unfaithful to him, and
so not have to be wary of another man's 'thing', or penis, nor that
he needs only to satisfy Nerissa physically in order to hold on to
her, but that the union of which the physical union is an inseparable

part is to be cherished and nurtured. This is a contingent resolution, resting on a continuously renewed relationship rather than a bond. A resolution of this sort is not possible in the issue between Shylock and Antonio because they are statically bound to each other. The relationship between the couples in Act V turns on the acceptance of the women's potency within the partnership of marriage. Where marriage was usually seen as a lord/vassal relationship, Portia suggest it is a lord/lady affair. Gratiano is saying that his fear of Nerissa's penis (potency) is as misplaced as Bassanio's bond with Antonio.

But we may see Portia in another light, while retaining the above. She has been described in glowing terms by most commentators; and perhaps the most damning thing said about her is that she fails to welcome Jessica when she arrives with Lorenzo in Belmont. She is the light bearer and the one who pleads for mercy, offering to Shylock the chance to redeem himself by being merciful. In Belmont, Portia's domain, music and harmony flourish. She is properly subservient to her father's will, and places herself in Bassanio's charge. She honours Antonio as Bassanio's friend, and restores everyone's fortune. But we must beware, in a play which has as one of its main themes appearance and reality, not to be deceived by such an appearance.

Portia is not quite any of these things. She destroys Shylock and castrates Antonio. Antonio sees her quite rightly, I think, in terms of the complete Medea myth, while Bassanio sees her only in terms of the golden prize. Medea, betrayed and furious, murders Jason's new wife, the daughter of Creon, and her and Jason's own two sons. In Antonio's eyes, Portia is as destructive and out of control: a description which also applies to his anima. Portia dismisses her suitors callously and depreciatingly. In spite of the way Portia is played in many productions, she is not an including figure, for she excludes from Belmont all except those who are there on her terms alone. More akin to a virago than a welcoming mother, she is aptly set opposite Shylock.

Portia is at first a young woman kept single and powerless by 'the will of a dead father'. In John Barton's 1981 production of *The Merchant of Venice*, Sinead Cusack tried to show how encumbered Portia is by having her take the caskets with her wherever she went, while wearing a coat clearly her recently dead father's (Brockbank, 1985, p. 34). So she was tied by the father's (external) command and by the mourning which came from within herself.

In Portia's and Nerissa's review of the suitors, Portia is contemptuous of all of them, and although this scene is obviously a knock-about comedy, satirizing the national stereotypes, it is more serious too. She cannot find a man among them who will meet her needs to be powerful *and* to be mastered. Thus Portia is prepared to rig the casket test should the sottish nephew of the Duke of Saxony attempt the ordeal, asking Nerissa to

> set a deep glass of Rhenish wine on the contrary casket, for if the devil be within, and that temptation without, I know he will choose it. I will do anything, Nerissa, ere I will be married to a sponge.
>
> (I,ii,78–81)

Thus she removes her destiny from drunken chaos and allows more structured chance its course.

I think there are two ways of understanding the father–caskets–suitors plot of the play. It would be possible to see Portia's father as an invading and intrusive figure, and her refusal of the suitors, both those who choose and those who do not, as a means of disposing of men to whom she refuses to be tied because, in some way, they too are invasive and raping. And yet, she says to Nerissa who suggests an outright rebellion against the terms of her father's will, 'If I live to as old as Sybilla, I will die as chaste as Diana unless I be obtained by the manner of my father's will' (I,ii,87–8). This prefigures Jessica's response to Launcelot Gobbo:

> Alack, what heinous sin is it in me
> To be ashamed to be my father's child!
> But though I am a daughter to his blood
> I am not to his manners.
>
> (II,iii,15–18)

Portia sees herself kin to her father's 'manner', to his method of trying suitors by a kind of projection test [5], thus seeing whether they can distinguish inside from outside, appearance from reality. This aspect of her character shows a second way of understanding this part of the play: Portia's father may have enough faith in his daughter's adult sexuality to know what it wants, and this, combined with his test, will sieve out the unsuitable suitors.

Only Morocco, Arragon and Bassanio take the step of risking the lottery. Morocco, a 'tawny Moor, all in white', begins his florid speech with a key theme: 'Mislike me not for my complexion'; we do not. What is dislikable about Morocco is his swaggering self-regard. His offer – 'And let us make incision for your love' (II,i,6) – brings to mind the blood-bond just sealed in the previous scene, but more than that, I think, it shows Morocco's misunderstanding of love and union. When Morocco contemplates the caskets, he who has said 'Mislike me not for my complexion' mislikes the lead casket; he reads the inscription, and expostulates:

Must give – for what? For lead? Hazard all for lead!
This casket threatens: men that hazard all
Do it in hope of fair advantages.
A golden mind stoops not to show of dross;
I'll then nor give nor hazard aught for lead.

(II,vii,17–21)

The idea that there is no necessary connection or ordinary correspondence between the material of the casket and the contents cannot lodge in Morocco, and I wonder why he has been so insistent, then, on others not judging *him* by his outward appearance. I think it is because he holds knighthood as an unrealized ideal, and is, as yet, unable to inhabit it. He would be a pure warrior, desiring heroic glory, loving knightly philosophy and endeavour, but he lacks experience to ground him in any kind of reality. One of the reasons that Portia rejects him lies, I think, in the idealization of the maiden implicit in the knightly tradition. The valuing of the maidenly aspect of women idealizes the vagina, while the knight idealizes the penis, expressed as his sword and lance. Portia sees the inevitable failure of such narcissism. But Morocco could make no other choice. For what else would he select, other than gold? It expresses his desire to aim for the highest and the best. He is 'rewarded' for choosing the golden casket with a death's head and a scroll which tells him, among other things,

> Had you been as wise as bold,
> Young in limbs, in judgement old,
> Your answer would not have been enscrolled.

(II,vii,70–2)

Despite his youth and ignorance, Morocco has in potential and in his aspirations qualities which Portia desires in a husband. Bassanio's narcissism is not so impenetrable as Morocco's, and so Portia is able to teach him in a way that she cannot teach Morocco.

But what makes Bassanio become capable of fitting with ('suiting')[6] Portia? One reason is suggested in the way Antonio has understood what Bassanio's quest really means even if Bassanio himself does not. If his departure from Antonio is also a breaking of some of the force of the bond between Bassanio and Antonio, Bassanio has then the need and opportunity to revise his ideas. He too begins to know that things are not what they seem, a good preparation for the casket ordeal. Bassanio makes a voyage in order to reach Belmont. Whether this is a symbol of the sea-change that overcomes him, I am not sure. But that he undergoes a transformation is certain. Perhaps a second reason lies in what Portia sees in Bassanio, whom we could describe on previous evidence as a shallow young fop. She says:

> Now he goes
> With no less presence, but with much more love,
> Than young Alcides when he did redeem
> The virgin tribute paid by howling Troy
> To the sea-monster.

(III,ii,53–7)

Portia sees Bassanio, with a properly enlivened Warrior (or knightly) archetype, as desirable. So Portia animates Bassanio with her own potency in the scene where he makes his choice, and she rescues him from Antonio in the final act.

Portia has ordered that music sound as Bassanio makes his choice, ostensibly so that if he loses, he 'may make a swan-like end' but also in order to give more of her clues. The song asks:

> Tell me where is Fancy bred,
> Or in the heart, or in the head?
> How begot, how nourished?

> Reply, reply.
> It is engend'red in the eyes,
> With gazing fed, and Fancy dies
> In the cradle where it lies:
> Let us all ring Fancy's knell.
> I'll begin it. Ding, dong, bell.
>
> (III,ii,63–71)

Fancy may mean a light passing whim of affection, more like a mild
infatuation with someone trivial, or it may mean a mistaken, foolish
calf-love. The question the song raises is how does love begin? Is it
rational or emotional? In a sense, it doesn't matter, because being
'engend'red in the eyes' tells us what we want to know. Eyes are
the first mirror in which we see ourselves, and loving the person
who contains the eyes, we mistake the picture of ourselves for the
person who carries the image. (Hence the necessary primary
narcissism of Shakespeare's Sonnet 4, which has not progressed
beyond the reflection of the self, taking it for a real encounter.)
Fancy, the shallow love, dies when gazing is *fed*, and being fed
requires a giving and receiving. It supposes two parties to the
enterprise; therefore it is not narcissistic.

Bassanio, musing about the choice before him, gives six
examples of the fact that 'the outward shows be least themselves',
from the fields of law, religion, valour, adornment of person or
house, and from travellers' tales. He will not be deceived by
appearance, but will choose what 'moves me more than eloquence'. Once Bassanio has made his choice and opened the casket,
the language still remains within fiscal realms but is transfigured by
the affect. The scroll itself sets the tone:

> If you be well pleased with this,
> And hold your fortune for your bliss,
> Turn to where your lady is,
> And claim her with a loving kiss.
>
> (III,ii,135–8)

Bassanio, understanding that a kiss means both to give and to
receive, says 'I come by note' and requires that Portia should give
him a sign, or else he cannot believe or take his fortune to be real:

So, thrice-fair lady, stand I even so,
As doubtful whether what I see be true
Unless confirmed, signed, ratified by you.

(III,ii,146–8)

Here he uses the language of commercial exchange[7], but it is transformed by the emotion. This is not metaphor alone, but involves a transformation which Shylock, for one, is unable to make. It is the same shift that allows the part to represent the whole, while knowing of the existence of the whole. I suppose it comes close to the sacramental, where symbol is more than emblematic device.[8]

Bassanio reminds us of the blood-bond theme, which could have disappeared in all this ecstasy, when he says: 'Only my blood speaks to you in my veins' (III,ii,176). This is a proper function of blood. Blood is all the wealth Bassanio has, as well as being the means of communicating his passion and affection to Portia, courtesy of Antonio. When Shylock is so desperate to have Antonio's 'blood' we see the travesty and distortion of Bassanio's usage, *and* the tragedy of the play. It is as though Shylock, frustrated and deprived of affection and inclusion, will have that which symbolizes them instead. It is the perverse form of desire. And then, Jessica's speech in Belmont, which may seem strangely placed, makes sense. The full revelation of Shylock's long-standing hatred of Antonio can only now be unveiled, when there is someone to carry its non-perverted form. Now that the real bond of blood is established, Jessica can reveal the depths of Shylock's hatred and distress:

When I was with him, I have heard him swear
To Tubal and to Chus, his countrymen,
That he would rather have Antonio's flesh
Than twenty times the value of the sum
That he did owe him; and I do know, my lord,
If law, authority, and power deny not
It will go hard with poor Antonio.

(III,ii,283–9)

At this point Portia seems not to understand the situation. There seems to be a simple matter of a debt which can be discharged very easily. She leaps into action, instructing that the couples should be married, and then that the men should be off to Venice with the money, galloping cavalry-style to the rescue. It is not possible from the text of the play to tell when Portia conceived her plan to become the lawyer and go to Venice. But although the text is silent, the structure is not. In between Portia sending the men to Antonio's rescue and her conversation with Lorenzo we have the short but vicious scene in which Antonio has been brought by his gaoler to Shylock in order to plead for mercy. If Portia can imaginatively inhabit this aspect of Shylock, she can understand the uselessness of ducats in salving Shylock's desire for the forfeiture of the bond. She has already heard, in Antonio's letter, a tone almost welcoming his defeat by Shylock, and has understood the nature of the bond between Bassanio and Antonio. Note that she makes pleasant comments about Antonio before she has heard the letter, but none follow it.

In the hearing between Shylock and Antonio, Portia as biased judge is necessary to be the warrior-shadow of Antonio, and so spike Shylock's guns by being for him the witch-figure that Antonio has hated from the beginning. She appears to be the messenger of mercy, but in this play which sets things topsy-turvy, she is the bringer of judgment and condemnation. This is why her famous speech about mercy is fraudulent. Her words have the appearance of mercy, but the reality lies in her sadistic desire for revenge. Portia has already given one reason why her speech will fail, saying to Nerissa in the first scene in which we meet them both:

> If it were as easy as to know what were good to do, chapels had been churches, and poor men's cottages princes' palaces. It is a good divine that follows his own instructions; I can easier teach twenty what were good to be done, than be one of the twenty to follow mine own teaching. The brain may devise laws for the blood, but a hot temper leaps o'er a cold decree – such a hare is madness the youth, to skip o'er the meshes of good counsel the cripple. *But this reasoning is not in the fashion to choose me a husband.* O me, the word choose . . .
>
> (I,ii,11–19, my italics)

She is not just saying that we may think of good sentiments and laws for ourselves, but it is another matter to follow them: she asserts that this will not 'choose me a husband', will not fulfil her primary conscious concern. The more she is consciously aware of her desire for a husband, the more her unconscious resentment at her father's envy of her emerging sexuality is activated. To achieve both her conscious and unconscious aims, she acts as the shadow* for the men. For Bassanio she is the heroic knightly rescuer; for Antonio she is the warrior he dare not be with Shylock and Bassanio; for Shylock she is the hysterical animus, the witch, destroying him completely.

For the Duke she is Logos, and here we have the reason why she rejects Arragon, the suitor who chooses the silver casket. Arragon will not 'jump with common spirits' even if this is what he really wants. His system of denial is motivated not by the need to protect himself (he is not mercantile) but by the need to be different, apart and therefore special. It is a form of envy, where the seeming propriety of 'I am special' really means, 'You may not have as well as me'. One reason for thinking Arragon wishes to deny the chance-ridden world is found in his choice of inscription that goes with the silver casket:

> 'Who chooseth me, shall get as much as he deserves.'
> And well said too, for who shall go about
> To cozen Fortune and be honourable
> Without the stamp of merit?
>
> (II,ix,35–8)

To 'cozen' means to claim kindred for advantage, and so by extension, to cheat. Arragon will not cheat Fortune as he supposes others to have done, but will rely on his deserving, rather than insinuating himself into Fortune's 'good books' to gain more than he deserves. He neither understands grace nor can imagine not deserving. His expostulation, 'let none presume/ To wear undeserved dignity' (II,ix,39–40), is addressed to others, but is primarily spoken to himself. As Morocco is the unformed Knight, so is Arragon the unformed Ruler or Prince. Such roles Portia must enact in the absence of these qualities in either Arragon or the Doge if her solution is to be potent. Arragon assumes desert and is rewarded with what is probably his most feared opposite: not so much a low person, but a 'blinking idiot'. Portia bids him farewell with the comment:

> Thus hath the candle singed the moth.
> O, these deliberate fools! When they do choose
> They have the wisdom by their wit to lose.
>
> (II,ix,78–80)

Arragon's name echoes arrogance, and it is this quality that makes him bereft of wisdom, that prime qualification of the prince. As ruler and father of the State, the Duke should have been able to make Portia's intervention unnecessary. But his failure is her opportunity. She enacts Arragon's potential for him. Here her word 'deliberate' refers to those who use reason to settle affairs of the heart. Arragon has worked on an inadequate set of premises and he has neither the courage nor the wisdom necessary to reconstruct them.

Launcelot Gobbo does what the Prince of Arragon speaks out against. He assumes nobility when there are no grounds for it, even though we may see the by-play with his father and '*Master* Launcelot' as the sort of comic routine expected from these sorts of rustic characters as well. It is interesting to note that this is the only example in the play of a father–son relationship. Launcelot says, 'Well, if Fortune be a woman she's a good wench for this gear: Father, come, I'll take my leave of the Jew in the twinkling' (II,ii,138–40). The close association with 'woman' and 'twinkling' may pick up the theme of transformation that Shakespeare is dealing with in Portia. There are two possible Biblical sources of 'twinkling'. One is from the Psalms as written in the *Book of Common Prayer* (the form of the Psalms with which Shakespeare would have been most familiar): 'For his wrath endureth but the twinkling of an eye, and in his pleasure is life: heaviness may endure for a night, but joy cometh in the morning' (Psalm 30: 6). This would fit with the overall scheme of the play. In Act V, Portia returns to Belmont as dawn breaks, and the new day figures the new harmony that is established there, of which Lorenzo and Jessica have just been speaking, and which the music prefigures. The second possibility is to be found in Corinthians:

> Behold I shew you a mystery; we shall not all sleep, but we we all shall be changed. In a moment, in the twinkling of an eye, at the last trump:

for the trumpet shall sound and the dead shall be raised incorruptible
and we shall be changed. (1 Cor. 15: 51–2)

This would take us to the notion of transformation, the dynamic
with which Portia is most concerned in *The Merchant of Venice*.
She is the one who transforms that which is transformable and
destroys that which is not.

SHYLOCK: THE EXCLUDED MIDDLE

The experience of seeing Shylock on stage is a disturbing one.
Perhaps he 'got as much as he deserved', but he is not simply villain
as is, for example, Iago. Shylock persists in our minds with the
irritation of an unresolved but intransigent issue of justice.

The root of the disquiet in *The Merchant of Venice*, so evident,
but so difficult to pin down in a supposed comedy, is that Shylock
is enmeshed by conditions which cannot, by their very nature,
provide for him ways to function as the kind of human being he
wishes to be. He is constrained both from the inside (by his own
character), and from the outside (by his relationship with the other
characters and the Venice they represent). These constraints are
part of his personal pathology and part of a skewed society which
imitates, mirrors and forms his pathology.

Shylock the Jew is not a merchant. How much Shakespeare knew
of the regulations and customs imposed on Jews is not easily
resolved. It is known that Jews were restricted to the trades they
were to follow, and with reference to the financial world they were
the means for Christians to circumvent the Church's uncertain
condemnation of usury. In this way Jews provided an arena for a
perverted form of transformation; it was legitimate for a Christian
enterprise to be financed by Jewish loans, and thus Shylock carries
the disapprobrium of the unacceptable nature of usury, while
enabling commerce. In miniature, this is parallel to the role he
performs in the play, the container for the unacceptable. In
Freudian terms, he represents the denied contents of the Ego. While
Shylock may not have chosen the form of his occupation, he has
chosen the qualities by which he enlivens it, and clearly has thought

about what he does. In the scene when the bond is sealed he offers a justification, typically witty and rabbinic, and points us to Aristotle, who made the distinction between that which organically increases, and therefore is a proper subject of usury, and that which is barren, like gold and silver. Shylock knows that money is not only an inert substance; it is more complex than that, and is capable of a meta-meaning which somehow becomes the equivalent of organic. Thus Shylock says, when asked whether there is a difference between money and animals, 'I cannot tell: I make it breed as fast' (I,iii,88). This is a defensive response to the society which has imprisoned him in a predisposition to anal withholding and impels him to spoil the opportunities there are to live the kind of life he wishes with the gifts he has. When he says to Antonio, 'I would be friends with you and have your love', he is not only, as Bassanio thinks, being the wily money lender, ready to be all things to all would-be debtors, but is speaking one of his truths. Alienated by the society in which he lives, and with no 'loved companion', Shylock's desire to be included is as reciprocally strong as the powers, internal and external, against him joining.

Correspondingly, both Antonio and Shylock operate within the mercantile system, but Shylock is not permitted to participate. In the trial scene, Portia points to the split when she asks, 'Which is the merchant here, and which the Jew?' (IV,i,170), making a separation which is endemic in the society: Shylock cannot be both merchant and Jew. He is granted a place upon the Rialto but he cannot belong.

Mercantilism is a means of protectionism of home trade: in psychodynamic terms I think it is akin to a 'best fit' where a fully mature stance is not possible. Mercantilism depends on a sense of nationalism (as opposed to nationhood), implying a consequent mistrust of others, believing them to be aliens and therefore enemies. It looks like an independent stance, bidding for self-fulfilment, but in the end it is not, because it repudiates a proper interdependence. A system that depends on division of labour, where this is based on more than a practical division of skills and raw materials, turns on a trusting attitude that 'once I have admitted I am not self-sufficient' (essentially a non-narcissistic stance) 'I trust others to supply for me in a non-exploitative way'. If the non-exploitative nature of others (states or individuals) cannot be trusted, then the best that can be achieved is a method of mutual self-interest which threatens damage to the self if conditions change. Mercantilism in England always had enough political and power-based protection from the Crown to identify it with political power, and therefore colonialism. It was not safe to admit need or lack; this was the sure sign of an open market and therefore an arena for exploitation. No country with a growing sense of itself and its worth could afford to make its lacks public. In psychodynamic terms this is like the plight of an individual who finds it hard to admit to need or dependence. Shylock is clearly in need, and his separation is not to be mistaken for independence. It is part of his tragedy that he cannot admit his need without fearing damage, and sustaining actual damage to himself. The Venetians round him, 'gentlemen' that they are, would be wolvish towards him while pretending that there was no conflict between money and love.

By the conventions of the time, any foreigner (and the Jew was the ultimate foreigner) was an outcast before he started. Therefore, whatever wishes he or she had for inclusion in the society, even on Venice's terms, could not be granted. And although mercantilism is inevitably linked with expansion of influence and the gaining of territory, it does not do so in the inclusive mode but in the mode of conquest and colonialism. So Shylock could be present and excluded at the same time. Was any way left then, for Shylock to find a way of belonging and of participation in the collective life? None at all, except that which perpetuated the split, and forced the ghetto to be both the place of residence and the dynamic of the life lived by any Jew.

In Kleinian terms, Shylock lives the 'paranoid–schizoid position'* because of the attitude of individuals and the pressures of society. He shows that he can occupy the more compassionate 'depressive position'* when he is asked why he would enforce the bond, and he replies in a way that shows he knows that the enforcing of the bond would be ridiculous:

> O father Abram, what these Christians are,
> Whose own hard dealings teaches them suspect
> The thoughts of others! Pray you tell me this:

If he should break his day what should I gain
By exaction of the forfeiture?
A pound of man's flesh, taken from a man,
Is not so estimable, profitable neither,
As flesh of muttons, beefs or goats. I say
To buy his favour, I extend this friendship.
If he will take it, so; if not, adieu,
And for my love, I pray you, wrong me not.

(I,iii,153–63)

I think Shylock uses 'buy his favour' and 'profitable neither' because this is the only language he is allowed to use. It is also the only language Antonio understands, but Antonio misses the irony, so typical of Shylock, who coins his humour from despair, like all great comics.

Shylock arrived at this impasse because law is the only mode he is allowed to operate in, and also the only mode he knows how to work, *without making himself too vulnerable to survive*. He is genuinely appalled in the court scene when Bassanio and Gratiano offer the lives of their wives for the rescue of Antonio: 'These be Christian husbands!' Here he sees the perversion of the Christian attitude of surrender and sacrifice.

He has encountered this perversion before, as he makes clear in the 'Hath a Jew not . . .' speech. This is not at all an intercession for tolerance and humanity, but explains that he has learned revenge from Christians, and, given the common humanity between Jew and gentile, if 'a Christian wrong a Jew, what should his suffrance be by Christian example? Why, revenge! The villainy you teach me I will execute, and it will go hard but I will better the instruction' (III,i,54–7). Later he blasts the Christian morality concerning slaves:

You have among you many a purchased slave,
Which, like your asses and your dogs and mules,
You use in abject and in slavish parts
Because you bought them. Shall I say to you,
'Let them be free! Marry them to your heirs!
Why sweat they under burdens? Let their beds
Be made as soft as yours, and let their palates

Be seasoned with such viands'? You will answer
'The slaves are ours.' So do I answer you.

(IV,i,90–8)

And there is no answer, except reformation of morality, which is
too hard for a society rooted too deeply in the comfort and service
given by slaves and servants to be able to countenance change. Here
Shylock understands the limitation of the language of money as the
Venetian society uses that language. Even in Belmont Portia and
Bassanio show how the economics of love should be conducted.
Shylock challenges the roots of a society that works on the basis
that money is the only mode of commerce between its members.
But he is not heard, nor has he the language with which to move
out of his own trap.

There *is* a requirement placed upon Shylock to change, however.
The most obvious example of this is in the demand for the forfeiture
of his bond. The Duke expects him to pity Antonio's losses:

Glancing an eye of pity on his losses
That have of late so huddled on his back,
Enow to press a royal merchant down
And pluck commiseration of his state
From brassy bosoms and rough hearts of flint,
From stubborn Turks, and Tartars never trained
To offices of tender courtesy.
We all expect a gentle answer, Jew.

(IV,i,27–34)

But the Duke's pun on gentle/gentile tells us that in his mind the
split will still exist. Shylock is required to act like a Christian, but
he will never be treated like one as far as acceptance is concerned.

More than that, 'stubborn Turks and Tartars' brings to mind the
Collect for Good Friday:

O Merciful God, who hast made all men, and hatest nothing that thou
hast made, nor wouldest the death of a sinner, but rather that he should
be converted and live; Have mercy on all Jews, Turks, Infidels, and
Hereticks, and take from them all ignorance, hardness of heart, and
contempt of thy Word; and so fetch them home, blessed Lord, to thy
flock, that they may be saved among the remnant of the true Israelites,
and be made one fold under one shepherd, Jesus Christ our Lord. (*Book
of Common Prayer*)

I think this is the clue to a stance Antonio does not dare to inhabit. Were he to believe the first sentence he would, like Shylock, have to abandon the hatred he holds for Shylock, and so would, as Shylock would, lose a part of himself that he cannot conceive of living without. The challenge is too much. To move into believing that he should replace the hatred of Shylock with love and gratitude would be more life-threatening, he believes, than the actual knife that, at this moment, Shylock is whetting on his sole.

Shylock knows the truth of the matter well. He has an example of the impossibility of being accepted by the gentile community in the attitude of Gratiano, who says to him:

> Thou almost mak'st me waver in my faith,
> To hold opinion with Pythagoras,
> That souls of animals infuse themselves
> Into the souls of men: thy currish spirit
> Govern'd a wolf, who hang'd for human slaughter –
> Even from the gallows did his fell soul fleet,
> And whilst thou layest in thy unhallowed dam,
> Infus'd itself in thee: for thy desires
> Are wolvish, bloody, starv'd, and ravenous.
>
> (IV,i,130–8)

But by the time of the trial words are lost on Shylock. He has shown himself a master of them in previous scenes, where he has been story-teller, allusionist and wit. I have explained why I think Portia's speech about mercy to be fraudulent. Yet it does raise an important issue for Shylock: mercy. There are no examples in the play of mercy being extended towards Shylock, and the sheer novelty of Portia's comment has no possibility of touching him:

> . . . consider this:
> That in the course of justice, none of us
> Should see salvation.
>
> (IV,i,194–6)

We may note here the only example in the play of an 'us' which includes Shylock.

Shylock can no more afford to be merciful than Antonio can give up his hatred. He would, then, be like other men, and one of the characteristics of the perversion into which Shylock is bound is the belief that 'I am not as others'. Partly, there is no concept of ordinariness available to Shylock which will preserve his 'special-ness'. Alienated and abandoned, it is no wonder that he projects his pain and loneliness, and then experiences them in a paranoid way once they are external to him.

Perhaps the most crucial scene for Shylock is his encounter with his 'friend' Tubal. Often in danger of conflating Jessica and his riches, he is unable to make the separation between them that he is usually able to do because Tubal plaits the two together too much. Tubal adds a third strand to the rope, Antonio's losses, and Shylock is undone. It is at this point that Shylock calls for an officer to take Antonio in charge, when the chance of repayment is nil. So the pound of flesh takes precedence, and his oral rage* returns. There is the spat-out reply when he is asked what is the good of Antonio's flesh: 'To bait fish withal', which shows he knows that Antonio's flesh will not meet his real needs. Yet Shylock has no alternative but to complete the murderous terms of the bond, for to absolve Antonio would leave Shylock weakened beyond what makes him able to live, his daughter gone, converted, and with her the larger part of his fortune.

Shylock's implacability is explicable within the terms of the understanding of Antonio I have suggested previously. Antonio attempts to relate to Bassanio in a maternal way, and the strength of his bond with Shylock is enough to make Shylock treat Antonio as a mother figure, and thus to direct his oral rage at 'her'. Antonio has demonstrated his continuing hatred of Shylock often enough: 'I am like to call thee so again,/ To spit on thee again, to spurn thee too' (I,iii,122–3). In the face of Antonio's stance towards him, Shylock's oral sadistic rage is directed towards the appropriate part, Antonio's breast. I think that Shylock cannot be merciful, not only because it will fatally weaken him, but because there is no hope of payment (money) that stands in for the gratitude Shylock should receive from Antonio, but knows will not be forthcoming. Shylock says in the scene with the Gaoler: 'Thou call'st me dog before thou hadst a cause,/ But since I am a dog, beware my fangs' (III,iii,6–7). His rage is expressed in the tearing and biting of which fangs are capable, and Antonio is right to fear for his life. For had Portia not been able to find a way of making his rage so evidently self-destructive, costing his own life too, Shylock would have consummated the bond. And 'consummated' is not an overstatement: it is the only kind of union left to Shylock.

Yet Shylock resembles Antonio in his hostility to a marriage and would have prevented Jessica from marrying Lorenzo had he any say in the matter: 'Would any stock of Barabas/ Had been her husband, rather than a Christian!' (IV,i,292–3) I think Shylock's hostility results from the fact that he is a widower, and so has no woman to carry his hysterically-prone anima. Before her elopement Shylock looked to Jessica to act as the carrier of his threatening, uncontrolled anima and therefore, in his phantasy, as his wife. This use to which he puts Jessica within himself, were she to collude with it, threatens *her* life as surely as Shylock threatens Antonio. One of the most poignant moments in the play is in the scene with Tubal when Shylock discovers the profligacy of Jessica and Lorenzo. His cry that he would not have given his turquoise 'for a wilderness of monkeys' cuts into the audience, and rings oddly, for while it encapsulates Shylock's pain, it does not give a coherent picture of Jessica who is not just a thief. It is not that she despises the value Shylock places on the ring, but that she *cannot* share it and survive. By giving the ring away lightly and not valuing it she repudiates the role she was required to play for him. Jessica's salvation inevitably implies also her father's loss, but the pain of Shylock's unmet needs sears through the audience.

Who is there to meet Shylock's need? Leah is dead and Portia cannot fulfil this function for him. Portia's requirement that he 'marries' mercy with his desire for revenge may provide him with a solution. But there is an insurmountable obstacle to this union.

For Shylock, to receive mercy would be too dangerous. It would involve gratitude towards the person being merciful, and so it would bring with it all the (thus far projected) desires with their attendant yearning,[9] which, in Shylock's case, had no chance of being met. This unrequited need, known and experienced, threatens Shylock's life as surely as the sentence Portia pronounces. Thus when he says, in response to Portia's judgment, 'I am content', it is a mocking, harsh and ironic version of his bereft state, compared to his desire.

Shylock has a framework, given by tradition and others, within which to live and, as long as he stays within that 'ghetto', he survives, and finds a way of (making a) living. But at the junction of the world of the given and the world which is out of his control, problems occur. Some of the trouble is not of his making. He has a fierce yearning to be included in an entire world, not one split into Ghetto and Venice, but to do so means for him, as it does for Antonio, abandoning the known for the seemingly unreliable and the unknown, where invention and inspection have to take the place of commandment. Thus it would require him to make real use of his masculine aspects, and in doing so would require him to question the power he gives to his anima, a power strengthened by the absence of Leah and compounded by his substitution of his daughter for his wife. The mysterious sympathy Shylock often evokes in audiences is rooted in the fact that he is the carrier of many of the split-off and denied parts of the other characters (and of course, of ourselves) and this too underlies our acknow-ledgement of him as tragic rather than merely malevolent.

Again, the interplay between the outside (Venice) and the inside (Shylock's psyche) is set in the context of reality and appearance. Stuck in a projection-dominated framework, which, by its very nature, makes distinguishing inside from outside impossible, how can either Shylock or Venice change? I think the answer to this lies in the model offered by Jessica. It is tempting to see Jessica's elopement and Portia's submission to her father's bond as two qualitatively different means of solving the same problem, as many have. Jessica, it is argued, makes a mockery of the casket test by throwing a casket to Lorenzo. He has no test to pass as Bassanio does, so his acquisitions are fraudulent, and their relationship needs as much redeeming as do the others in the play. I am sure this is not so. The contrast is not between the caskets, or the rings, but between the methods by which Portia, Jessica and Lorenzo make themselves powerful in a world which would, unchallenged, leave them without a means of impinging upon it. Lorenzo has already passed the appearance/reality or outside/inside test. He has seen beyond the cultural, religious, psychological and family ties that would make Jessica impossible to contemplate, and he has recognized there is no kinship between Jessica and Shylock beyond the most sterile and trivial. Jessica frees herself from the world of her father's projections and imaginings. She says:

> But though I am daughter to his blood
> I am not to his manners. O Lorenzo,
> If thou keep thy promise, I shall end this strife,
> Become a Christian and thy loving wife.
>
> (II,iii,17–20)

She has to escape because there is no collaborative way to find, with her father, her own life and its fulfilment. And she, too, uses disguise as the means of making her escape certain. Jessica experiences the shame of her disguise more than Portia does. I think this is because she feels the sadness that comes because such a counterfeit measure must be adopted. Shylock does not have room in his thought-world for friendship, even, between Jessica and Lorenzo, although such a friendship between himself and Antonio is one of *his* deepest desires. Thus Shylock has no alternative but, in phantasy, to kill off Jessica. Jewish tradition demanded that he regard her as dead, but he does not need tradition to tell him what to do; it comes from the heart of him. Solanio reports the stricken cries of Shylock:

> I have never heard a passion so confused,
> So strange, outrageous, and so variable,
> As the dog Jew did utter in the streets:
> 'My daughter! O my ducats! O my daughter!
> Fled with a Christian! O my Christian ducats!
> Justice! The law! My ducats and my daughter!
> A sealed bag, two sealed bags of ducats,
> Of double ducats, stolen from me by my daughter!
> And jewels – two stones, two rich and precious stones,
> Stolen by my daughter! Justice! Find the girl!
> She hath the stones upon her and the ducats!'
>
> (II,viii,12–22)

It is this 'passion so confused' which prevents Shylock from having a relationship with his daughter which would have made the means of her escape unnecessary.

Thus Jessica faces a choice: apparent loyalty and soul-death, or apparent treachery and life. So she too has her equivalent of the casket test, a test of projections. Staying within her father's standpoint, she would have to assume guilt along with her escape. Only by abandoning that standpoint, and living within her own, may she have life, and experience not guilt, but sadness. In contrast, Portia takes another path in dealing with her father: that of destructive revenge, with the ill-founded hope of finding satisfaction that way. Unless Bassanio inhabits his knightly role, she will destroy him too.

By asking who Shylock's heroes are, we may know more about the Shylock who wishes to emerge but who fails to do so, for they will also be his ego-ideals*. His major references are to Jacob, a sharp-dealing patriarch whose life was transformed by the wrestling match at the ford Jabbok (which means emptiness). Before Jacob is able to be reconciled with his brother, he is confronted with the Almighty. Jacob's omnipotence is broken (the dislocation of his hip), and he is able, then, to be blessed and renamed Israel. Shylock stands in need of the reconciliation with his 'brother' Antonio, and it is both with the Almighty (omnipotence within) that he wrestles, and with the external, corrupt society which while advocating mercy shows him none. He is forced to live by a legal system which guarantees his safety but which does not meet the requirements of his heart. There is no place for mercy, and none for charity. Worse still there is no room for grace in individuals or in their society.

It is left to the clowns to point ironically to the truth of Shylock's poverty of grace. Launcelot says, 'The old proverb is very well parted between my master Shylock and you, sir: you have the grace of God, sir, and he hath enough' (II,ii,124–6). Onlookers know that Bassanio is granted grace, not by God but by Portia, who has given him enough clues to solve the casket riddle. The gift is in herself, which he accepts and is thus enlivened by her animus.

The final act would seem the obvious place to look for grace. In Portia's Belmont, music rules the house, and harmonies are the order of the day – and of the night. But even here there is exclusion. Shylock is absent, and Antonio, although present, is not within one of the couples. Lorenzo unconsciously speaks the truth in this scene when he and Jessica antiphonally speak of the wonders of the night and of figures in *The Legend of Good Women*, and then praise the heavenly harmonies:

Such harmony is in immortal souls
But whilst this muddy vesture of decay
Doth grossly close it in, we cannot hear it.

(V,i,63–5)

The examples Jessica and Lorenzo use are all of lovers divided from each other, and of unconsummated union. Given this speech, why is Lorenzo not as melancholy as Antonio? If it is true that we are prevented by 'this muddy vesture of decay' from hearing the music which would enrich and transform us, what hope is there? Lorenzo tells us, I think, by using the phrase 'close it in' when we expect 'close it *out*'. He avoids the trap of making a split between transcendence and immanence.[10] Both Shylock and Antonio grossly close harmony in: the one in outrageous behaviour, and the other in fastidious refinement. Excluded Shylock longs for union. He hates the 'unthrift' of his daughter's love, but this is the only way for love to thrive. Shylock's only hope is to brave the non-narcissistic stance. To do so requires an attitude of faith in the world for which he has no model and no justification for taking as true.

But the Jacob-narrative is about transformation, and Shylock needs such an experience. Portia is the means by which other characters are transformed, so why does she fail Shylock? I think she fails him because she is too much like him. She too wields a knife. She splits Antonio from Bassanio by the cutting edge of her wit and intellect, and she out-bids Antonio at every point. She impales Shylock on his own envy, and by so doing destroys him. There is no possibility of transformation because there is no place either in the collection of characters or in the society to hold him, and to allow him to thrive. Thus he is a victim, made a sacrifice by Portia, so that she may play out her transference* revenge towards her father on Shylock. For him alone her penis is barbed, as she inhabits the destructive paranoid projections Shylock places on to her.

When Shylock begins the Jacob analogy, he notes, perhaps rather wistfully, that 'his wise mother wrought in his behalf'. Were Shylock to have had such a mother, things may have gone very differently. Certainly Portia cannot be this for him, and Antonio, for all his maternal leanings, is not wise, nor will he do anything on

Shylock's behalf. Perhaps the person who comes closest (albeit in a perverse way) to producing potency in Shylock is Tubal. When Shylock says to Tubal, 'Thou stick'st a dagger in me', he is right, for Tubal's intervention forces Shylock into feeing an officer, and this is a mocking and perverted form of potency.

I have called Shylock 'the excluded middle', an image borrowed from some formulations of classical logic. The Law of the Excluded Middle states that either p is true or p is not true and I suggest that a possible solution to the Shylock 'problem' lies here. The axiom is usually sound, but leaves problems in the areas of future events, of category confusions, and, most importantly, of change and transformation. If Shylock has but one way to escape from his narcissism, that of believing that the world will receive him, then he has no method of knowing whether this belief is true (nor does any one else), and so 'either p or not-p' cannot be tested, except in the execution of a projective faith for which he has no grounds and no experience. It is as much a condemnation of Venetian society as of his pathology that he is so bereft.

I think that Shylock, for all his envy and hatred, attempts to find an ethical way of being. His essays at adulthood are rebuffed and his morals mocked. He is head and shoulders above the rest of the characters, and heroic in his attempts to join with Venice and to strive for a meaning commensurate with his instinctual sensing of society's form and existence. In this sense, Shylock may have a kind of projective faith, but he is blocked by pathology and people from its flowering.

This is, in my view, one of the reasons why our experience of the play leaves us disturbed and feeling all is not well, despite the harmonies of the final act. Shylock makes a plea for a kind of plurality to exist in Venice in which he can thrive without recourse to envious reprisals and implacable hatred. Hatred is love without an outlet; either the object of the love will not receive it, or the lover cannot forgive wrongs. To acknowledge the existence of the other is perforce to move from a narcissistic position. Were Shylock to do so, he would be overwhelmed by the yearning for inclusion, which Venice is not ready to offer. I sometimes wonder if we do any better, either as individuals or as a community.

GLOSSARY

Anal stage: descriptive of a physiological preoccupation in an infant's development which, by analogy, is a stage of ego-development characterized by striving for control and mastery and concerned with creativity. It has both positive and negative aspects.

Anima: in Jungian psychology the female aspect of the male. This is determined in two ways: by experience through upbringing by specific women, and the consequent internalization of such figures and their characteristics; and through an archetype* which needs 'enlivening', by which I mean identifying those qualities in another, then recognizing them as part of the self and owning them as such.

Archetype: a Jungian term meaning patterns of instinctual behaviour, inaccessible to conscious experience except in a symbolic and personified form. For example, the instinct to mother and be mothered are both aspects of the Mother Archetype. Behaviour governed by archetypes is driven and compulsive in character, and out of touch with reality.

Denial: an unconscious, defensive activity which keeps unacceptably painful experiences out of consciousness. It is also applied to the rebuttal of aspects of the self which are equally unacceptable, but are not necessarily pernicious. Antonio has a great investment in keeping the reality of his relationship with Bassanio and his attitude towards money separated (one he appears to value above life, the other he treats as unimportant). Their similarity is masked from him by a process of denial.

Depressive position (see also **Paranoid-schizoid position**): Klein's view that in successful development the infant negotiates the paranoid-schizoid position by a growing understanding that the previously split object is, in fact, one. The hostility perceived as coming from the object is acknowledged as being of a personal origin, and this leads to depressive anxiety which is ameliorated by reparation, gratitude and a sense of the fruitlessness of revenge. It implies that ambivalence is present.

Ego-ideal: in contradistinction to the super-ego. A positive and aspiring component of the ego recognized in others to have reached fruition, and taken by the individual as a loved model. Whereas conflict with the super-ego produces guilt, conflict with the ego-ideal results in shame.

Masculine protest: a social–psychological Adlerian term which describes a way in which some women choose to overcome attitudes in others and themselves which assume women to be inferior to men by imitating and over-valuing traditionally 'masculine' behaviour. It may be argued that Portia and Nerissa do not use the masculine protest because they knowingly employ the device of disguise, but Jessica's case is not so clear, as her discomfort shows.

Narcissism: a normal state for a young infant who has not developed the concept of others, despite experience. When it persists in humans it is usually a defence against the terror of not having one's needs met – against greed and gratitude.

Oral rage: from the stage of physical and emotional development when oral experiences are the main or only source of contact. Oral rage is expressed through biting and tearing and accompanied by phantasies of destroying the other by these means.

Paranoid–schizoid position: a term used by Melanie Klein to describe a normal stage of infantile development which defends the ego against unpleasant and threatening emotions and experiences by attributing the 'good' to one object and the 'bad' to another, although the proper origin of both kinds of experience is one and the same object, either the self or the breast or both in union. She uses the term 'position' to emphasise the fluidity of the stance and the contingent nature of the dynamic. It is not a stage in the Freudian sense. It is paranoid in that unacceptable feelings are projected out of the self and then are experienced as hostile towards the self, and schizoid because it rests on splitting the whole object into parts.

Projection: an unconscious mechanism by which unacceptable emotions and motives are hurled into another and perceived as originating from that person.

Projective identification: a Kleinian term, originally (1946, pp. 182–4) in only an aggressive form, where parts of the infant's ego are 'projected' into (usually) the mother in order to rob or control the contents. An extension of this idea (for example, in W. R. Bion (1957)) includes a benign form of projection which leads to empathy and is a primitive form of communication.

Reaction formation: part of the repertoire of the unconscious, obsessional defences. The original impulse (such as greed) is mastered and disguised by an exaggerated form of the opposite (such as generosity).

Reparative act: reparation is consequent upon an acknowledgement of destructive impulses, regret and a belief that the harm done is not irreversible because the infant is good enough to be able to repair the phantasied damage from his own sources of goodness. It is rooted in compassion and Winnicott's idea of 'ruthfulness'.

Shadow: a Jungian term often mistaken for the 'bad' parts of the self. It is better thought of as that which is unacceptable to the conscious and cannot be lived. 'The unfulfilled desires of the virtuous are evil; the unfulfilled desires of the vicious are good,' aptly remarked Edwin Muir. For Bassanio, the concept of 'blood' contains ideas of nobility, wealth and his own life-spring which is properly possessed. The shadow of his conscious attitude is to be found in Shylock's revengeful desire for blood to deprive Antonio of life.

Transference: an unconscious process of displacement from a figure from the past on to a figure in current life. It is swift and unjust, although in normal neurotic behaviour there are enough 'hooks' for it to not to disregard reality entirely. Portia displaces her desire for revenge on her father on to Shylock. One of the characteristics of transference activity is that it does not satisfy the original impulse, but only placates it. This is why I say that Bassanio also stands in danger of being destroyed.

NOTES

1. Mercantilism arose from: 1) a growing sense of national identity where attachment which derived from status or occupation was replaced by attachment to the nation state; 2) the consequence of national awareness, which was a mistrust of the 'other' where hostility was presumed rather than friendship, even though Western Europe was theoretically joined by virtue of the Christian faith; 3) a need to ensure power over the other, which led to a kind of colonialism. Merchants had erstwhile been members of a 'gentleman's club' where commerce between them turned on trust and their bond, but with the shift to the primacy of the interests of the state, where self-sufficiency is the aim, international co-operation and interdependence are replaced by an exchange system designed to preserve the state. In terms of the individual psyche, this is like a retreat to narcissism when not enough bonding has been established, or when fear of possible bonding becomes too great.

2. The irony here is poignant: she *is* the judge.

3. As the scene with Tubal is Shylock's turning point, so, for Portia, is Antonio's letter to Bassanio, I believe.

4. I think that Antonio's move from 'body' to 'soul' evokes both Faust and the Medea legend. Antonio's view of Portia is that she is both the Devil and a murderous enchantress. The Medea theme is clear from the Jason allusions surrounding Bassanio's quest, and the Faust stories were available in English in 1592. (See my section 'Portia: "sweet madam"?')

5. Perhaps part of the requirement made by Portia's father was that the prospective suitors know themselves well enough to be able to 'see' Portia without the intrusion of their own projections.

6. This is not only a shallow pun. The interesting range of meanings of 'to sue' include to follow, to beseech and to prosecute. To 'make suit' means to try your luck with a lady, and also to match.

7. Bassanio has described Portia to Antonio in terms of commerce and gain. I think he does so, in part, to defend himself against Antonio's envy and misplaced affections, and also because, for all his fine words, it is the only language Antonio understands (cf. I,i,160ff). Gratiano retains the same mode in III,ii,240.

8. See Klein (1929, 1930, 1931, 1935) on the aetiology of symbol formation and part and whole object relationships. In Klein's view, the move from part-object relationships is defended against as it brings the person to know his or her ambivalent feelings about the whole object,

and to understand the sadistic and unjust relationship with it. Achieving the depressive position is what Shylock strives towards, although he is blocked by society, and what Antonio flies from, lest he know his own savagery, which he believes to be without possibility of reparation.

9. I see yearning and longing as a gratitude-based state, having faith as its dynamic. Here faith is in the form of projective identification. The appeal is made to the outside world that needs be met simply on the grounds that the needs exist and their satisfaction is somehow due. This yearning may be frightened or blocked by not getting what is due, and then it becomes envy and shifts into phantasies of control and, eventually, destructiveness. Shylock has human needs which are not met and he is unable to find nourishment and acceptance; therefore he has no alternative to an envious state and so becomes sadistic towards Antonio; and both are bound together in a destructive course from which neither may profit.

10. The inside/outside problem, which theology states in the form of the simultaneous transcendence and immanence of God is essentially a narcissistic problem. Narcissus was unable to find a bridge between the inside and outside worlds, and so is trapped in his inner world, only able to regard himself. Narcissus says, 'My very plenty makes me poor', to which idea Lorenzo alludes, I think, in the words 'doth grossly close it in'. There needs to be transaction and commerce between the inside and outside worlds (Ovid, *Metamorphoses*, iii and Graves, vol. 1, p. 126). See note 9 above for a parallel shift in the nature of Nemesis.

5 SOILED MOTHER OR SOUL OF WOMAN?: A RESPONSE TO *TROILUS AND CRESSIDA*

ANGELA SHEPPARD

> Only the poet can make a whole picture of the unity of joy and sorrow, departure from self and absorption in self, devotion and self-assertion.
>
> Lou Andreas-Salomé, 'The dual orientation of narcissism'

Following the 1987 production in Stratford, Ontario of Shakespeare's *Troilus and Cressida* I became aware that my response to Cressida was different from that of others and I was curious to discover what might be learned from these varying reactions through the use of psychoanalytic tools.

Here is a brief summary of the play, and excerpts of passages relevant to my discussion. The beautiful Helen has been abducted from her Greek husband Menelaus by the Trojan, Paris, and the resulting war has reached a stalemate after seven years. Troy is under siege. The Trojan leaders dispute the value of continuing the war merely for the sake of Helen. The greatest Trojan warrior, Hector, declares her not worth the lives she costs, but abandons this argument to support his brother Troilus' view that 'manhood and honour' demand they continue to fight for her. In the course of his argument that persuades Hector, Troilus says, 'Reason and respect/ Make livers pale and lustihood deject' (II,ii,49–50); there is a parallel between this idealization of honour and his later devaluation of Cressida when she rejects the conventions of courtly love.

All Shakespeare citations are from *The Complete Works*, Peter Alexander, ed., London: Collins, 1961.

Against this background Troilus has fallen in love with Cressida. Her father is Calchas, a Trojan defector to Greece, and her mother is never mentioned in the play. Her uncle Pandarus helps in the successful wooing, but Cressida, despite her desperate protests, is sent to join her father in the Greek camp in exchange for Antenor, an important Trojan held by the Greeks. She is put in the charge of the commander Diomedes who brings her to the general and his other commanders. Cressida meets their sexual banter and flirtatious kisses with playful wit. After she leaves the older commander, Nestor says she is 'A woman of quick sense' (IV,v,54), but Ulysses disagrees:

> Fie, fie upon her!
> There's language in her eye, her cheek, her lip,
> Nay, her foot speaks; her wanton spirits look out
> At every joint and motive of her body.
> O these encounterers so glib of tongue
> That give a coasting welcome ere it comes,
> And wide unclasp the tables of their thoughts
> To every ticklish reader! Set them down
> For sluttish spoils of opportunity,
> And daughters of the game.
>
> (IV,v,54–63)

Ulysses then brings Troilus to see what passes between Diomedes and Cressida, and he comments on the scene for Troilus: 'She will sing any man at first sight' (V,ii,9).

I will now 'dispresent', rather than mispresent, the dialogue between Cressida and Diomedes, omitting the frequent comments of the three eavesdropping characters, present to Shakespeare's audience, but not to the two participants. My purpose is to separate their actual encounter from the varied reactions to it in this doubly theatrical scene. The dialogue (with ellipses indicating the omitted commentary) begins thus:

> *Dio.*   How now, my charge!
> *Cres.*   Now, my sweet guardian! Hark, a word with you . . .
> *Dio.*   Will you remember?
> *Cres.*   Remember? Yes.
> *Dio.*   Nay, but do, then;
> And let your mind be coupled with your words . . .

Cres.   Sweet honey Greek, tempt me no more to folly . . .
Dio.   Nay, then –
Cres.   I'll tell you what –
Dio.   Fo, fo! come, tell a pin; you are a forsworn –
Cres.   In faith, I cannot. What would you have me do? . . .
Dio.   What did you swear you would bestow on me?
Cres.   I prithee, do not hold me to mine oath;
Bid me do anything but that, sweet Greek.

                                                        (V,ii,7–27)

Already there is a sense of Cressida trying to be friendly but asking Diomedes to leave her alone sexually. It is impressive that Diomedes is not forcing her, as she is 'his' to do with as he wishes, which she knows too. She seems earnest and afraid, not teasing. The dialogue continues:

Dio.   Good night . . .
Cres.   Diomed!
Dio.   No, no, good night; I'll be your fool no more . . .
Cres.   Hark! a word in your ear . . .
Dio.   And so good night.
Cres.   Nay but you part in anger . . .
Cres.   Guardian! Why, Greek!
Dio.   Fo, fo! adieu! you palter.
Cres.   In faith, I do not. Come hither once again . . .
Dio.   But will you, then?
Cres.   In faith, I will, lo; never trust me else.
Dio.   Give me some token for the surety of it.
Cres.   I'll fetch you one . . .
Cres.   Here, Diomed, keep this sleeve . . .
Cres.   You look upon that sleeve; behold it well.
He loved me – O false wench! – Give't me again.
Dio.   Whose was't?
Cres.   It is no matter, now I ha't again.
I will not meet with you to-morrow night.
I prithee, Diomed, visit me no more . . .
Dio.   I shall have it.
Cres.   What, this?
Dio.   Ay, that.
Cres.   O all you gods! O pretty, pretty pledge!
Thy master now lies thinking on his bed
Of thee and me, and sighs, and takes my glove,

And gives memorial dainty kisses to it,
As I kiss thee. Nay, do not snatch it from me;
He that takes that doth take my heart withal.
Dio.   I had your heart before; this follows it . . .
Cres.   You shall not have it, Diomed; faith, you shall not;
I'll give you something else.

(V,ii,28–85)

Cressida is in an agony of uncertainty as how best to proceed and
keep her captor a friend, without agreeing to sex. She gives the
sleeve, token of her love with Troilus, to appease Diomedes, to hold
him off with promises of future sex, but then cannot go through
with this, calls herself a 'false wench', and takes the sleeve back.
There is even a sense of her trying to share her loss as one would
with a friend (as if to say, 'Look at this sleeve! He really loved me!').
They continue:

Dio.   I will have this. Whose was it?
Cres.   It is no matter.
Dio.   Come, tell me whose it was.
Cres.   'Twas one's that lov'd me better than you will.
But, now you have it, take it.
Dio.   Whose was it?
Cres.   By all Diana's waiting women yond,
And by herself, I will not tell you whose.
Dio.   Tomorrow will I wear it on my helm,
And grieve his spirit that dares not challenge it . . .
Cres.   Well, well, 'tis done, 'tis past; and yet it is not;
I will not keep my word.
Dio.   Why, then farewell;
Thou never shalt mock Diomed again.
Cres.   You shall not go. One cannot speak a word
But it straight starts you.

(V,ii,86–99)

She is telling Diomedes that she does not intend to mock him. She
is seeking a way to hold onto her love for Troilus and somehow
keep her word that she would never be false to him, while still
relating to Diomedes. They continue:

Dio.	I do not like this fooling . . .
Dio.	What, shall I come? The hour –
Cres.	Ay, come – O Jove! do come. I shall be plagu'd.
Dio.	Farewell till then.
Cres.	Good night. I prithee come.

(V,ii,100–4)

Diomedes exits and then comes her final speech, about women:

> Troilus, farewell! One eye yet looks on thee;
> But with my heart the other eye does see.
> Ah, poor our sex! this fault in us I find,
> The error of our eye directs our mind.
> What error leads must err; O, then conclude,
> Minds sway'd by eyes are full of turpitude.

(V,ii,105–10)

Troilus, who has been one of the eavesdroppers, is overwhelmed, and tries denial:

> Was Cressid here? . . .
> She was not, sure . . .
> Let it not be believ'd for womanhood.
> Think, we had mothers; do not give advantage
> To stubborn critics, apt, without a theme,
> For depravation, to square the general sex
> By Cressid's rule. Rather think this not Cressid.

(V,ii,123–31)

Ulysses, another overhearer, is puzzled by these remarks and asks what this all has to do with mothers: 'What has she done, Prince, that can soil our mothers?' (V,ii,132) Troilus replies: 'Nothing at all, unless that this were she' (V,ii,133).

Then follows Troilus' speech telling of his agony and confusion; in analytic terminology we would say he is not able to maintain a split between the good, loving, faithful Cressida, and 'Diomed's Cressida'. He is unable to use successfully the defence of keeping versions of perfectly good and totally bad apart in order to avoid the painful disillusionment of a realistic human mixture.

> This she? No; this is Diomed's Cressida.
> If beauty has a soul, this is not she;
> If souls guide vows, if vows be sanctimonies,

If sanctimony be the gods' delight,
If there be rule in unity itself,
This was not she. O madness of discourse,
That cause sets up with and against itself!
Bifold authority! where reason can revolt
Without perdition, and loss assume all reason
Without revolt: this is, and is not, Cressid.
Within my soul there doth conduce a fight
Of this strange nature, that a thing inseparate
Divides more wider than the sky and earth;
And yet the spacious breadth of this division
Admits no orifex for a point as subtle
As Ariachne's broken woof to enter.

(V,ii,135–50)

Not even the finest strand of a spider's web can fit between the two Cressidas. So he concludes:

Instance, O instance! strong as Pluto's gates:
Cressid is mine, tied with the bonds of heaven.
Instance, O instance! strong as heaven itself:
The bonds of heaven are slipp'd, dissolv'd, and loos'd;
And with another knot, five-fingered-tied,
The fractions of her faith, orts of her love,
The fragments, scraps, the bits, and greasy relics
Of her o'er-eaten faith, are bound to Diomed.

(V,ii,151–8)

Diomedes can have her! She is totally devalued and hence is no loss. We hear no more of Cressida. The story finishes the next day as Hector goes into battle where he is treacherously murdered by Achilles. With Troy's fall certain, Troilus assumes Hector's role as the leading Trojan champion.

Now let us listen to the 'audience' of critics who have given Cressida such bad press.

Stephen Reid, in one of the rare psychoanalytic papers on this play, writes of the 'speed and ease' with which Cressida accepts Diomedes (1970, p. 266).

Fritz Wittels gives Shakespeare's Cressida (along with Delilah, Helen of Troy, Cleopatra, Lucrezia Borgia, and Brunhild) as an example of the woman of destructive beauty, the narcissistic woman who cannot turn her love to objects outside herself: 'They conquer – they cannot be conquered; they possess – they cannot be possessed' (quoted in Holland, 1966, p. 277). Judith Cook in her book *Women in Shakespeare* feels that Cressida's act of 'betrayal' reflects that of Shakespeare's Dark Lady, and that the play was written following a period of bitterness and disillusionment. She quotes Jan Kott:

> Cressida . . . has many aspects and cannot be defined by a single formula . . . She is inwardly free, conscious and daring . . . She is cynical or rather would-be cynical. She has seen too much. She is bitter and ironic. She is passionate, afraid of her passion, and ashamed to admit it. She is even more afraid of feelings. She distrusts herself. She is our contemporary because of this self-distrust, reserve, and need of self-analysis. She defends herself by irony . . . there is no place for love in this world . . . she already knows that she will become a tart. Only before that happens she has to destroy everything so that not even memory remains. (In Cook, 1980, p. 118)

Then she reminds us that Shakespeare has Cressida write to Troilus but he tears the letter up unopened (as against Chaucer's version of the story, in which he reads it).

Muriel Bradbrook describes the 'quicksands of Cressid's faith' and her 'maudlin tears' in the scene with Diomedes. She writes:

> . . . the suddenness and completeness of this metamorphosis destroys more than the image of Cressid; it destroys [Troilus'] whole world. Chaos is come again . . . If beauty have a soul – if the outward and the inward ever correspond to each other – this is not she; the existence of truth, of the womanhood that was in our mothers, of sanctimony itself is questioned. (1984, p. 107)

The literary consultant to the BBC/PBS Shakespeare Productions, John Wilders, seems more ambivalent in his evaluation of Cressida:

> Her infidelity is, considering her shallowness and the circumstances in which she finds herself, entirely understandable. She is a victim of international diplomacy, powerless to prevent herself from being snatched away after her one night with Troilus, a vulnerable girl alone in an enemy camp, flattered by the attentions of the strong man, Diomedes, needing his protection, and as instinctively responsive to his

sexual advances as she had been to those of Troilus. When she commits herself to becoming Diomedes' mistress, she does so not without a last thought for her former lover and a twinge of guilt . . . She fails partly because she has no confidence in her strength to be constant . . . Her betrayal creates a shock to Troilus' youthful idealism from which he never recovers. Unable to believe that she was unworthy of his love, or to understand that circumstances have changed and that she has adapted herself to circumstances, he finds relief for his pain only in revenge, and he plunges into battle determined to destroy his rival. (1988, pp. 179–80)

In using the words 'shallowness' and 'fails' Wilders is closer to agreeing with Troilus that Cressida is 'unworthy of love' than believing in his own idea that she is 'vulnerable', a true 'victim' (she has not masochistically engineered the situation) who has 'adapted herself to circumstances'. The first is a moralistic super-ego judgement while the second is a realistic ego judgement. This distinction, and the underlying ambivalence towards Cressida which blurs it, is central to the question of women's strength and the female ego-ideal.

Northrop Frye in *The Myth of Deliverance* says she is a 'slithery deserter', but makes room for an alternative response:

When Shakespeare's Cressida deserts Troilus for a Greek lover, she is being very sensible in a way: the fate of captive women in a conquered city will not be hers. But few audiences would find her slithery survival tactics as appealing as the desperate fidelity of Juliet. (1983, p. 42)

Why do most audiences find Cressida not just unappealing, but in fact worthy of contempt? I felt there might be some insights gained by comparing different reactions, including my own, and wondering what generated them. Norman Holland in *Psychoanalysis and Shakespeare* holds that the psychoanalytic critic 'finds bedrock' when he deals with the audience's mind, as opposed to Shakespeare's mind or the mind of a fictional character (1966, pp. 309–10).

Overall, the critical reaction to Cressida seems to be one of angry devaluation. Is this because the woman who assertively finds a way to take care of herself arouses envy and/or a sense of abandonment and rejection? Is there a universal fury and fear linked with being left to our own devices by the first and most important woman in our lives, our mother? Are we especially moralistic when we learn that her absence is so that she can enjoy/nurture herself, either with a man or by herself? Our first expectations of women are highly idealized. They are based on the mother we felt was our due, the mother of our childhood who should be available and all-giving, the mother who should never frustrate or humiliate us by introducing life's limits, who should shield us from any sobering inkling of all the resources that have gone into our growth. A more realistic appreciation of mother, and women in general, calls for much disillusionment and mourning both for men finding a mate and for women becoming mates and mothers in their own turn. A more factual sense of women emerges, an awareness that they are not simply mothers, nor are mothers only tender and bountifully nurturant! Do we so insist on the image of woman as self-giving and sacrificing because we won't accept a very different version of a woman's strength? What does a woman look like who is waking up to a need to take care of herself? Has morality for women been defined in terms of taking responsibility for others, giving to others? What happens if a woman starts to take responsibility for herself? Does she become Cressida, rather than Juliet? Will this be seen as hurting others, as rejecting, as selfish? Does the development of self-love mean learning to live with the hate and envy of others?

I am going to try to pursue these questions, and in the process, elaborate some thoughts on the female super-ego and the formation of the female ego-ideal. There is a growing consensus in the psychoanalytic literature on the question of the essence of the female ego-ideal – or the ideal (as opposed to idealized) woman. This emphasizes valuing the awareness of being both separate and connected, and of the constant interplay between these two states of being, and emphasizes the importance of learning to judge which is more crucial and to whom, at any particular moment, and of being able then to make choices (Chodorow, 1978; Gilligan, 1982; Herman, 1989).

In classical Freudian theory, the super-ego is described as the heir of the Oedipus complex in that it is constituted through the internalization of parental prohibitions and demands (Laplanche and Pontalis, 1967, p. 436). The little boy at about the age of five gives up his claim on mother and accepts his ultimate exclusion from the parental couple and their creativity together. Freud felt this is based on the boy's fear of his father; that is, he gives up mother because of castration anxiety. The internalized father's prohibition thus forms the basis of his super-ego. Freud remained puzzled about how this process happens for women, since in his understanding of them they are already castrated. What induces them to give up father, and what kind of super-ego would they be able to form? What is the threat for the little girl? He wrote that the woman's super-ego 'is never so inexorable, so impersonal, so independent of its emotional origins as we require it to be in men' (1925, p. 257).

There is no hard-and-fast meaning for the term ego-ideal in Freud. At times in his writing it appears to be synonymous with the super-ego, whereas in other texts the function of the ideal is assigned to a substructure within the super-ego. Many authors now distinguish between the ego submitting to the super-ego out of fear of punishment, whereas the ego-ideal guides the ego by love. The origin of the super-ego is based on dreaded figures, while the ego-ideal is formed on the model of loved objects (Laplanche and Pontalis, pp. 144–5).

André Lussier has spoken of the ego-ideal as structurally differentiated from the super-ego, describing the ego-ideal as constituted by an almost endless series of hierarchical layers of idealized self-representations, from the most archaic ones (unconscious omnipotent and grandiose ideas of ourselves and of our creative and destructive powers) up to the ones closest to reality (the more mature ego-ideal, closer to the conscious 'conscience') (1985).

In his introduction to Melanie Klein's *Love, Guilt, and Reparation*, Money-Kyrle describes her concept of this psychological process as the ego-ideal being added to the archaic super-ego and archaic ideal ego:

> The child's earliest super-ego, containing his own projected destructiveness turned against himself, is a paranoid–schizoid construction which, as Freud discovered, operates as an archaic internal god with an archaic morality of an eye-for-an-eye kind. This is not ego-syntonic, and a major aim of analysis is to weaken it. But at around four months old the

appearance of the depressive position ushers in the possibility of a different and far more ego-syntonic morality based no longer on a specific form of a paranoid delusion, but on depressive guilt at the injuries inflicted both in reality and phantasy on loved objects outside and inside the self in the earlier paranoid–schizoid position. In so far as these damaged love objects are mourned, they are felt to come alive inside as internal mentors who help and sustain the ego in its struggle against remaining bad objects inside and real external enemies. (1975, pp. x–xi)

While intra-uterine life offers the foetus optimal conditions, growth as effortless bliss, so, ideally, the pregnant mother becomes sensitized to that life, enabling her to provide the nearest possible approximation to it after childbirth. This responsive, adaptive mother can gradually let the baby be introduced to the world. She can help maintain the illusion of blissful unity while allowing the discovery of the difficult reality that she is not part of the baby, does not belong to the baby, that she is a separate person not under the baby's control, and has to be shared with others! Intense feelings of frustration and pleasure, envy and gratitude, love and hate have their beginnings here. If the child is able to feel that mother can withstand all the passionate feelings directed towards her then there will not be a fear that she has been damaged by the child, and that she will retaliate; just because we might wish that she would 'drop dead', that if we 'step on a crack', we might 'break her back', we won't be so powerful and dangerous in fact as we are in phantasy. (This spelling 'phantasy' is meant to differentiate conscious daydream fantasy from unconscious mental content. See Isaacs, 1948.) What Melanie Klein found in the phantasies of children was that the basic fear of retaliation by a destructive envious mother, the witch of fairy tales, is the fear that she will rob the child of all of its good things, of all the pleasures inside. An eye for an eye, a tooth for a tooth. Retaliation is feared because of all the feelings the child has had about mother's apparent ownership of everything and her omnipotent power over all things. Included in the things mother has that are attacked in phantasy are all her inside babies, always waiting to be born as usurpers to the claim for exclusive possession. And if all our good things are removed by her in retaliation, we are left at the mercy of all our bad monstrous contents. This would be the archaic, primitive super-ego. As we develop the capacity to remember good things (about ourselves or some other part of the world) that have disappeared or been spoiled in some way, and to wish for their return, we will try repair with measures available to us (in our dreams and/or waking fantasies, and with loving acts) and will also try preservative measures. This is the start of an ego-ideal. We can then begin to have a real impact on making our dreams come true and no longer only be confined to magical wishing.

The super-ego thus unconsciously monitors the phantasies behind our actions and thoughts to be vigilant about how the bad is spoiling the good. This results in feelings of dread of retaliation and of despair that all might be lost, when any signs of damage or destruction are found. What can help in the face of this moralistic hopelessness? This is the role of the ego-ideal – to show how the good can change the bad into something good (or even better!) or at least how it may contain the bad and prevent it from getting worse – the role of the creative caring capacity which tries to discover realistically what the matter is and what's to be done about it. Is the reality that of a complete loss, of something which needs to be buried and mourned so that we can go on with life after death? Or is some kind of recovery or resuscitation possible and with what resources at what costs? This is how we make the best of bad or sad jobs (Scott, 1987). There may be conflict between our super-ego and our ego-ideal, depending on their contents and their relative forcefulness. This brings us back to Cressida. Is it better to be dead than in bed (with Diomedes)? Should she remain true to her Troilus even unto death? Or might she make the best she can of a bad and sad situation and try to stay alive?

Piers and Singer bring another perspective in their differentiation between shame and guilt: shame arises out of a tension between the ego and the ego-ideal; guilt arises out of tension between the ego and the super-ego. Thus shame is a later emotion related to not 'being true to ourselves', in contrast to guilt for trangressing the boundaries of the super-ego, displeasing the prohibiting parent (1971, pp. 23–4).

What is this moralistic response to Cressida that has made her name synonymous with womanly infidelity? She did not become adulterous, criminal, perverse, or promiscuous, and may even have found a better man in Diomedes! The negative response arises from our tendency to see all women as if they were mother and to respond accordingly. As we have seen, Shakespeare draws our attention to this in the dialogue between Ulysses and Troilus, when Ulysses asks 'What has she done, Prince, that can soil our mothers?' Shakespeare is telling us the disagreeable truth about mothers; he confronts us with the pain of the knowledge. They do not belong to us. This is the bad news (or seems to be!) We have become aware of the separateness of 'the other' and experience loss. There is good news. We do belong to ourselves and have our own resources; we gain a greater sense of having ourself for ourself.[1]

There is much aggression and mourning involved in this process of becoming separate and individual. In the black-and-white world of the unconscious, when we are the one 'doing' the separating, telling the other to 'get lost', this is like 'doing away with' or killing the other. Also, the process is linked with the emotions and the memories of how we have felt when told to wait, go away, 'go to sleep now', or do without. Winnicott describes the early, infantile capacity for excited loving, and the emergence from a state of 'pre-ruth' (before a state of 'ruth' or capacity to care for the other and hence the even later possibility of being 'ruthless') to the realization of the fact of the other who is not under our omnipotent control, who must be able to survive on their own. Then we can not only relate to the other, but can also make good use of them and what they have to offer; we can gobble them all up, in our phantasy, and there will still be more. At first, the other is there only because we put them there; the world starts when we open our eyes, and stops when we close our eyes. This is an important illusion that needs to be maintained for a while, until we can begin to bear discovering that things are not as we would have them, that we are not in charge of the world. We begin to find the world as it is, and in the process we are making all those things 'not me', sorting out the me and the not-me. Making things not-me is equivalent to destroying them in the unconscious. It is then crucial that the 'other' has a liveliness of its own, does not experience this shift as a killing rejection, and does not respond by retaliating. When the baby bites the breast, the mother does not react moralistically. This is crucial for all development in which growth is related to dependence. To the extent that the other is outside of our omnipotent control and we can truly use (not exploit) them we can be fed by their substance (see Winnicott, 1988, pp. 67–83).

As we learn to tolerate mother's separateness and our dependency on her, a nurturant ego-ideal emerges and the power of the omnipotent super-ego diminishes (Mancia and Meltzer, 1981). In one convention of love Cressida (mother) should have died like Juliet, and been forever 'with' Troilus, and certainly not with anyone else; his omnipotent possession of Cressida would have been intact. Her sin was to be separate, alive, and with another.

There is a powerful re-emergence of these issues in adolescence. Winnicott's description is one of the most lucid in psychoanalytic writing:

> The same problems loom at puberty that were present in the early stages when these same children were relatively harmless toddlers or infants. It is worth noting that, if you have done well at the early stages and are still doing well, you cannot count on a smooth running of the machine. In fact you can expect troubles. Certain troubles are inherent at these later stages. It is valuable to compare adolescent ideas with those of childhood. If, in the fantasy of early growth, there is contained *death*, then at adolescence there is contained *murder*. Even when growth at the period of puberty goes ahead without major crises, one may need to deal with acute problems of management because growing up means taking the parent's place. *It really does*. In the unconscious fantasy, growing up is inherently an aggressive act. And the child is now no longer child-sized. (1971, p. 169, author's italics)

I have been addressing the question of the negative response to Cressida, and was originally drawn to my particular line of thought by the words Shakespeare gave to Troilus linking Cressida and mothers. If a positive response to Cressida is possible, then we return to thoughts about what ideal of being a woman she might represent, how this relates to a woman's strength and potency, and how it is gained in the development of the girl becoming a woman.

What do women want to be (to have within themselves) and what do women want to be able to do with what they have? One issue at stake here is a woman's capacity to feel herself separate from mother, without feeling bereft, and to know that what she has is her own, and not mother's. It helps to have a strong mother who knows what she has as a woman and who enjoys the creative possibilities in competition with her daughter. It also helps to have a sense of a multiplicity within oneself, to have many different and separate parts that may each be remembered and made available at the appropriate moment, and be integrated in such a way that they do not interfere with one another (this is similar to Lussier's notion of 'endless series of hierarchical layers' in the development of the ego-ideal). The ideal of aggression plays a major role here since others will have their own idea of which 'part' they would like! This is why people don't like Cressida. (Henryson's *The Testament of Cresseid*, written a century before Shakespeare's play and a continuation of Chaucer's *Troilus and Criseyde*, has Diomedes grow tired of Cressida and cast her off. She rails against Venus and Cupid and is stricken by them with leprosy! (Henryson, 1968))

Did Cressida survive in order to find her ideal? Or was her ideal empowering her survival? Was she struggling valiantly with each new turn of events to know how to respond, how to survive when deprived of all her previous external sources of support and care, and in the process discovering her own strength and courage? Or had she already an ideal that she could call on, of how a capable but vulnerable woman could deal with a frightening situation? There is no mother or mother-substitute mentioned in the play and hence no role model for Cressida. Nor am I trying to analyze a fictional character, but rather our response to her. For me this is a story of a struggle to find a new ideal, of how the good can change the bad, of how Cressida is making the best of both a 'bad job' (the circumstances of war, no family or community support) and a 'sad job' (the loss of her lover). Cressida has enough capacity to mourn the lost good to be able to move on to making the best of it, whereas Troilus remains moralistically mad.

Nancy Chodorow in *The Reproduction of Mothering* elaborates 'The Psychoanalytic Story' of how a little girl becomes ready to be a mother, emphasizing the issue of enduring connectedness or attachment to mother, rather than the concomitant aggressive issue of becoming separate. (This is the heart and soul of the matter for women: how we manage to integrate in a creative way our separateness and our connectedness to each other, what our responsibilities are to all involved, and on what basis we will make that decision.)

> Because of their mothering by women, girls come to experience themselves as less separate than boys, as having more permeable ego boundaries. Girls come to define themselves more in relation to others. Their internalized object-relational structure becomes more complex, with more ongoing issues. These personality features are reflected in super-ego development. (1978, p. 93)

I would interpret the super-ego to include the ego-ideal for Chodorow. Later in the book she writes:

> For a girl there is no single oedipal mode or quick oedipal resolution, and there is no absolute 'change of object'. A girl's libidinal turning to her father is not at the expense of, or a substitute for her attachment to her mother. Instead, a girl develops important oedipal attachments to her mother as well as to her father. These attachments, and the way they are internalized, are built upon, and do not replace her pre-oedipal attachment to mother. (p. 127)

For boys, the process of giving up mother is facilitated by the capacity to identify with father. The boy has a penis which makes him different from mother, and through the sense of difference, a sense of separateness and identity is likely to emerge. For men, much pride and strength is found in this being separate and autonomous. But girls have an intrinsic difficulty. They are not 'different'. From the little girl's point of view she is merely an inadequate version of mother (with no breasts and no babies, as opposed to the little boy who has a smaller version of father's penis which at least can pee potently). For both, if the same-sex parent is lively and well overall, much hope can come from the sense that becoming a grown-up someday will be possible and worthwhile. But the problem remains that even when the girl enjoys a positive sense of having a vagina, and a growing sense of her own creativity, she still has to try to get a sense of how she is different from mother. During childhood she remains fairly attached to mother and this may be linked to Gilligan's findings about the value for women of 'being connected' – the value and importance of relationships with others. The Oedipus complex is not 'resolved' since the girl can't 'give up' the person she must identify with; she must 'become like' and yet find also who she is uniquely.

Ernest Jones describes this dilemma:

> The girl's task of coping with her sadistic attitude towards the contents of the mother's body . . . and the anxiety it gives rise to . . . has two reasons for being harder than the boy's. In the first place her anxiety essentially relates to the inside of the body and has no external organ on which to concentrate as the boy's has . . . In the second place, the boy has another personal lightning-conductor for his sadism and hate, namely his sexual rival, the father. The girl, on the contrary, has as her sexual rival and the object of her sadism the same person, the mother, on whom the infant is completely dependent for both libidinal and all other needs of life. To destroy this object would be fatal, so the sadism, with its accompanying anxiety, is pent up and turned inwards far more than with the boy. In a word, the girl has for two reasons less opportunity to exteriorize her sadism. This explains the remarkable attachment to the mother, and dependence on her. (1935, p. 266)

By adolescence these issues take on a new urgency. There may be huge battles with mother, or the aggression may be directed against the process of growth as in anorexia nervosa or suicide. Many daughters are inhibited in the process of becoming more separate by the guilt involved in 'murdering' mother, especially if mother is depressed because she never achieved a real sense of herself as a valuable woman and person. The guilt may be complicated by envy of mother's creativity and a wish to murder her babies; the daughter may be unable to tolerate having come from mother, or the fact or possibility of siblings. Part of the trouble will be that the daughter still needs a mother who can help her find her own resources. She may find a substitute who can help (teacher, sister, grandmother, aunt) but she often turns instead to a man, believing that the penis will define her vagina. This may take the form of promiscuity and/or despairing, angry, disappointed battles with her mate, when the solution fails. She may make a pact with peers, and be able to gang up on mother without feeling so guilty. The pack of peers may have an orgy or break up into couples.

If mother is a woman who has integrated her sexuality and her aggression well enough to enjoy being herself and sharing herself with others, this will mean that she knows how to nourish herself for her own sake and for the sake of others. Hers is not a selfish or destructive aggression when she sometimes has to 'get tough' in looking after herself. Many women don't know this, but instead become guilty and feel they must be only giving, never denying or withholding. They might be more comfortable becoming aggressive in the service of another. This is likely to be an unwelcome gift if it carries the unconscious denial of their own needs. But it might also appear with great strength. The wife of a colleague once remarked soon after the birth of a son: 'I'd die for my husband, but I'd kill to protect my baby.' If mother can manage such powerful feelings, including the discovery that she could also kill her baby when her own self is threatened in some way, she is more likely to do something constructive for everyone. She will also make it much easier for her baby to tell her to 'get lost' without guilt when that baby just wants to be alone. This will be a much easier mother to kill in the internal world of phantasy, since she will be strong enough to survive the rejection and be resurrected in the form of a new relationship.

This brings us back to Cressida, and how she deals with needing to take care of herself. Her danger lies in remaining isolated and separate; she must make connections as part of taking care of herself. Carol Gilligan's book *In a Different Voice* makes a strong argument that men portray attachment as illusory and dangerous, while women portray autonomy this way. So women stress continuity and reconfiguration ('work with whatever you have') in response to loss, while men stress separation and replacement, thus diverging in their metaphors of growth. For women, autonomy does not have as much value as a sense of self in relation to others, a separateness that is not distant. Here is the issue of men and women having different ego-ideals. It may be that autonomy tends to be overvalued by men (or by feminists) and represents unintegrated ideals that leave no room for also valuing dependency. As Winnicott said, there is only relative independence (1988, pp. 158-9). This is related to the stage when we can leave mother but we must know where she is, and she must not leave us!

There is no implication in her dialogue with Diomedes that Cressida does not love Troilus any longer. Rather, there is a deep sense of her agony. It is Troilus' distortion, since he cannot conceive of any other explanation, that Cressida has betrayed their love. She remains connected to him and aware of her loss. To quote again from Northrop Frye:

> Cressida may be 'faithless', but fidelity would be impossibly quixotic in the world she is in, a world where heroism degenerates into brutality and love itself is reduced to another kind of mechanical stimulus, as Thersites points out with so much relish. When at the end of the play Pandarus shrivels into a contemporary London pimp, professionally concerned with the spreading of syphilis, there is very little sense of shock or incongruity: we have already realized that this play is about us, if not about the aspect of us that we want to put on exhibition. It is by a final irony of language that we call the portrayal of such a world 'disillusioned', and associate the term pejoratively with a weary pessimism. Being disillusioned with a world like that is the starting point of any genuine myth of deliverance. (1983, pp. 85-6)

Cressida is the vehicle for this disillusionment. There is a sense of painful surprise when it comes in the play. There is in the audience a perplexed feeling that begins when she enters the Greek camp, intensifies during her last scene, and is left for us to resolve within ourselves.

Cressida as the personification of disillusionment – as the one who must face reality and both conceptualize and resolve the inherent moral dilemma – recalls much of the work to be done by an analytic couple. In each analysis this must usually be done first in the person of the analyst. It also falls to the mother to be the disillusioner for her children. They are not her first love. She must disabuse them of false hopes. Even if father embodies the prohibition, the 'no', mother can completely negate his position. She must be the final 'no-sayer' to others, the final keeper of her own body, the final 'yes-sayer' to herself. And if she is exuberantly alive and full of potential babies, we might get over our envy and fear of her, and discover our own creativity.

NOTE

1. Another approach to understanding Troilus' need to split Cressida, and
    to Ulysses' questioning what has Cressida done 'that can soil our
    mothers?', is considered in a paper by Janet Adelman which I found
    late in the preparation of this paper. Adelman says:

    > Her betrayal becomes in effect the assertion of her status as a
    > separate person, not simply the creature of Troilus' fantasy. But we
    > might also answer that Cressida has done nothing – that the agent
    > of soilure is in fact Troilus himself. For ultimately, I think, it is not
    > the rupture of the union but the consummation of the union
    > [between Troilus and Cressida] that soils the idea of mother for
    > Troilus. (1985, p. 134)

    She adds in a footnote on the same page: 'At issue here is, I suspect, a
    primitive fantasy in which separation *is* infidelity: for the infant, the
    mother's separateness constitutes the first betrayal; insofar as she is not
    merely his, she is promiscuously other.' Adelman misses the crucial
    concept of the envy behind spoiling, envy of mother's power to say to
    us 'yes' or 'no' about herself and her resources. It is the dilemma
    involved in the exercise of this aggression that leads women to identify
    with the devaluing projection, since they are women as mother is, and
    therefore guilty of the very sin they accuse her of committing. If the
    daughter mourns the idealized mother, and is inspired by, rather than
    envious of her mother, she will form a more realistic ideal, and is more
    likely to find the courage to retain her own strength and her own
    creativity in the face of the envy of others.

6   THE PERILS OF PERICLES

RUTH NEVO

A thing which has not been understood inevitably reappears; like an unlaid
ghost, it cannot be laid to rest until the mystery is solved and the spell broken.
Sigmund Freud, 'Little Hans'

Pericles, first of Shakespeare's four romance narratives of vicissitude, loss and restoration, is usually regarded as the most tentative,
fumbling or inchoate of the four, or not entirely Shakespeare's at
all. Critics have been made unhappy not only by a text probably
transcribed in part from memory, but also by the Gower narrator's
laboured tetrameters, the jerky tempo of frame narration and
dramatized episode, the curiously 'phlegmatic' or 'passive' character of the protagonist, and the outlandish events. It is only, it is
widely felt, in Act III, with the death of Pericles' wife and the birth
of his daughter, that the true Shakespearian fire breaks forth from
the flint.

It is certainly a very weird play. Severed heads, more storms and
shipwrecks than most readers can confidently count, the miraculous preservation of persons alive under water or dead and unburied
on land, a denouement which mixes, if not hornpipes and funerals,
at least brothels and betrothals, and a remarkably accident-prone
protagonist. 'Most critics', says Ernest Schanzer,

Unless otherwise indicated, all Shakespeare citations are from *The
Riverside Shakespeare*, G. Blakemore Evans, ed., Boston, MA: Houghton
Mifflin, 1974.

are agreed that, while Acts III, IV and V are substantially Shakespeare's, Acts I and II are not. The questions to be asked, therefore, are: Who is the author of Acts I and II? And how did the non-Shakespearean first two acts come to be joined to the Shakespearean last three acts? (1965, p. xxi)

I would like to ask quite other questions of this text, which seems to me, so far from being fractured, to possess a degree of unity bordering on the obsessive. I shall hope to show that a reading *of*, rather than round, *Pericles'* strangenesses, a reading attentive to the oneiric dimension of its symbolism and the dream-like aspects of its representations, will give the play a rather different specific gravity than is usually attributed to it, and will enable us to find it, once again, convincing. 'Till the closing of the theaters in 1642,' Ernest Schanzer tells us, '*Pericles* seems to have been one of Shakespeare's greatest stage successes' (p. xli). I would like to return the presently undervalued *Pericles* to the canon, finding it, precisely because it is closer to primary process, more anomalous, 'crude', absurd, strange, a representation of elemental and universal fantasy of great power.

The story of Pericles is impossible, of course. So, André Green reminds us, is the tragedy of Oedipus. 'How can the life of a single man pile up such a set of coincidences?' (1979, p. 18) He continues: 'It is not for the psycho-analyst to answer; but rather for the countless spectators of *King Oedipus* who might say, with Aristotle, "a convincing improbability is preferable to what is unconvincing even though it is possible".' What is 'convincing'? Green's answer is implicit in his account of his project: 'The aim of a psycho-analytic reading is the search for the emotional springs that make the spectacle an affective matrix in which the spectator sees himself involved and feels himself not only solicited but welcomed, as if the spectacle were intended for him.' It is with the identification of this matrix, and with the investigation of the symbolic activity which allows us access to it, that I shall be engaged.

The questions I would ask, then, emerge from the following reflections. It is not in dispute that the father/daughter theme in the play is its dominant concern, repeated time after time and, in the reunion scene, treated with an admirably expressive pathos, not granted, for example, to Rosalind's father, or Hero's, who also have their lost daughters returned to them. Why then is the axis of the play's action skewed? It is after all the story of Pericles, but Pericles does not become a father until Act III. At the peak of his fortunes his hard-won wife is snatched from him, his newly-born daughter left motherless in his charge. Then indeed he rages against the storm in language reminiscent of Lear, man of sorrows, and daughters. But the child is immediately abandoned to the care of foster parents. And what of his role up to that point? Is it really a kind of marking time, or fragments of a cobbled-together or corrupt text, or the work of an inferior collaborator? Or rather a chapter in what Coppélia Kahn sees as Shakespeare's lifelong pursuit of 'a dramatic and psychological strategy for dealing not only with our common ambivalence toward our families but specifically with the male passage from being a son to being a father' (1980, p. 217)? This is useful for the situating of Pericles in the life cycle of sons; but when she continues, 'He found it [the strategy] through the romance, in one of its typical patterns of action that I shall call "the providential tempest" . . . this pattern is that of a journey . . . the individual's passage from emotional residence within the family to independence and adulthood' (p. 218), I believe her invocation of the archetypal symbol of the journey blinds her to a false distinction. 'Independence and adulthood' is surely not the opposite, but rather the authentication and clarification of 'emotional residence within the family'. Do we, in other words, ever 'reside' elsewhere than within the family? The 'providential tempest' in the story of Pericles will, I believe, reward closer examination, as will the role of the son in the triad father, daughter, suitor which appears again and again in the play.

Pericles is tragicomedy *comme il faut* according to Renaissance theory, which demanded both extreme peril and happy solution; and Pericles' saga of preposterous and totally fortuitous misfortunes can be moralized without difficulty into a vision of longsufferingness (Barker, 1963), princely excellence (Schanzer, 1965) and the wondrous ways of a mysterious Providence. In this, I suggest, traditional criticism is swallowing the bait of secondary revision which camouflages, or is even itself blind to, the insights that it nevertheless makes available. Traditional criticism characteristically judges the responses of characters to the events which happen to them in terms of ethical, theological or didactic value systems, or interprets them methodically by means of allegory. It is therefore flustered by the gaps, awkwardnesses, inconsequentialities, archaisms it encounters in a text. Indeed, unless we can read in 'the progressive, educative "official" plot' the threatening 'repetitive process obscurely going on underneath or beyond it' (Brooks, P., 1980, p. 511), we will very probably find 'no solution to the problems of *Pericles*' (Edwards, 1976, p. 41), no alternative to the dismissal of *Pericles* as a mere blueprint, or rehearsal, for the greater plays to follow.

T. S. Eliot once said that 'meanings' in poetry were like the meat the burglar throws to the house-dog to keep him quiet while it gets on with its proper business. He was, perhaps, paraphrasing Freud, who remarked, drily, that 'it is the much abused privilege of conscious activity, wherever it plays a part, to conceal every other activity from our eyes' (1900b, p. 774). We need to cap these gnomic sayings with the programmatic Lacan, who, intent on that 'other activity', that 'proper business', says, 'every unsuccessful [verbal] act is a successful, not to say "well turned", discourse . . . and exactly in the right quarter for its word to be sufficient to the wise' (1966, p. 58). The passage of interpretation from signifier on the stage – perhaps odd or crude to the rationally disciplined eye – to signified of 'that other scene' – and 'Is it not that the theater is the best embodiment of that "other scene", the unconscious? It is that other scene' (Green, 1979, p. 1) – requires a reading 'wise' to the 'tentacular network' of the normally forgotten or repressed, for, and I quote Green again, 'in the long succession of signifiers in linked sequence which constitutes the work, the unconscious signified rises . . . from the gulf or absence in which it resides . . . not in order to express what has to be said, but in order to indicate, by veiling it, what needs to be hidden' (1979, p. 28). 'Every literary narrative', says Geoffrey Hartman, 'contains another narrative . . . discontinuous and lacunary' (1978, p. 102). In order for 'the outward movement of the plot to become an inward movement of the mind' (Skura, 1980b, p. 212) it is this other narrative that we must attempt to pursue.

One cannot do better than to begin at the beginning, for this is a play which begins with a bang. The presenter, Gower, puts the audience in complete possession of the ugly facts, and the quite extraordinary circumstances in which the young pretender to the hand of the Syrian princess makes his suit. There is a riddle to be explicated and the cost of failure to do so is graphically depicted by a gruesome row of severed heads: the remains of previous contenders in this risky enterprise. This is not an inviting scenario. It is, as the audience knows, a classic double-bind: if he solves the riddle he falls a prey to Antiochus' rage at being discovered. If he doesn't, he dies. Freudian symbologists will immediately identify a castration fantasy. Traditional criticism has chosen to ignore or play down any such specificity in the threat, repressing its terrors and regarding it simply as a rather melodramatic launching pad for Pericles' adventures. It is, for example, simply 'by the discovery of hidden evil', according to Traversi, that Pericles is 'driven . . . to abandon his first dream of felicity' (1969, p. 265).

Traditional criticism, in fact, has not taken the opening quite seriously. If we do take it, and the fantasy that it represents, seriously, however, if we decide not to detach so startling an opening from its unconscious moorings, we will at once discover a great deal else that suddenly figures in Pericles' responses, much as Napoleon's hat will suddenly emerge from among the leaves of a tree, in the children's puzzle game used by Leclaire and Laplanche as a model for the absent presence of unconscious representations (Skura, 1980b, p. 204). Note, for example, the timbre, and the content, of Pericles' opening speech at his first sight of the beautiful daughter of Antiochus, 'apparelled like the spring' (I,i,12), in whose face, it seems, 'sorrow were ever ras'd, and testy wrath/ Could never be her mild companion' (17–18). Conventional enough, no doubt, on the face of it, these praises, but not every young lover admires in his mistress the absence of attributes (sorrow, wrath) not usually associated with youth and love at all. More is to come. Where Antiochus likens his daughter to the golden apples of the Hesperides, defended by 'death-like dragons' (27, 29), Pericles associates the gratification of his desire with the dangerous and forbidden fruit whose eating is the source and origin in Genesis of sexual guilt, and of death:

> You gods, that made me man, and sway in love,
> That have inflam'd desire in my breast
> To take the fruit of yon celestial tree
> (Or die in th'adventure), give me your helps
> As I am son and servant to your will . . .
>
>   (19–22)

What, in this context, can we make of the homiletic meekness with which he turns to Antiochus:

> Antiochus, I thank thee, who hath taught
> My frail mortality to know itself,
> And by those fearful objects to prepare
> This body, like to them, to what I must;
> For death remembered should be like a mirror,
> Who tells us life's but breath, to trust it error.
> I'll make my will then, and as sick men do,
> Who know the world, see heaven, but feeling woe,
> Gripe not at earthly joys as erst they did . . .
>
>   (41–55)

Is this not, Christian–stoical though it may seem, somewhat cold for an ardent lover? Is there not the trace of more than a conventional *contemptus mundi* here? A dyspepsia, a melancholy, a lassitude of the will to live and love? This young lover, it seems, is preternaturally ready to envisage his own body in the image of an (already) severed head, preternaturally ready to 'make his will . . . as sick men do'. He bequeaths, he says, his 'riches to the earth from whence they came;/ But [his] unspotted fire of love' to the Princess (52–3). The odd splitting and the opposition draw attention to an unspoken tension within the rhetoric. The riches that he bequeaths to Mother Earth can only in the context be his body – rich to him as to any man – and it is this body that stands in opposition to the 'unspotted' fire of love. It, therefore, by implication, is what is spotted. The sense of carnal taint is the stronger for the evasive displacement. This suggestion of a sexual anxiety in Pericles' deference to the father of his hoped-for bride magnetizes the apparently banal figures of speech in Antiochus' warning: 'because thine *eye*/ Presumes to reach, all the whole *heap* must die . . . / Yon . . . princes/ Tell thee, with speechless *tongues* . . . / And with dead *cheeks* advise thee to desist' (32–9 *passim*; my italics). The body imagery speaks a subtle and menacing sexuality, at once desire and threat.

It is upon this textual ground, so to speak, that the seed of the riddle falls. We, of course, know the answer to the riddle because we have been told of the incest; and for that reason we may miss its central symbolic import, its own crucial condensation. Let us recall it:

> I am no viper, yet I feed
> On mother's flesh which did me breed.
> I sought a husband, in which labour
> I found that kindness in a father.
> He's father, son, and husband mild;
> I mother, wife – and yet his child.

(64–9)

The riddle, it will be noticed, is a riddle because it introduces a third, complicating term into the incest relation between father and daughter: the absent mother. Antiochus is father and husband to his daughter quite literally. How is he her son, she his mother? The expression 'feeding [like a viper] upon mother's flesh' is metaphorically tenable for the daughter whether taken to mean simply 'taking that which belongs to my mother', or whether relayed through the prior metaphor which makes man and wife one flesh (cf. *Hamlet*, IV,iii,52). Shakespeare's innovation was to make the implied speaker the daughter rather than Antioch as in older versions of the tale.[1] There is a moment during which the solution of the riddle hovers indeterminately between father and daughter: the viper might pick up the previous Eden associations and so keep the riddle's 'I' within the feminine orbit, or it might be phallic and so masculinize the whole grotesque image. That Pericles himself is the reader of the riddle, hence our conduit to it, is important in this respect, especially in the theatre. There is a certain double-take, therefore, in the deciphering of the riddle. The daughter feeds upon her mother's rightful possession – her own father; but Antiochus too can be said to feed upon mother's flesh – the issue of the mother who is (or was) his own wife. Antiochus is father and husband to his daughter literally but it is only by trope that he is her son, she his mother. It is just this metaphorical condensation that the riddle performs, making Antiochus' daughter/wife his surrogate mother: 'he's father, *son*, and husband mild' (my italics).

The riddle is constructed like a dream as Freud expounded the dream work. It is the dream work methodized: condensation, displacement, representation in pictorial image all cunningly tricked out by secondary revision into the form of the conventional riddle. The absurdities, or catachreses, are instantly penetrated by Pericles, as if the enigma were to him transparent. As indeed it is. 'All love the womb that their first being bred' (I,i,107), he says, summing up the meaning of the King's evil; but how is this the meaning? Philip Edwards says, 'This puts the incest the wrong way round, son and mother' (1976, p. 145) and suggests textual corruption. Is it not possible that 'the wrong way round' is the right way up, the essence of the matter, a parapraxis if you will, or slip of the text – the desire of the mother being shared, in unconscious complicity, by these two mirror-image oedipal contenders?

The traumatic experience at Antioch precipitates Pericles' return home, causes his subsequent flight, hence his first shipwreck, hence his arrival in Pentapolis and so forth; but its function as causal event in a linear series does not exhaust its significance. Indeed, we can read the play's events as causing the Pericles story, but we can also read the Pericles story as motivating the events. Drama is peculiarly the art of the present tense, but in its present, as in all presences, is contained the unrecognized past, the other 'uncensored draft' of the history (Lacan, 1977, p. 51). As psychoanalysis teaches us, 'What is forgotten is recalled in acts.' Lost to conscious memory the past reproduces itself as an unmastered force in the present. We 'follow' the fable unfolding before us 'with cunning delays and ever-mounting excitement' (Freud, 1900b, p. 363) as a tissue of surprises, as if their end were undetermined; at the very same time we move backwards through a retrospective succession of partial recognition scenes. We move back and forth in a shuttle which enables us to find relationships between the end towards which we progress and the beginning to which we return ('to know the place for the first time'). Drama, the supremely metaleptic art, resembles, as Freud observed, the 'remembering, repeating and working through' of psychoanalysis more than any other form of narrative.[2]

Interestingly, in *Pericles*, because of the narrator Gower, the dual textual functions of relating and enacting are separated. Gower is the only continuous narrator/presenter in Shakespeare. Like the chorus in *Henry V* or Time in *The Winter's Tale*, but unlike other mediating or parabastic figures, he *only* addresses the audience, never the dramatis personae.[3] This has the effect of distancing or framing the events, and creating a split in the audience between empathetic participation and critical awareness somewhat as in the Brechtian alienation effect. Only here, since Gower is a character accompanying the whole play, and since the historical Gower has already told the story before in the *Confessio Amantis*, the effect is of a *mise-en-abyme*, a telling within a telling. What is shown and what is told seem fairly arbitrary. Events (some of which we have ourselves witnessed) are recapitulated, other events are anticipated in narrative discourse; a nodal change-producing occurrence is mimed; further events, unrepresentable practically speaking, like the storms and shipwrecks, are reported. Gower's punctuation of the sequence of direct dramatic enactment by alternating narration and dumb-show foregrounds the question of selection and deletion in narration itself; for that matter the question of the authentic as against the authenticated – the re-told. The Gower figure offers his tale to the audience 'for restoratives'; he steps out on stage between the audience and the dramatis personae; he interferes. He constantly requests his audience to conjure up for themselves events anticipated or recapitulated: 'In your imagination hold/ This stage the ship' (III,Chorus,58–9). I suggest that we can regard him as a kind of threshold figure – indeterminately analyst and censor, a mediator both vehicle and obstacle. It is as if either the unconscious of the text, like an analysand, strove to communicate a deeper, more inward substance, but was constrained by some inner resistance to offer a processed or pre-packaged version. Or, as in Peter Brooks's notion of 'the erotics of form' (1987), as if the text was leading us on with pre-images to some anticipated consummation or resolution, yet delaying progress by returns and repetitions. We are sensitized by Gower's mediation to levels of consciousness, and to functions of the telling. Gower remembers, and recounts the story; Pericles re-enacts it; and the re-enacting itself, *en abyme*, is a compulsive repetition.

What Antiochus thus triggers in Pericles, by way of the condensations of primary process fantasy, is, we intuit, a repetition of himself, an unconscious recognition. Antiochus is his uncanny double; and the progress of the play is the haunting of Pericles by the Antiochus in himself, the incest fear which he must repress and from which he must flee. For Pericles, who, it will be recalled, referred to himself as 'son' to Antiochus (I,iv,24,27), already at the outset is, as we have seen, in the grip of the oedipal guilt which Freud, in *The Ego and the Id*, characterizes as 'the pure culture of the death instinct . . . [which] often enough succeeds in driving the ego into death, if the latter does not fend off its tyrant in time by the change round into mania' (1923, p. 394). Pericles is indeed very nearly driven into death or mania as the play proceeds, but we are not, I submit, to see this as a matter of contingent circumstance alone. Rather, to understand *Pericles* is to see that the Pericles figure – the Periclean fantasy – is always already death-driven.

Let us once more attend to the drama's text as it proceeds with its articulation of the fantasy it both veils and reveals. The predicament presented in Act I, scene i, produces a delayed action, like a time bomb. Pericles abandons his courtship, of course, flees Antioch, and goes back home to Tyre; but there he falls into an inexplicable melancholy. He is surrounded by courtly pleasures; his thoughts have 'revolted' against the 'sweetest flower' once, but no longer, desired; danger is at a distance, in Antioch, and yet he can find no peace.

> Why should this change of thoughts,
> The sad companion, dull-ey'd melancholy,
> [Be my] so us'd a guest as not an hour
> In the day's glorious walk or peaceful night,
> The tomb where grief should sleep, can breed me quiet?
>
> (I,ii,1–5)

Why, indeed? On the face of it he does have a plausible reason for fear, and for the flight he decides upon. The long arm of the King, whose secret he discovered, will surely pursue him and

With hostile forces he'll o'erspread the land,
And with [th'ostent] of war will look so huge,
Amazement shall drive courage from the state,
Our men be vanquish'd ere they do resist,
And subjects punish'd that ne'er thought offence.

(I,ii,24–8)

The apparent plausibility of this argument must strike us as
disingenuous. Its worst-case reasoning is exaggerated, unnerved. It
is surely odd for a prince so avidly to envisage defeat, and critics
have been properly dismayed at such strangely unrulerlike
behavior. How can we account for it? The speech continues thus:

Which care of them, not pity of myself –
Who [am] no more but as the tops of trees,
Which fence the roots they grow by and defend them –
Makes both my body pine and soul to languish,
And punish that before that he would punish.

(29–33)

The disavowal of self-pity suggests its presence, and we note the
insistence on the notion of punishment (as opposed for example to
revenge or retaliation). Why so much punishment? What crime has
been committed (by Pericles) that his thoughts should be so full of
punishment? What, moreover, in this deviant syntax, is the subject
of the first 'punish' in line 33? It is, or it should be, 'care of them',
which precedes the embedded subordinate clause. 'Care of them',
however, requires a third person verb. The absence of such a form
derails the syntax at that point and generates a search for a possible
alternative. If we read 'punish' as an infinitive (correlative to 'to
languish') our alternative subject becomes 'soul'. Thus: 'Care of
them makes my body pine, and my soul to languish and to punish
that (myself) before he (Antioch) does.' Pericles needs the
remonstrances of his loyal and candid counsellor (51–124) to
crystallize the decision to set sail from Tyre, and to justify the
decision as the action of a noble Prince ready to remove himself, a
casus belli, from the scene; but the packed syntax reveals to us that
it is a self-inflicted punitive suffering from which he flees. Why? A
powerful potential enemy is an ostensible reason for his flight. That
that potential enemy is an intimidating father-figure, law-maker, and

beheader, possessed of a (significantly nameless) daughter/ mother/bride – 'an O without a figure' (*Lear* I,iv,193) – is suggestive of preliminary conditions; but the immediate precipitating source of his dread – an archaic energy at work like Hamlet's old mole – is specific: it is that *he has uncovered* the King's terrible secret. The primal scene of the play – Act I, scene i – triggers a primal-scene fantasy for Pericles, which powers thenceforth his guilt-stricken, haunted drivenness.[4]

But his sallying forth is not only fugue. At all events, as it turns out, it acquires major value and virtue through the role of feeder and saviour he is enabled to play in famine-stricken Tarsus. There, Cleon reports, once fastidious palates now beg for bread, man and wife draw lots to decide who shall die first, there is scarcely strength left to bury the dead, and

> Those mothers who, to nousle up their babes,
> Thought nought too curious, are ready now
> To eat those little darlings whom they lov'd.
>
> (I,iv,42–4)

These are dismaying, and resonant, images to appear in the description of the plight of Tarsus.[5] And he is not permitted to remain a saviour for long. These devouring mothers mark the oscillation of longing and fear, fight and flight which is the rhythm of Pericles' wayfaring. The next phase of the action is introduced by Gower again recounting the initiating incest story, and by his dumb show, in which bad news is delivered of pursuit from Tyre. Act II opens with Pericles' address to the elements when he finds himself cast up upon the shore at Pentapolis after the wreck of his escape ship.

Bred on the thunderous eloquence of Lear we may find these lines at first somewhat threadbare; but it is a speech worthy of remark in several respects.

> Yet cease your ire, you angry stars of heaven!
> Wind, rain, and thunder, remember earthly man
> Is but a substance that must yield to you;
> And I (as fits my nature) do obey you.
> Alas, the seas hath cast me on the rocks,
> Wash'd me from shore to shore, and left [me] breath

Nothing to think on but ensuing death.
Let it suffice the greatness of your powers
To have bereft a prince of all his fortunes;
And having thrown him from your wat'ry grave,
Here to have death in peace is all he'll crave.

(II,i,1–11)

Pericles has every cause for distress at this point – 'All perishen of man, of pelf,/ Ne aught escapend but himself' (II,Chorus,35–6) – but it will be noticed that there is no reference in his lament to the loss of the ship, or the sailors, nor any reference to the trauma of the wreck itself; nor for that matter is there any rejoicing or thanksgiving, however qualified, regarding his own escape. It is a total submission, a capitulation, that he expresses, and the powers to whom he capitulates are given, by the nature and the configuration of the imagery, a distinctly familial cast; the paternal, wrathfully punitive sky elements which it is 'his nature' to obey; the maternal ocean from which he has emerged. We note the casting upon rocks, immediately displaced by the rocking motion ('wash'd me from shore to shore') suggesting a cradle, or womb; but he is a castaway upon this rocky shore, breathless and bereft, and it is a 'wat'ry grave' from which he has been thrown. The passage is indissolubly ambivalent: whether he wishes or fears this womb/grave is impossible to determine – the condensation is, precisely, a compromise formation. The parent–child configuration gives a particular tinge to the melancholy he expresses, the deep depression, the dispirited craving for death. We discern the backward drift of an unresolved, unnamed preoccupation. We perceive the stance of a son whose rebellious rage against a parental couple – sky-father and sea-mother – has turned inward against himself.

This is the first of the play's sea journeys, which mark the pendulum swing of desire and dread, outgoing and withdrawal in the psychodrama which we follow. The play enacts its complex fantasy by repeated emergings from the sea, repeatedly foiled by the sea tempests themselves – a collusion of both parental figures in a rejecting fury. Pericles is dogged by mischance, but do not these chances as Freud said 'reflect the destiny which has decreed that through flight one is delivered over to the very thing that one is fleeing from'? That the sea, Pericles' constant refuge, and betrayer, giver and taker, destroyer and restorer, is a powerful presence in the play, has escaped no interpreter but its import has been found bewildering. 'The unlikelihood of the events,' says Philip Edwards,

> the lack of cause-and-effect in the plot, make the play a presentation of images which, while individually they expand into wide and general meanings, yet as a whole sequence withdraw from asserting how things run in this world. We are offered ideas or propositions about love and suffering and chastity, and the relation of them to a divine will, but we are not offered a clue to any meaning lying in the progression of events. The sea, therefore, remains a mystery. (1976, p. 31)

Yet his own description of 'the sea of life, the flow of unaccountable circumstances in which we drift' contains more of the clue he seeks than, it seems, he realizes: 'The sea threatens and comforts, destroys and rebuilds, separates and unites' (p. 17). Archetypal symbol of vicissitude in human life – yes; but 'oceanic', it will be recalled, was Freud's term for those fantasies of merging, union and dissolution which are rooted in yearnings for the primal symbiosis of infant and mother; and it is not without relevance to remember the interesting image used by the melancholy wandering Antipholus in *The Comedy of Errors:* [6]

> He that commends me to mine own content,
> Commends me to the thing I cannot get:
> I to the world am like a drop of water,
> That in the ocean seeks another drop,
> Who, falling there to find his fellow forth
> (Unseen, inquisitive), confounds himself.
> So I, to find a mother and a brother,
> In quest of them (unhappy), ah, lose myself.
>
> (I,ii,33–40)

The mere identification of a symbol is no more than is available in any dictionary of symbols. Simply to name is to vivisect, as Freud himself warned (though he often sinned himself in this respect (see Freud, 1900b, pp. 496–529), failing to distinguish between hallucinatory infantile visual symbolization and subtly complex verbal derivatives). The sea has been with us, and in our iconologies, for a very long time, but there is a pre-Freudian and a post-Freudian way of attending to symbols. In 1899, in his Notes to *The Wind among the Reeds*, Yeats speaks of 'some neo-platonist [who] describes the sea as a symbol of the drifting indefinite bitterness of life'; in 1932, in his Notes to *Fighting the Waves*, 'a German psychoanalyst', he says, 'has traced the "mother-complex" back to our mother the sea – to the loneliness of the first crab or crayfish that climbed ashore and turned lizard' (Yeats, 1899, p. 66; 1932, p. 571). Yeats makes my point. What the play *Pericles* wonderfully captures, obsessively reiterates, is, indeed, the rhythm of vicissitude in human life, the rhythm of maturation: separation, dispossession, return, under the cross of guilt, where three roads meet. The original loss, or lack, or absence, psychoanalytic theory tells us, is always the same; but its individual manifestations are always different, for it is through an endlessly varied chain of displaced signifiers that we strive, in language, to reconstitute the ever-receding, forever lost state of undifferentiated wholeness that was the bliss, and the fate, of the speechless infant.

Yeats's note treats evolutionary biology with considerable poetic licence, but let us, adopting his metaphor, pursue the adventures of our 'lizard'. It is the sequence of his recovery at this point which is particularly worth remarking.

Pericles climbs ashore at Pentapolis, and meets fishermen who have acerbic and foolish–wise things to say about the inequalities of the worldly world, where 'the great ones eat up the little ones' (II,i,28) like whales, who would swallow all, 'parish, church, steeple, bells, and all' (34). The Third Fisherman caps this parable with his own: 'when I had been in his belly, I would have kept such a jangling of the bells, that he should never have left till he cast bells, steeple, church, and parish up again' (40–3). What the 'whale', or sea, casts up is in fact the dripping Pericles: 'What a drunken knave was the sea to cast thee in our way!' (58)

Ancient paradigms have suggested themselves as models for the wanderings and sufferings of Pericles, in particular Ulysses, and the long-suffering Job; but in the light of the imagery in which the fishermen's observations are cast, Jonah would seem to be no less suitable a candidate (see Nathan, 1956). Not that these figures need be mutually exclusive. Texts wander about the world in each other's company, as we know, no less than romance protagonists.

But, it will be remembered, Jonah too fled from commitment, sank deeper and deeper into withdrawal during his three days aboard – a fugue which culminated in the belly of the whale – and was spewed forth to take up his mission again willy-nilly. Once again it is such derivatives of the primal oral infantile fantasies of eating and being eaten which lend support to the theory of 'the other story', the repressed or censored draft. Pericles' first response to the fishermen's questions is that of a passive victim – mere tennis ball (like Bosola) to the waters and the wind; 'a man throng'd up with cold' (73), he envisages death and imagines his own burial; but when the good King Simonides is referred to, and the joust that he plans, at which suitors will 'tourney for the love of his fair daughter', Pericles regains a will to live. 'Were my fortunes equal to my desires,' he says, 'I could wish to make one there' (111–12). Whereupon, hey presto, what should emerge from the sea in the fisherman's net but – his dead father's armour! This is a blessing, obviously, since it provides Pericles with the means to pursue honour, and a bride, at the court of Pentapolis; but for this purpose any treasure chest, or for that matter any suit of armour from the sunken ship would have served. Pericles' father's armour is talisman and symbol as well as blessing. Bequeathed in the father's will, it defended the father as the latter hopes it may defend his son. In the dream language of condensation, wearing it, blessedly belched forth out of the sea, Pericles both is, and is safe from, his dead father. He 'becomes' his father, legitimately, even obligatorily, as he sets forth upon his second courtship adventure.

In *Pericles* the psychomachia – the motivations at war within the protagonist, the bonds and bindings, the desires and fears which constitute for him his impossible choice – is not explicit, not immediately to be perceived. We are listening with the third ear, catching the unspoken filtering into discourse in the underhand ways the unspoken has of speaking. Ostensibly what Pericles contends with is the weather, the ocean, the winds and the waves, or competing knights at a tourney; but consider the scene of the tourney, or rather the scene which, significantly, takes the place, and at some length, of any staged combat.

The actual tourney, which takes place off stage, is prefaced by a procession of the contender knights each bearing a shield with an emblematic device and an explanatory Latin tag. On the face of it, and at the level of the represented world of the fable, what we are presented with here is simply a piece of chivalric decoration. We may entertain ourselves (as do the courtiers – the hermeneutic game of emblems was very popular in the seventeenth century) checking the match of tag to enigma, wondering what riddle will come next and what Pericles' contribution will be. The emblem game consisted of pictorializing epigrams or sententiae of extreme and uncontextualized generality: 'a black Ethiop reaching at the sun . . . *Lux tua vita mihi*' (II,ii,20–1); 'a hand environed with clouds,/ Holding out gold that's by the touchstone tried . . . *Sic spectanda fides*' (36–8); and so on. The connection between image and idea was often enough conventional, but the game became popular and interesting, worth playing indeed, in so far as the images were derived from the motto by rebus-like or arcane associations of one kind or another, or by what we would call today 'free' association. The resemblance to the techniques of dream, here as in the first riddle, is again striking: condensation, displacement, pictorialization and secondary revision; and we have a context – threatening parental figures, an imagery of bodily injury, menace and engulfment, which, if not repressed by readers, will magnetize the whole semiotic environment.

We can read the knights, minimally identified and all identical in aim, as essentially all one knight – projections of Pericles himself. We can read these images as mirrors in which Pericles reads himself, or as signifiers given meaning in Pericles' dream. The anomalies, paradoxes or absurdities at the level of the signifier solicit *our* interpretation; the ulterior signifieds, his. The devices are all configurations of ambivalence, the repressed unconscious fear concealed by the decorous mask of the mottos' secondary elaboration which expresses the conventional devotions and tribulations of courtly desire. Thus, while '*Lux tua vita mihi*' suggests an appropriate knightly ardour, the Ethiop in the emblem is (also) a black, or blackened, or shadowed Icarus, an overweening son against the sun. The armed knight that is conquered by the lady bears the unexceptionably courtly message: '*Piu per dolcezza che per forza'* (27), but this could be taken literally (as is the way of dreams) as referring to an actual conquest by a woman, and so articulates ambivalent wishing and fearing. In the symbology of dreams, crowns and wreaths, metamorphoses of that most fertile of all figures, the circle, are genital displacements upwards (see Willbern, 1980, pp. 244–64). The burning torch turned upside down, to show that 'beauty hath his power and will,/ Which can as well inflame as it can kill' (34–5), has for motto '*Qui me alit, me extinguit*' ('Who feeds me puts me out') – again a thralldom of desire and dread, which plugs, with splendid overdetermination, into oral, filial and sexual anxieties. The image of the hand holding out gold from amidst clouds to be tested by the touchstone (36–7) is surely very strange and obscure unless we can see an (anal)ogy to infantile anxieties about producing and withholding, while the 'country knight's' own phallic device, a withered branch with a green tip (43), once again marvellously symbolizes an irresolvable ambivalence of hope and fear.

Pericles, despite his rusty armour, wins the tourney and Thaisa's heart; and Simonides, good king, not bedazzled by outward show, recognizes the inner worth of his impeccably courteous future son-in-law: but is it courtesy, or a humility bordering upon a surrendering self-abasement? Perhaps the most revealing moment in these scenes is the melancholy knight's own aside immediately after his victory at the tourney. A triumphant winner at this point, what he says is as follows:

> [Yon] king's to me like to my father's picture,
> Which tells [me] in that glory once he was;
> Had princes sit like stars about his throne,
> And he the sun for them to reverence . . .
> Where now his [son's] like a glow-worm in the night,
> The which hath fire in darkness, none in light.
>
> (II,iii,37–44)

At the point of winning his fair bride Pericles' self-estimation has, strangely, never been lower, nor his guilty self-abasement more explicit. If we reverse the son/sun homonym, moreover, the tempting/frightening possibility of usurping the father-figure comes again into view: 'And he the son for them to reverence . . . /

Where now his sun's like a glow-worm in the night.' Danger – of supplanting the father – is inherent in success. That which is dangerous – *pericoloso* – is embedded in Pericles' name.[7] Moreover the play reiterates its obsessions in other figures besides Pericles. Simonides, despite his acceptance of the match, is not immune to paternal jealousy.

> By Jove, I wonder, that is king of thoughts,
> These cates resist me, he but thought upon.[8]

$$(28-9)$$

This pang of resentment is at once dissimulated as a testing of his daughter's feelings for 'but a country gentleman' who has 'done no more than other knights have done' (33). Scene iii concludes with the utmost amity on his part towards Pericles, yet scene v repeats the whole premarital testing sequence, with Simonides acting out a Brabantio-like rage towards Pericles – 'Thou hast bewitch'd my daughter and thou art/ A villain' (II,v,49-50) – and a blocking father's tyranny to his daughter:

> I'll tame you; I'll bring you in subjection.
> Will you, not having my consent,
> Bestow your love and your affections
> Upon a stranger?

$$(75-8)$$

Whether we read Simonides' dissembling as simply for the purpose of testing Pericles' character, or as an acting out of his own fatherly ambivalence ('Nay, how absolute she's in't,/ Not minding whether I dislike or no!' (19-20)) is immaterial. The question is how this unwilling son will respond to Simonides' assault. Pericles' initial response is to abase himself, to disavow all aims or claims to Thaisa's hand, to plead like a scolded child. Yet suddenly, at the charge of treachery, he rises to defend his honour at sword's point.

Pericles, it would seem, is a kaleidoscopically wavering character. He oscillates between listlessness and energy, withdrawal and outgoingness, defence or flight and attack. He seeks a wife, a family. He is a responsible king. He can rouse himself to courageous action despite his diffidence, as we have seen, and phonemic ambiguities (son/sun) may serve as cover for a considerable urge to self-assertion. Yet he withdraws, gives up, wanders away, evades, or is foiled. What happens to him is invariably what he fears, not what he hopes, as if the elements conspire with a self-fulfilling prophecy. The chorus which opens Act III images sexual fulfillment, achievement, but at once comes terrible reversal. Pericles loses his wife in a tempest at sea as his daughter is born. In terms of tragic structure this is as it should be: a fall from a height of power and prosperity. But the constant repeat or reiteration of such events is itself a message which solicits our attention. These vicissitudes of fortune can be read, at one level, simply as such. Ostensibly they represent the turn of Fortune's wheel, now up, now down, testing Pericles' powers of endurance with its mutations; but if, at a level more covert, the sea is a displaced signifier of the maternal oceanic, then Pericles' tale is very easily retold. 'If what Freud discovered and rediscovers with a perpetually increasing sense of shock has a meaning,' says Lacan,

> it is that the displacement of the signifier determines the subjects in their acts, in their destiny, in their refusals, in their blindnesses, in their end and in their fate, their innate gifts and social acquisitions notwith-standing, without regard for character or sex, and that, willingly or not, everything that might be considered the stuff of psychology, kit and caboodle, will follow the path of the signifier. (1972, p. 60)

Pericles travels out and away and back. He cannot escape, cannot cut the umbilical cord, and cannot resolve the later oedipal guilt. The sea is indeed his beloved enemy, as the sun–father is his envied and hostile rival. Antiochus represents at the outset the threatening father-figure, and whatever person Pericles seeks is a symbolic personage representing the mother, lost and forbidden. It is therefore always by the incest fear that he is haunted. Derivatives of these primal constellations erupt in language and situation throughout: the very name he gives his daughter is the name of the sea.

It is as such a haunting fantasy, I think, that we can read the report of Helicanus in Tyre of the exposure of Antiochus' incest with his daughter (it is the third time we have been told of it) and of their terrible fate. This report is apparently arbitrarily intercalated between the two scenes in which Simonides plays the role of a

threatening father, rather as in a film when shots from another time
and place are interpolated into a sequence to represent an image in
the mind. Seated in a chariot with his daughter:

> A fire from heaven came and shrivell'd up
> Those bodies, even to loathing; for they so stunk,
> That all those eyes ador'd them ere their fall
> Scorn now their hand should give them burial.

(II,iv,9–12)

The blocking father and the incestuous daughter are dead, indeed,
but their nightmare image continues to haunt; the shrivelled bodies
stink to high heaven, unburied, preserved mysteriously as images
of fear and horror and loathing as yet unexorcized.

The nightmare is the obverse of the oceanic dream; the
prohibition of its siren lure. It is the tempests at sea, with their
lightning and thunder, that repeatedly overthrow him. It is perhaps
not without significance that Pericles' address to the storm recalls
that of Lear, who would have set his rest upon Cordelia's 'kind
nursery'.

> O, still
> Thy deaf'ning, dreadful thunders, gently quench
> Thy nimble, sulphurous flashes! . . .
> . . . [Thou] storm, venomously
> Wilt thou spet all thyself?

(III,i,4–7)

The jealous, tempestuous sea takes Thaisa, yet once again the sea
spews its victims (Pericles himself, or his wife, or his daughter)
forth, in the struggle to be born again. The mortal combat between
Thanatos and Eros is given in the second part of the play with a
verbal felicity and resonance to which no critic can fail to respond.
Consider the peculiarly evocative speech in which he consigns
Thaisa to the waves, which contains within its compass ('A
terrible childbed hast thou had, my dear;/ No light, no fire' (56–7))
the Jonah death-wish, the great desire to be, at last, at peace,
beneath the 'humming water' and 'the belching whale', 'lying with
simple shells' (62–4). (On shells see Bachelard, 1964, chapter 5.)

The recovery of Thaisa in Act III, scene ii is manifestly a
compensatory birth or rebirth fantasy: out of the chest/coffin

emerges a sweet-smelling 'corse'. Why does the play need a birth fantasy, and a nourishing father (in the life-giving physician Cerimon: 'hundreds call themselves/ Your creatures' (III,ii,44-5)) when it has the real birth of Marina?; and how can we account for his leaving the babe, that 'fresh new seafarer' (III,i,41), to be reared by Cleon and Dionyza while he retreats into the monkish garb of a Nazirite? The tragic reversal of Act III, culminating in the tempest which kills Thaisa, is transformed by amazing happenstance into a happy reunion, with the sea giving up its 'dead' and a reconstituted, benign family configuration replacing the monstrous union of the first act. However, this comic resolution is due to happenstance only in terms of the 'official' or exterior plot. If we read 'the repetitive process obscurely going on underneath or beyond it' (Brooks, P., 1980, p. 511), expressing itself indirectly through the very means which veil it, much of great interest becomes apparent.

The recovery of Thaisa, belched forth from the sea, is a rebirth fantasy in the text, to which we, the audience, are privy, but in the progress of the fable her loss at sea represents regression in Pericles. As his abandonment of his baby daughter to the care of others also indicates, he is still not enfranchised, not ready to accept fatherhood, still haunted by the spectre of incest. Lear, as the Fool tells him, made his daughters his mother; Pericles cannot permit himself to love his daughter, lest he desire her – and when he dares, it is too late.

Years later, he 'again thwart[s] the wayward seas . . . / To see his daughter, all his live's delight' (IV,iv,10-12) and to bring her home. He finds her, as he believes, in her grave. That Pericles will suffer grievously over this loss hardly needs explanatory comment, but Gower's comment points interestingly to the relation between mourning and melancholia which was in due course (three hundred years and a decade later) to become a Freudian theme. 'He swears', Gower informs us, 'Never to wash his face, nor cut his hairs;/ He [puts] on sackcloth, and to sea. He bears/ A tempest, which his mortal vessel tears,/ And yet he rides it out' (27-31). Tempest-tossed, death-possessed, he has become fixed in the mortified posture which acts out the wish to die that is born of the conviction that he deserves to die.

The play's remedial and recognitive last two acts will tell us that what Pericles needs is not the return of his wife or the birth of a child but a rebirth for himself. Not until Pericles' lost and found daughter 'beget'st him that did [her] beget' (V,i,195), as he puts it, is the tempest which his mortal vessel tears at last stilled. But is it? And how shall we integrate into our reading the grotesqueries of Mytilene?

The 'absolute' Marina, it will be recalled, is done away with by her jealous foster mother – a figure who reappears as Imogen's stepmother in *Cymbeline*, and, as the witch Sycorax, lurks in the background of Prospero's island. Her own daughter is put in the shade, so she feels, by Marina's surpassing excellence in the womanly arts and virtues. Cleon protests, but is overborne by his Goneril-like queen. This weak and recessive father cannot save his step-daughter from the assault of the dominant mother, since he is undermined by Dionyza's taunts of cowardice. Is Cleon, proxy father for Pericles, also his masochistic self-image? 'In the dream,' André Green reminds us, 'when the dreamer's representation becomes overloaded, the dreamer splits it into two and sets up another character to represent, separately, one or more of his characteristics or affects' (1979, p. 2).[9] This will prove a useful principle with which to approach the next phase of the play.

Act IV, which follows the adventures of the fatherless Marina (orphaned also of her faithful old nurse), is, it will be noticed, quite conspicuously full of surrogate parental or quasi-guardian figures including the brothel 'family' – the pandar, his bawd wife and their servant Boult – and Lysimachus himself, who, though his age is never mentioned, seems, as governor of the city, authority-figure and Marina's patron, more a father than a lover until their betrothal. It is also conspicuously full of imminent rape. Leonine expects the rescuing pirates to ravish Marina; the brothel 'family', for whom Marina's virginity at first presented itself as a commercial asset, are later intent upon disabusing themselves of her 'peevish' intractability ('We must either get her ravish'd or be rid of her . . . she would make a puritan of the devil' (IV,vi,5–9)); the two gentleman customers are put by her 'quirks, her reasons, her master-reasons, her prayers, her knees' (8) 'out of the road of rutting forever'

(IV,v,9) and the disguised governor Lysimachus is – what? unmanned? derailed? converted? (we shall return to Lysimachus presently) by what the Bawd calls Marina's 'virginal fencing' (IV,vi,57).

The classic recourse, in psychoanalytic theory, of the maternally fixated libido is a debased sexual object – prostitute or courtesan. The transformation of Marina into such a figure liberates sexual fantasy, the brothel scenes providing a screen through which the deeply repressed sensuality of Pericles can find release. Thus the remedial fourth-act exorcism-through-exacerbation which characterizes Shakespearian comedy can be seen to be effected through the brothel scenes.[10] Pericles, himself absent from the stage, a monk in his mourning and his melancholy, is replaced by these fantasized figures, whose bawdy eroticism can be allowed free play within the constraining limits, or off-limits, of Marina's charismatic chastity. What strikes us in the sexual metaphors here is that they are sadistic, rather than comic. The overriding theme is not reciprocal sexual play, cheerfully spilling over into verbal play as in the early comedies, or in Mercutio's jesting, nor even the wry consequences of sexual play in the form of venereal-disease punishment which is also usual in Shakespeare. The overriding theme is simply defloration, and the metaphors are fantasies of injury, force, mutilation or cannibalism too threatening to amuse. They at once titillate and alienate by appeals to a voyeurism or sadomasochism not veiled but provoked by the euphemism or metaphor: 'Marry, whip the gosling, I think I shall have something to do with you. Come, you're a young foolish sapling, and must be bow'd as I would have you' (IV,ii,86–8); 'if I have bargain'd for the joint – Thou mayst cut a morsel off the spit' (130–1); 'For flesh and blood, sir, white and red, you shall see a rose' (IV,vi,34–6); 'Boult, take her away, use her at thy pleasure. Crack the glass of her virginity, and make the rest malleable . . . And if she were a thornier piece of ground than she is, she shall be ploughed' (141–5).

The brothel sequence fulfills its exorcist function despite, or within, the control of secondary revision. The drama's seductive fable ensures that the physical act, through the wit, wisdom and self-possession of Marina, the protective bounty of Lysimachus and the good offices of Boult, does not in fact come about. The whole brothel sequence takes something of the form of a protracted, though in the end frustrated, initiation ritual: 'My lord, she's not pac'd yet, you must take some pains to work her to your manage,' says the Bawd (IV,vi,63–4); she is to be initiated into 'our profession' (7). This, because it is parody of a sort, serves as a species of legitimization; even the commercialization of sex does this. One notes that it is this theme which is made to yield the Shakespearian humour of Boult's final grumbling protest at Marina's excoriation of his trade: 'What would you have me do? Go to the wars, would you? where a man may serve seven years for the loss of a leg, and have not money enough in the end to buy him a wooden one?' (171–3); but read at the level of primary process Marina is a depersonalized sex object for the release of deeply repressed and traumatized libido.

It is at this point that we can take up two nagging questions that have troubled the critics. Why, it is asked, does Thaisa, retrieved from a watery grave by Cerimon, become a vestal in Diana's temple instead of setting forth in search of her husband? 'The plot of romantic fiction will have it so', says Hallett Smith (1974, p. 1481). It is the answer, not the question that, I suggest, is naive. If we read, not the plot of romance narrative, but the plot of 'the other scene', we can see that it is necessary for both Marina's parents to be sexually in abeyance, neutralized, while the screen fantasies of the brothel scenes are taking place. The psychic burden is shifted, so to speak, to the shoulders of the surrogate figures. It is upon similar lines that we can address the second nagging question: What was Lysimachus doing in the brothel in the first instance?

The text is poker-faced. We cannot make out whether he is caught out in a visitation the like of which it is his custom to make – he is certainly familiar enough to and with Boult – and subsequently converted by Marina's spirited virtue; or whether he is covertly investigating – what? – the state of morality in the stews of his city? 'I came with no ill intent' (IV,vi,109), he says. Then with what intent did he come? This unsolved mystery is more serious than it seems because it puts into question his relation to Marina, making this brothel–betrothal seem a rather hugger-mugger affair, to say the least. This problem too cannot be solved by appeal to comic genre conventions such as marriages all round or sudden conversion and the like because, first, too much emotional interest is invested in protagonist figures for us to be content with mere plot devices to round off a play. In the second place it is never made clear whether Lysimachus was in need of conversion or not. He remains therefore a split character, indeterminately ravisher and protector. This split, or anomaly, is our clue. For if the dream burden has been displaced to other figures in the way Green describes, and we can read Lysimachus as a representation, or extension of Pericles, then the split in Lysimachus is the unconscious split in Pericles. If therefore, the archaic turbulence of ambivalent desire and dread has been played out in the fantasy, and Marina has been saved by a fatherly figure (and/or a brotherly figure if we see Boult as her immediate saviour), when the young girl is brought to the ailing King, in Act V, to warm him back to life there is a double indemnity against the threat of incest. Pericles and Marina are safe and the way is clear for rebirth and restoration.

When the reunion occurs therefore it is truly miraculous – thaumaturgic. The King's grief has brought him to the point of death; now his healing is enacted before us. His initial resistance as he pushes Marina away, her resemblance to Thaisa, the gradual dawning of his recognition, the reluctance to believe lest it not be so, the fear of too great joy:

> O Helicanus, strike me, honoured sir,
> Give me a gash, put me to present pain,
> Lest this great sea of joys rushing upon me
> O'erbear the shores of my mortality,
> And drown me with their sweetness. O, come hither,
> Thou that beget'st him that did thee beget . . .
>
> (V,i,190–5)

these draw their power not only from finely observed human behaviour, but from our intuition of the entrenchedness of defence and repression that has had to be broken through. We must love, said Freud, in order not to fall ill. The pleasure we feel is the measure of the depth of the need, and the deprivation:

> My dearest wife was like this maid, and such a one
> My daughter might have been . . .
>   . . . another Juno;

Who starves the ears she feeds and makes them hungry,
The more she gives them speech.

(V,i,107–14)

We witness the paradigmatic moment of the late romances which, in Barber's felicitous formulation, 'free family ties from the threat of sexuality', whereas the early comedies had freed sexuality from the ties of family (1969, pp. 59–67). 'Thou that beget'st him that did thee beget' is, as Barber notes, the secular equivalent of Dante's theogony: 'Virgine madre, figlia in tua figlio', and is 'the rarest dream that e'er dull'd sleep/ Did mock sad fools withal' (V,i,161–2).

Here, clearly, the play cannot remain. For a totality of psychic value in one beloved figure – mother and daughter at once – reproduces the spectre of Antioch. The play offers us a solution to this impasse in the recovery of Thaisa, and the betrothal of Marina to Lysimachus. There is even a separate kingdom available for both the generations, since the recent death of Thaisa's father leaves the throne of Pentapolis vacant for the parental couple.

And yet there is an unresolved indeterminacy in the text which makes it possible to read the ending of *Pericles* not as a mandala closure but as a dizzying return to square one. Consider the strange ambiguities of Pericles' final speech to the restored Thaisa:

No more, you gods, your present kindness
Makes my past miseries sport. You shall do well
That on the touching of her lips I may
Melt, and no more be seen. O, come, be buried
A second time within these arms.

(V,iii,39–43)

Eros? Thanatos? Can we say? To die upon a kiss was a common Renaissance metaphor for consummation; but how shall we read these words? Does the text crumble to its own deconstruction at the end, with nothing resolved or exorcized, but all to be done again? I turn once more to André Green. 'We shall often feel a renewed disappointment', he says, 'faced by [the text's] refusal to take us anywhere except to the point of origin from which it took its own departure' (1979, p. 23). Is this the case in *Pericles*? And is it disappointment that we feel? Or is this refusal simply a sign that the play has put us in touch with the familiar ghosts – the desires and the terrors – that habitually haunt our minds?

NOTES

1. P. Goolden (1955, p. 251) reviews the history of the riddle from the Latin prose *Apollonius*, where involuted in-law relations provide the clues, through Gower's Middle English version to Shakespeare's adaptation in *Pericles*. He notes that Shakespeare's innovation allows for simplification; he ignores, however, the oddity that catches our attention. R. E. Gajdusek (1974, pp. 109–30) has recourse to a Jungian Triple Goddess both for the riddle and the play which he reads as a mythical contest between the feminine (all-devouring) and the masculine (separative) principles. Dr Rivka Eifferman, in the course of a seminar on Psychoanalysis and Literature held at the Hebrew University Centre for Literary Studies in 1985, suggests the possibility that 'All love the womb that their first being bred' could paraphrase as 'All love the daughter that they first [in their youth] raised', thus providing a literal solution to the riddle and obviating recourse to the unconscious.

2. The riddle contains metalepsis in Quintillian's sense: the metonymical substitution of one word for another which is itself figurative. But I am using the term in the sense made familiar in narratology: transpositions of past and present, foreboding and retrospection. Both senses offer paradigms for the psychoanalytic process.

3. For an account of levels of representation in Shakespeare – the use of choric figures, plays-within-plays, actors acting actors, on-stage audiences and other parabastic devices, see Aviva Furdi (1984). See also the interesting earlier account of 'multi-consciousness' given by S. L. Bethell (1944).

4. See F. D. Hoeniger's Arden edition (1963) for an account of the textual problems in this passage. I am indebted to Dr Rivka Eifferman for the primal-scene insight.

5. Alan B. Rothenberg (1973, p. 215) notices the image of maternal devouring in I,v,41–3, and points out that in the 1609 and 1611 Q texts of *Pericles* 'nousle' (to nurse) is spelled 'nouzell' (our 'nuzzle' – to thrust the nose into). The composite neatly condenses feeding and projective threat, mother and child.

6. *The Comedy of Errors*, derived from the same literary source as *Pericles* – the popular fifth-century *Apollonius of Tyre* – is evidently a younger oedipal fantasy in which the threatened father, Egeus, is

rescued by his son. See Freud on rescue fantasies in 'Family romances' (1909).

7. I am grateful to Dr Paul Gabriner for suggesting this onomastic possibility.

8. This difficult line has been glossed in many ways. The 1609 Q text has 'not', which is followed by Hoeniger's Arden edition (1963), and by Ernest Schanzer in the Signet edition (1965). Philip Edwards' emendation (1976) is 'but', which makes good sense for the reading here advanced. Edwards suggests that the aside be given to Thaisa, which however would destroy the repartee effect of her 'Juno' to Simonides' 'Jove'.

9. As Robert Rogers says, 'Whenever decomposition (splitting, doubling or multiplication of personae) takes place in narrative, the cast of characters is never quite as large as it would appear to be' (1970, p. 63).

10. In Nevo (1980) I have attempted to develop a cathartic, or 'exorcist' theory of comic form.

7 THE TEMPEST, 'ALL TORMENT, TROUBLE, WONDER AND AMAZEMENT': A KLEINIAN READING

B. J. SOKOL

Not only the mariners in, but the critics of Shakespeare's last play [1] cry 'We split' and are dissevered. Despite wide critical divergences, I think the truth must have it both ways. *The Tempest* is still a reparative comedy although the 'wonder' expressed in it is a product of misapprehension and illusion. The play calls for a complex judgement also because its themes of forgiveness and reparation are poised against a frequent vein of hate and disgust.

Harsh tones in *The Tempest* often express imperfectly repressed conflicts or half-suppressed seething. Only when Caliban is in question is the great anger in the play presented simply and explicitly. Symmetrically, only Caliban's rebellion expresses fully the turmoil of his supposed 'betters'. They in various ways complicate the issue because they cannot frankly admit, as he can, to what W. H. Auden has described in his poem 'Canzone':

> Our dreadful appetite demands a world
> Whose order, origin and purpose will
> Be fluent satisfaction of our will.

The fallen courtiers of *The Tempest* exceed Caliban in rapaciousness, illustrating how appetite dresses up in civility. But hidden appetite appears more poignantly in the unfallen mage Prospero, whose sufferings derive from the guilt of desires denied and repressed.

Unless otherwise indicated, all Shakespeare citations are from *The Tempest*, Frank Kermode, ed., The Arden Shakespeare, London: Methuen, 1961.

Repression in Prospero causes a choking off of awareness, and this in turn poses a great threat to his project of Art. The danger is increased by one of Prospero's apparent advantages, his magical power of surveillance. Too much outer sight makes it easy for him to indulge in the self-deception, even the hubris, that deflects from insight. Our own insight is also threatened because we are invited to share with Prospero an omniscience that misleads. Thus we may miss how *The Tempest*, like *The Winter's Tale*, presents at first the threatened tragedy of its self-blinded protagonist. The Folio stage direction '*Prosper on the top (invisible)*' suggests a safe and detached viewpoint which we the audience must, as must Prospero, struggle to overcome.

Our perspective, like Prospero's, does reveal ironies, as when Miranda on meeting rogues and would-be murderers cries out 'O, wonder!' But what to make of such knowledge is not answered by omniscience alone. With only one exception, which we will explore, Prospero never fails to react immediately and accurately to the actions and secrets of all the others during the play. So in contriving his deceptions Prospero never flounders, and hardly ever needs to improvise. This leaves intact the image of Prospero's full omnipotence, which has often created difficulties of response to the play.

But Prospero's omnipotence in *The Tempest*, and his apparent knowledge of all significant circumstances, are themselves illusions presented by the play specifically to be seen through. How they are seen through generates their meaning. That is to say, the true purpose of the presentation of Prospero's power in *The Tempest* is to enable our discovery of the invisible limits that lie within it.

Such a reading of Prospero's power accords with Shakespeare's text, but lies athwart both of the two opposed schools of interpretation of the play recently dominant – which will be discussed at some length presently. This reading, in which Prospero is self-impeded, finds its main support in the play's dramatic tone. Although the magic fable in *The Tempest* imposes very few outward impediments to Prospero's magian role, the play's actual text suggests its performance should be high in tension and urgency. Explicitly this is connected with the pressure on Prospero to complete a project of spiritual alchemy constrained by 'a most auspicious star' (I,ii,182). But this time-limit on his life's 'zenith' does not fully account for a feeling throughout the play that he is straining against difficult odds. Here, as often in *The Tempest*, cause in the form of explicit motivation is unequal to the implicit emotional effect.

Prospero's complex passion concerns basic problems of action itself. From long passivity he moves directly to confront external resistance and rebellion, and must backtrack to deal with internal rebellion. Prospero's role is not the only expression of this theme, and *The Tempest* sounds the gamut of ways to live rebelliousness: from loving self-control, through slips of 'forgetfulness', to other-deceiving treachery, self-deceiving hypocrisy, and drunken or berserk riot.

Yet it is usually appreciated that the play's outcome is not seriously endangered by rebellion, and indeed it is often said that the plot of *The Tempest* lacks all suspense (Kermode, 1963, p. 42; D. G. James, 1967, p. 141).[2] This then makes an enigma of why Prospero, entirely lacking practical impediments, undergoes emotional struggles. The very structure that replaces traditional plotting with evolutions of a myth of omnipotence, omniscience, and triumphal destiny draws us to question what Prospero battles with, and what he overcomes.

The answer I will propose is that he battles with dangerous inner rebellions, which he must overcome to ensure that his 'charms crack not'. This answer suggests a less shimmery and indefinite understanding of the magic island than is usual. Yet *The Tempest* always keeps its ability to surprise. Indeed exploration of the play leads again and again to incongruities in its articulations of motives, tones, and conventions – incongruities which are synthesized to yield 'something rich and strange'.

1

One of the ways *The Tempest* synthesizes opposites is in combining a characteristic Romance plot with natural-seeming portrayals of character and interaction. This spans two axes at once, from convention to uniqueness and from symbolism to verisimilitude. Thus the play is by turns bold and subtle, mannered and direct.

A fit audience must be able to attend simultaneously to compressed realistic nuances and large conceptual gestures. All four late Shakespeare Romances make this demand; it corresponds to the development Inga-Stina Ewbank has demonstrated in *Pericles*, the first of them: 'with Marina Shakespeare discovered there does not have to be a conflict between the demands of Romance plot and the demands of characterization' (1980, p. 117). Within the fantastic framework of *The Tempest* we find a similar aptness of portrayal. For example, as Coleridge perceived, 'the scene of the intended assassination of Alonso and Gonzalo is an exact counterpart of the scene between Macbeth and his lady, . . . exhibiting the same profound management . . . ' (quoted in Kermode, 1961, p. 53n).

The 'profound management' most interesting in *The Tempest* is of conflicts in and around Prospero's magical project. So I will first offer a brief discussion of conflict in the play as a whole, and then attempt to analyse some of the compressed and fine-grained portrayals that make Prospero and his fellows appear lifelike in their inner and outer conflicts, even though they inhabit a fantastic Romance world.

Of course all Romance stories contain elements of conflict and even evil, but these typically need no more underpinning than story-book conventions. The jejune motivations of Shakespeare's own evil-stepmother-figures such as Dionyza in *Pericles* or the nameless Queen in *Cymbeline*, or of his deceptive foreigner-figures including Antiochus' nameless daughter, and Iachimo in the same pair of Romance plays, illustrate this. But in *The Tempest* hate and harshness imply far more than bald convention allows.

Despite this I will maintain against many recent critics that conflict is not, and certainly cynicism and disillusion are not, the limiting finalities of the play. These critics believe the play concerns only power and oppression and deny the genuineness of its themes of forgiveness and reconciliation.[3] I believe that conflict, hate and bitterness are central in the play and are not all eradicated there, but I think *The Tempest* incorporates also themes of love and tolerance. In this way again the play spans bold opposites, as it does in confronting ironic experience with hopeful innocence, habitual harshness with fresh tenderness, worldly disillusion with lasting art.

What makes it possible for the play to join together such wide opposites is that it dramatizes a genuine synthetic process. This is a process in which real gains of freedom and autonomy are achieved by means of internal struggles which are, moreover, implicitly not final but painfully recurrent in continuing cycles. These are, in short, the cyclic processes of psychic growth described by Melanie Klein. If Kleinian cycles do appertain to *The Tempest*, much recent criticism properly identifies extreme hatred and anger in the play, but fails when it presents these as contradictory to a theme of growth.

Earlier twentieth-century critics brought to *The Tempest* an interpretation centering on reconciliation, seeing it as an 'amazing work' triumphantly and fully transcending the pain of Shakespeare's tragic phase, and thus crowning his life's achievement and summing up 'the poetic essence of the whole Shakespearian universe'. These phrases are from G. Wilson Knight's *The Shakespearian Tempest* (1932, p. 247). Their point of view persisted, according to Frank Kermode, in the 'general interpretation of *The Tempest* now current' at least until 1961, when Kermode revised his admirable earlier preface (1954) to the New Arden edition (1961, p. lxxxiii). And indeed readings of the play as essentially affirmative as Wilson Knight's are found in the work of Tillyard, Traversi, Frye, and many others.

An opposite view, often repeated recently, is that *The Tempest* is exclusively a record of violent political contradictions and consequent falsifications of consciousness. This school of thought usually sets itself up as 'revising' the work of what it calls 'essentialist' criticism. Often Wilson Knights's and E. M. W. Tillyard's readings in particular are singled out as politically naive. Members of 'revisionist', 'new historicist' or 'cultural materialist' factions typically dismiss earlier twentieth-century critics by alleging they found in late Shakespeare only sweetness-and-light, and accepted uncritically the propaganda of a well-ordered 'layer-cake' universe, an 'Elizabethan World Picture' (see Tayler, pp. 45–6).

But extraordinarily, the typical revisionist reading of *The Tempest* as a play concerned with colonialist oppression is found in a late essay of Wilson Knight himself. In this essay Wilson Knight reverses his earlier patriotic defence of benefits of British colonialism he saw in *The Tempest* (1947, pp. 253–5) and claims that the exploitation and oppression of the new world Red Man, in the guise of Caliban, gives *The Tempest* a political theme of struggle between cultures and value systems (1980, pp. 205–21). As Wilson Knight acknowledges in his notes, a similar view was proposed in 1972, with added fascinating psycho-sexual speculations concerning miscegenation, by Leslie Fiedler (pp. 167–212).

These older critics do not work from such rigid political presuppositions as the 'revisionists'.[4] I do not think it unfair or reductive to say that revisionists begin by assuming that the only human relations having real significance are relations of power. The whole realms of affection, subjective perception, and any kind of transcendent value or belief, are held by them to be parts of a mere 'superstructure' built on the genuineness of a material 'base'. So creative literary texts for many revisionists become one of a range of so-called 'discourses' unequal only in bourgeois prestige to 'lit-crit', journalism, advertising, and propaganda.

'Discourse' is defined in the notes to Paul Brown's revisionist essay on *The Tempest* as 'a domain or field of linguistic strategies operating within particular areas of social practice to effect knowledge and pleasure, being produced by and producing or reworking power relations between classes, genders, and cultures' (1985, p. 69). The essay draws attention to the 'discourse of colonialism' in the play, and focuses on Prospero's remark regarding Caliban, 'this thing of darkness I acknowledge mine'. Brown sees this as Prospero's assertion of a property relation 'when apportioning the plebeians to the masters' (p. 68).[5] Then he discusses how the remark suggests an identification between Prospero and Caliban which points to ideological contradictions implicit in the 'colonialist project'. But even with such irony acknowledged this reading stresses relations of power alone. In order to achieve this the essay disregards aspects of Shakespeare's text. The context of Prospero's remark is complex and indeed disputed (see the notes to the Arden text), but surely 'apportioning the plebeians' is untrue to the tone in which Prospero ruefully admits to being master of a worse rogue than the roguish followers of his despised enemies. Brown's reading also requires the word 'acknowledge' to take on a meaning not found anywhere else in Shakespeare: the many Shakespearian instances of the word all carry the meaning 'admit to' and most further imply the (for a revisionist, probably unacceptable) notion 'with individual responsibility'.[6]

Let me continue to focus on Prospero's 'acknowledging' of Caliban, using this passage to test other modes of reading the play. Its difficulty reveals a typical deficiency in the sorts of allegorical reading of *The Tempest* that Wilson Knight's influential first interpretations displaced. Pure allegory makes no more sense of Prospero's rueful 'acknowledge' and possessive 'mine' than putative 'discourses of colonialism'. For how can Prospero acknowledge as *his* a Caliban representative of some principle or part of nature such as earth, water, matter, the vegetive soul, or libido? As A. D. Nuttall concludes after carefully considering the possibility of strictly allegorical readings of *The Tempest*, something more is required by the play than an assumption of 'stony' allegory, or of a contrasting 'rigid' cynicism (1967, p. 159). Otherwise a passage such as 'this thing . . . I acknowledge mine' will mean nothing.

Finally let me consider a third reading of Prospero's remark 'acknowledging' Caliban, in D. G. James's *The Dream of Prospero*. This book traces the earlier Elizabethan fascination with exploration and plantation derived from accounts of the voyages of the 1570s and '80s, and then it treats the use in *The Tempest* of more contemporary accounts of real events (*c.* 1610) including storm, shipwreck, misrule and mutiny in Bermuda and Virginia. By giving a detailed historical context for the 'Bermuda pamphlets' James is able to contrast the 'sweetness of the first meetings' of Englishmen and Indians which included 'humane' intentions, with the slightly later colonists' frequent rapaciousness and violent conflicts with each other and with native Americans (p. 77). Once having established this properly complex context in which Shakespeare worked, James is able to see the possibility of more than colonial oppression in the depiction of the bad relations of Prospero and

Caliban. He sees Prospero 'harsh and intransigent to Caliban', but adds:

> Prospero is not only the Virginia planter; and the time will come when he will say: 'this thing of darkness I acknowledge mine'; as St Augustine in his *Confessions* knew well the darkness was in *him*, set over against the light before which he trembles in love and awe. (p. 121)

For me the great suggestiveness of this lies in the comparison with a confession like Augustine's. The reference to the *Confessions* suggests that there is in Prospero, at the moment he acknowledges Caliban, both a voluntary awareness of guilt and a strong intimacy of feeling. If his acknowledging Caliban truly suggests such a mode of being in Prospero it can have nothing to do with abstractions of an allegorical sort, and even less with a cold struggle for dominance in a world of power alone.

2

If Prospero achieves such authenticity of being near the play's end, he has in my belief come an immense way during the bare three hours of time portrayed in *The Tempest*. I would agree, of course, that his achievement is made plausible by the indication of his long period of arduous study preceding the play's action, for the Renaissance closely associated a spiritual quest with intellectual pursuits.[7] But however intense his preparation, the play gives distinct evidence against views that Prospero has already achieved at its start a personal 'comprehensive view of spiritual reality' (Traversi, p. 322) which can be simply transferred to others.

Success in spiritual alchemy leading to 'projection' or the creation of a spiritually healing elixir is a development requiring: the mage's long and arduous intellectual preparation; a rare combination of auspicious stars; a proper admixture of earthy substance or manure (Caliban) with subtler fiery substance (Ariel); an ambience of chastity (Ferdinand's and Miranda's); and the immediate good spiritual condition of the mage. Because of the last of these especially, no alchemical 'project' is certain before the event not to 'crack'. Prospero's project, I maintain, is certainly chancy, for the play presents ever-increasing evidence that he is and has long been self-ignorant, self-thwarting, and a great self-deceiver.

To prove this I will proceed like a crafty prosecutor and arraign Prospero by stating first a 'mitigating circumstance' that is in reality damning. In the Milan of his early manhood Prospero seems to have lacked any obvious goad (like the immorality of Vincentio's Vienna) forcing him from studiousness. So his trust in his brother's over-capable administration was not a criminal neglect of duty. Young Prospero's less obvious disgrace was that, unlike Hamlet, he failed to notice or to care when merely efficient administration took the place of the just exercise of authority. (This is not fanciful speculation, – we will see that these past circumstances, *and how they are misrepresented*, are central to the play's first act.)

The same dishonourable collusion with unjust efficiency is still widely current when the play begins. Among the courtiers Antonio's crime of usurpation is conveniently forgotten by all. Not only is there no murmur against this old crime, but all courtiers except Gonzalo (whose acceptance of the *status quo* will be considered later) are confidently expected by Antonio to be ready and willing to accept its repetition: 'They'll take suggestion as a cat laps milk' (II,i,283).

The illegitimacy of Antonio's power is obscured by the glitter of his alliance with the powerful King of Naples, who was implicated in his manoeuvres. That Antonio has bought Naples' friendship with tribute extracted from the Milanese people has the invisibility of a non-thought for Antonio's and Alonso's well-off 'councellors'. Despite only three villains being specified by Ariel disguised as the Harpy, all of the ruling classes are 'men of sin'.

In my belief Prospero at the start of *The Tempest* also deserves this judgment. He also is guilty of averted scruples and convenient lapses of memory. To argue this I will consider details of the beginning of the play's marvellous 'establishing' scene (I,ii), in which Miranda is informed of her past and prepared for her debut in the wicked world.

In this scene Prospero paradoxically mixes his harsh insistence that he be understood with a tense reluctance to communicate. This contradictory behaviour is matched by other evidence of confused attitudes. Although the storm scene first shows Prospero as a powerful mage, he immediately afterwards presents himself as the scholarly and contemplative recluse that, in his own view, is a superior sort of man. Although nearly omnipotent in purveying illusions, he takes pains to describe himself to Miranda as entirely different from 'the deceiver', his vigorous worldly brother.

Prospero's long sequestering away from responsibility may remind us of Montaigne's voluntary withdrawal to his philosopher's tower in plague-time, when he was the mayor of Bordeaux. There may even be a sarcastic reference to this in *The Tempest* when Gonzalo offers a muddled paraphrase of some of Montaigne's idealistic social ideas.

In any case there is much irony, evidencing inner conflict, in the establishing scene of *The Tempest*. In it Prospero reveals embittered attitudes which ill serve his attempts to inform and prepare Miranda prior to her encounter with civilization. Also he himself deliberately contrives the means for an introduction of contagious 'infection' (his own metaphor for Ferdinand's effect on Miranda) to his sanctuary.

Language in the scene reveals that Prospero is passionate in his complexly motivated behaviour. He first tenderly says to Miranda that he acts only 'in care of thee'. Yet in the scene he shows repetitive verbal harshness to her. This contradiction is worthy of the closest attention. It would seem initially that Prospero's hectoring tone is motivated by his concern lest Miranda remain too innocent. She does seem at first potentially gullible. She pityingly assumes the false-dealing shipwrecked rogues are 'poor . . . fraughting souls', and soon after greets them with the, for the Renaissance, highly questionable emotion of 'wonder' (see Sokol, 1980). But anxious tender care for his 'loved darling' cannot fully explain Prospero's battering and staccato demands for her mindfulness. Indeed it is a bit uncanny to see, in the scene in which Prospero actually hypnotizes his daughter/pupil, how he repeatedly and violently expresses doubts that he can even hold her attention. These incongruities imply undercurrents in the scene contrary to a motive of care, and far beyond its structural function of conveying necessary background information to launch the following action.

In fact it is not possible to excuse Prospero's browbeating on account of a real fear that Miranda is incapable of imagining sophisticated worldly evil. Gentle Miranda is not at all unapt, bland, or mindlessly serene. Even before Prospero makes his main point Miranda anticipates it, asking 'What foul play had we' (I,ii,60). Later she goes beyond simply accepting the rhetorical point of his 'then tell me/ If this might be a brother', replying:

> I should sin
> To think but nobly of my grandmother:
> Good wombs have borne bad sons.
>
> (I,ii,118–20)

Here (unlike disastrously married Desdemona) she shows a mature capacity to imagine betrayal and sexual infidelity, and shows moreover an understanding that evil need not be mechanical or hereditary.

Some of Miranda's responses satisfy Prospero. Particularly when she asks why outright fratricide and child-murder did not serve the purpose of the usurper better than exile, she draws Prospero's applause: 'Well demanded, wench' (I,ii,139). Nevertheless there is conflict between Prospero and Miranda throughout the establishing scene. While he continues to speak of deceits and misfortunes he has suffered, she seeks evidence of loyalty or concern that countered the ill-treatment. Her cross-questioning elicits Prospero's narration of the people's great love for their Duke, of the 'cherubin' behaviour of her baby self, of the charity of old Gonzalo, and of the Providence that brought them ashore 'blessedly holp hither'. But Prospero repeatedly returns to bitter recollections, recalling his brother's underhanded behaviour, the perfidy of the King of Naples, the ungenerous reason for their exile rather than assassination, even the wretched boat given them.

Prospero is clearly obsessed with the evil in the outside world that betrayed him. His educative intention is nearly overwhelmed because it falls under the sway of an anger not of the present time and place. Some of this anger glancingly strikes undeserving Miranda. Prospero exhibits an ill-motivated exasperation with her, similar to the fallen courtiers' vividly portrayed animosity to the Boatswain in the preceding storm scene. Neither the Boatswain's profanity nor the supposed incapacity of Miranda is the real cause. Thus Prospero repeats 'Obey, and be attentive','Dost thou attend me?', 'Thou attend'st not!', and so forth, until Miranda her-gracious-self sounds slightly testy: 'Your tale, sir, would cure deafness' (I,ii,106).

It is not an attempt to cure deafness or any other incapacity of Miranda that causes Prospero to be so peculiarly insistent. His fractious tone in the scene expresses rather his own bitterness, and in alleging her incapacity he describes his own incapacitating conflicts.

The division within Prospero is expressed by his use of three distinct voices. With one he lushly recalls his lost dignities, describing himself (in the split-off third person) as 'A prince of power' and as 'Prospero the prime duke, being so reputed/ in dignity, and for the liberal Arts/ Without a parallel'. This schizoid voice of idealization finds another side in Prospero's voice of paranoid belittlement, heard in the barking tone of his spite against Antonio and also in his harsh suspiciousness about Miranda's inattention. Thirdly, Prospero uses a language of deliberate obliquity:

> *Pros.*   Being once perfected how to grant suits,
> How to deny them, who t'advance, and who
> To trash for over-topping; new created
> The creatures that were mine, I say, or chang'd 'em,
> Or else new formed 'em; having both the key
> Of officer and office, set all the hearts i' th' state
> To what tune pleased his ear; that now he was
> The ivy that had hid my princely trunk,
> And suck'd my verdure out on 't. Thou attend'st not?
> *Mir.*   O, good sir. I do.
> *Pros.*   I pray thee, mark me.
> I, thus neglecting worldly ends, all dedicated
> To closeness and the bettering of my mind
> With that which, but by being so retir'd,
> O'er-priz'd all popular rate, in my false brother
> Awak'd an evil nature; and my trust,
> Like a good parent, did beget of him
> A falsehood in its contrary, as great

As my trust was; which indeed had no limit,
A confidence sans bound.

                                                                (I,ii,79–97)

Despite his repetitive demands that Miranda 'mark' him, Prospero's language is convoluted here to the point of obfuscation. Its choppy rhythm goes in fits and starts, its diction is unsettled by neologisms, and its plain meaning is hobbled by a constant preference for metaphor. This style of expression allows the passage to describe minutely the faults of Antonio's 'man management' while glossing over Prospero's failed responsibility. It seems likely that Prospero speaks this way mostly to mislead himself. Surely his showy style is inappropriate to an intimate conference with his daughter, and moreover, this style informs very badly.

Prospero's seeming explanations have in fact the marked effect of leaving important questions unanswered. For example, why could his 'creatures' not seek some protection from the 'prime duke' against being 'trashed'? Use of a style that evades, confuses, and glides past uncomfortable questions implies a deceiver within Prospero's own self in league with (or which 'did beget of him') a deceiver in his ambitious brother. Indeed some collusion of deceivers must have gone into making a 'confidence sans bound'. So present behaviour and old history both confirm that Prospero has and has long had tendencies to glossing-over and self-deception. Prospero's half-awareness of this, implied by his account to Miranda which half reveals it, explains why such great bitterness persists in him despite his having projected out all blame; self-spite underlies his extreme loathing of the perfidy of others. Unconscious projection and psychic splitting of good from bad has disabled Prospero. Thus we may understand his extended stay on his island as a kind of self-exile from self.

3

Prospero's vital concern for Miranda provides the only plausible reason why he would ever abandon his scholarly exile. Paradoxically, fear of deceptive men, like himself, causes him to mix reluctance with urgency when preparing to present Miranda to 'the world'. Prospero can only win past his impasse at the cost of suffering a full realization of the cause of his reluctance, which means acknowledging dreaded and heavily denied inner rebellions.

Before examining these rebellions I want to make Prospero's suffering more evident by contrasting him with the play's putatively good old man, Gonzalo.

First I want to point out that Gonzalo is ribald. When Samuel Pepys saw the Restoration version of *The Tempest* for the first of many times, he thought it 'no great wit, but yet good above ordinary plays' and 'the most innocent play that ever I saw' (p. 847).[8] Searchers after sexual innuendo in Shakespeare concur with Pepys and classify *The Tempest* among the very 'cleanest' of the plays, in which 'bawdy has little to do' (Partridge, pp. 54 and 53; Colman p. 155). So much the more we may note a peculiar indecency of Gonzalo's (see Colman, p. 155 and Partridge, pp. 139-40). In the storm scene, this 'honest old Councellor' (as he's listed in the First Folio) makes the only misogynist reference to menstruation in all of Shakespeare[9], offering to: 'warrant [the Boatswain] for drowning, though the ship were no stronger than a nutshell, and as leaky as an unstanched wench', for 'He'll be hang'd yet,/ Though every drop of water swear against it' (I,i,46-8, 57-8).

This obscenity is not accidental, but multiply functional. For one thing, it vividly shows two favourite taboo subjects, hanging and sexuality, breaking out in the face of threatened violent death. Leaving for later consideration the foreshadowing reference to a 'wench', we may note that it mirrors the psychological mechanism of gallows humour, and so provides a natural touch to counterpoint the magic storm's symbolism of mental ferment.

Indeed Shakespeare's lifelike portrayal of speech gives his storm scene more verisimilitude than the true account by William Strachey of his actual experience of a 1609 Bermuda tempest, citing: 'panting bosoms . . . Prayers . . . in the heart and lips, but drowned in the outcries of the Officers' (in Bullough, p. 135). It is possible that Shakespeare used Strachey's letter of 1610 concerning the wreck for a source of *The Tempest*, although it was not published until 1625. At any rate many similarities suggest that *The Tempest* was influenced by some account of the *Sea Venture* wreck of 1609. Strachey's reports a leaking ship, a despairing crew, wreck on a strange island, rebellion there, and the miraculous salvation of nearly all the company. Shakespeare's variations on the likely source are as usual fascinating. Among them are his disparaging portrayal of the behaviour of the leading men on board. Thus Gonzalo and his fellows 'mar' the labouring mariners, even 'assist the storm' (I,i,13–14); whereas, far from hindering the sailors, the highborn of the *Sea Venture* are reported by Strachey to have striven willingly to save the ship and company. Thus all ranks helped bail out, while one of the leaders, Sir George Summers, was first to sight landfall, and the other chief, Sir Thomas Gates, was said to have undertaken on land a share in '"every meane labour" dispensing "with no travaile of his body"' (in Brockbank, 1966, pp. 191–2).

By contrast, all the shipwrecked nobles of *The Tempest* offer words alone, and no physical 'travaile'; the best ones pray, the worse mouth maledictions, plot murder, blaspheme and scoff. It seems Shakespeare does not subscribe to the Renaissance aristocratic (and artistic) distaste for physical work noted by Castiglione, Leonardo, and Sir Philip Sidney. For Shakespeare's Marina in *Pericles* (published in 1609 before reports of the Gates and Summers shipwreck) is proud of her father, who in a wild storm

> did never fear
> But cried 'Good seamen!' to the sailors, galling
> His kingly hands, haling ropes . . .
>
> (IV,i,52–4).

Gonzalo and his fellows are galling in quite another sense when they interfere with and harass the Boatswain. Worst is the verbal violence of Sebastian and Antonio, who call him 'blasphemous, incharitable dog', and cry 'Hang, cur! hang you whoreson . . .' Their pretended outrage at the sailor's salty language is a vent for their fear, only dressed up in the language of piety. For these men who object to lower-class profanity also ignore Gonzalo's suggestion that they join the King in prayer below.

Gonzalo's own extemporaneous prayer during the storm, concluding, 'The wills above be done! but I would fain die a dry death', indicates superior courage, resolution and humour. Gonzalo is, relatively, 'a noble Neapolitan', as Prospero tells Miranda. But in the recognition scene at the end of *The Tempest* Gonzalo shocks us. He is greeted as 'Holy Gonzalo, honourable man', and pronounces a moving blessing on Ferdinand and Miranda to which King Alonso says 'Amen'. He then sums up the adventure by expressing gratitude for its full closure in Claribel's marriage, the resurrection of all the lost selves, and the crowning restoration of Duke Prospero and his daughter (V,i,201–13). Then, with so much dignity acquired, just after pronouncing his own 'Amen!', Gonzalo greets the miraculously restored, now gently-spoken Boatswain. He abandons all sense of reconciliation and thanksgiving and lapses into: 'I prophesied, if a gallows were on land,/ This fellow could not drown' (V,i,216–17), returning to abusive snobbery at a sacred moment.

In addition to insensitivity there is a significant incongruity in Gonzalo's remark. He insists that a gallows awaits the Boatswain when the ship connecting them with Italy is still believed lost. Thus Gonzalo assumes that with Alonso again sane and Prospero restored the punitive social *status quo* is re-established. This assumption shows no change from the way Gonzalo represents authority at the play's start when, as Terence Hawkes says: 'Unless and until he learns that "these roarers" care nothing "for the name of King" (I,i,16) Gonzalo and the depersonalized "authority" represented by his language will find great difficulty in adapting to the demands of the new world into which they are about to be cast' (p. 201). Gonzalo shows he has learned nothing new when he imagines there will be gallows on Prospero's island (as there were indeed on Gates's and Summers's Bermuda). He cannot realize that Prospero's project aims to replace, in C. L. Barber's terminology, 'everyday' with convention-inverting 'holiday' (1959, pp. 6–10); or aims, in the terms of Shakespeare's anthropological reader Marjorie Garber, at the anti-structure of a ritual of 'liminality' (1981, pp. 7–8 and 243–4). By clinging to 'everyday' language and ideas Gonzalo evades liminality and shows his inability to accept the island's flexible reality as a means of mental growth.

Gonzalo receives no physical punishment; even his courtier's clothes are kept clean. Yet it is stressed how he suffers: 'His tears run down his beard, like winter's drops/ From eaves of reeds', says Ariel (V,i,16–17). These are said to be tears of pity for the others, but again the emotion outruns the stated cause. His excessive tears indicate also that Gonzalo, although the best of the courtiers, suffers guilt. This arises because he has accommodated himself to a corrupt world. Of course he could not have resisted the command when he was appointed 'Master of [the] design' to destroy innocents, no more than could Shakespeare's Leonine, Pisano, and Antiginous before him. In fact he risked then as much charity as he dared. But twelve years later, when we meet him, he readily joins in the usurper's fleering 'superior' abuse of the Boatswain, in defensively attacking a 'rogue' who can be their only salvation.

Gonzalo is also associated with the unthinking carry-over of 'courtly' tendencies wherein Antonio and Sebastian view shipwreck as an opportunity for usurpation. They are blind to how circumstances make 'the name of King' hollow (much fun is made of this in Dryden's and Davenant's version of *The Tempest*). Instead they attempt to perpetuate in the wilderness a fine old court tradition: fratricidal seizure of power. Although Gonzalo doesn't share their motives, he too clings to a courtly ethos. Thus his utopian dreams are correctly if unkindly mocked by fleering Antonio and Sebastian, for Gonzalo imagines himself a *King* of a Golden Age commonwealth with 'no sovereignty'. This comically shows his unshakeably narrow social conceptions. His ideas for a renewed society share none of the true cultural relativity of Montaigne's essay 'Of the Caniballes', from which their expression is borrowed.

Although he is not sinister, we may find in Gonzalo the sin of accidie, or at least a vice of severe moral inattention. He entirely lacks a strenuous view of virtue, so in his imaginary commonwealth all good things come 'without sweat or endeavour' (II,i,156). And after his actual tears and sweat have been extracted by the eventful magic island Gonzalo seems only pathetically emotionally exhausted, begging: 'some heavenly power guide us/ Out of this fearful country!' (V,i,105–6).

Gonzalo is usefully paralleled with Gloucester in *King Lear*. Both elderly courtiers appear in the first scenes of their plays participating in scurrilous banter, Gloucester by squalidly boasting in the presence of his bastard Edmund 'there was good sport at his making', and Gonzalo by alluding to an 'unstanched wench'. Gloucester later serves to focus Lear's immense capacity for suffering by presenting a contrasting inability to confront his own disaster: Gloucester's final hope is to attain an oblivion in which 'woes by wrong imaginations lose/ The knowledge of themselves' (*King Lear* IV,vi,281–4). Similarly, as we shall see, Gonzalo's response in mute tears and fatigue contrasts with Prospero's ability to learn through suffering.

Indeed Gonzalo at the end of *The Tempest* may still demonstrate a courtier's temporizing conscience, for it is only after powerful King Alonso acknowledges Prospero that Gonzalo says he is glad to see him restored, excusing his unusual silence on stage with: 'I have inly wept,/ Or should have spoke ere this' (V,i,200–1). If we do suspect Gonzalo of a politic silence, we will note that Prospero himself makes no comment on this, nor on the many sins of omission of others. This I think is because Prospero's tolerance for others' lapses grows as he becomes aware of unstated aversions of his own. Next I want to explore Prospero's aversion to recognizing his own baser humanity.

4

Rather like Gonzalo and the others who abuse the Boatswain, Prospero shows scant respect for physical work. Both the revelation of his all-engrossing pursuit of knowledge before the start of *The Tempest*, and the vehement expression of exclusively pro-cerebral attitudes in the play, indicate he habitually acknowledges only the part of himself that resembles the incorporeal Ariel. Split off from Prospero, like a part-object, is the rejected earthy Caliban: Prospero insists repeatedly on Caliban's utter and unbridgeable difference from himself.

Caliban and Ariel are often seen as symmetrical allegorical figures. Certainly, in the background story, the harms they inflict are reciprocal: Caliban's tribe has oppressed Ariel and bound him in matter, and Ariel helps Prospero to enslave Caliban. But, as A. D. Nuttall put it, although 'Ariel and Caliban of all the characters in the play come nearest to being allegories of the psychic processes . . . it would certainly be a mistake not to realize that they are very much more besides' (1967, p. 159). Even the psychological master Henry James has indicated that Caliban's fantastic 'conception and execution' show the height of 'ineffable delicacy' (in Palmer, p. 88).

We are made to feel from the start the absoluteness with which Caliban angers and disgusts Prospero. D. T. Traversi senses that 'The intensity of Prospero's reaction ("*Filth* as thou art") is a clear indication of the gravity of the issues involved, and of the tension which so persistently underlies the moralizing harmonies of this play' (p. 332, author's italics). Exactly so: Prospero's calling Caliban 'filth' in the play's 'establishing' scene (I,ii,348) establishes just where they start from. Prospero's relations with Ariel are somewhat more benign, but still very intense. He describes Ariel with possible ambiguity as 'my tricksy spirit' (V,i,225). 'Tricksy' was in 1611 a term of endearment which meant 'spruce, fine, smart', but Ariel may also seem a deceptive or deceiving spirit, 'tricksy' in its somewhat later developed sense of 'crafty, cunning, cheating'. In one way at least Ariel is definitely inclined to cheat; we learn in the establishing scene that 'once a month' he becomes impatient and wants to evade his commitment to a term of willing service to Prospero.

Not only does this periodicity echo Gonzalo's menstrual theme, but it also introduces a theme of cycles of resentment, rebellion and suffering. Such repetitive cycles can lead to freedom, or to madness, according to Melanie Klein (see especially Klein, 1946).

Longer cycles apply as well: Ariel was punished in a cloven pine 'a dozen years', then served Prospero twelve more years, and is now in danger of twelve years of further torment unless he serves his master well (I,ii,294-6). Prospero also approaches the end of a twelve year's captivity, and shows a sense of danger which, as I've said, is only partly attributable to his 'auspicious star'. These patterns may indicate correspondences of Ariel with parts of Prospero, but if so they go beyond the allegorical because their full meanings are developed in exchanges of tenderness, anger, and pride evidencing a genuine relationship (or object relationship) between the two of them.[10] Ariel's desire for freedom I would say resembles Prospero's own less evident need for release from the isle. It recalls more obviously also the demands of Miranda's womanhood requiring independence from Prospero after twelve years of intimacy. Miranda and Ariel, as loved objects, must both be set free despite Prospero's beautifully tender regrets: 'But yet thou shalt have freedom: so, so, so' (V,i,96).

But Ariel is sharply differentiated from Miranda as well. He is entirely 'dainty' and spiritual, having pointedly refused the witch Sycorax's 'earthy and abhorr'd commands' (I,ii,273). Miranda on the contrary is a sexual being, desirable in varying ways to Caliban, Stephano, Ferdinand and others. Her recent sexual maturing is foreshadowed in Gonzalo's remark on an 'unstanched wench'. 'Wench' is a term Prospero uses also to address Miranda, and he is well aware it is time she is married. Thus he raises a tempest to bring Ferdinand to her. But then he makes the way to this marriage far less smooth than it need be, and this implies a reluctance in him with deepest importance to the play.

Prospero suffers from a problem found in all four of Shakespeare's last plays: the problem of imagining any man worthy of the marvellous young heroines of these plays. So the future son-in-law Lysimachus in *Pericles* is caught creeping in a brothel, Posthumus in *Cymbeline* is incredibly boastful, gullible and mistrusting, and Florizel in *The Winter's Tale* when fleeing paternal wrath becomes uselessly seasick. Ferdinand arrives on Prospero's island literally wet, being the unheroic first to jump overboard from the wreck. All this is to say that the perspective in Shakespeare's Romance plays seems close to that of a possessive father-in-law, for these plays tend to belittle son-in-law figures, and to adore daughters.

A shadowy incest motif also appears in each of Shakespeare's four Romance plays. In each case it is played down. In *The Winter's Tale*, as compared with the source novel, Greene's *Pandosto*, Shakespeare greatly attenuates the prominence of Leontes' desire for his unrecognized daughter. Gower's *Confessio Amantis*, the source of *Pericles*, also gives a much fuller account of Antiochus' incest with his daughter than does Shakespeare's play. The incest motif is also adumbrated in *Cymbeline* where Imogen resists the frank lust of her ludicrous step-brother Cloten only to arouse desires in her unrecognized real brother Guiderius (III,vii,42). Here one taboo replaces another, and the desire that would have made

Guiderius 'woo hard' is sublimated because Imogen 'cross-dresses' as the boy Fidele. Thus, unlike his bold contemporary John Ford, Shakespeare cautiously treats incest in plays. Yet where he might easily have done so he does not eliminate this motif, which according to the Arden editor of *Pericles*, 'some people regret' (Hoeniger, p. xv). I believe we should not regret this, nor conversely regret Shakespeare's discretion in presenting the incest motif, for in his Romances it acts like a homoeopathic dose which is most powerfully where it is most subtly incorporated.

This motif appears most subtly in *The Tempest* in a negative form, as repression. Prospero repeatedly shows his absolute disgust concerning the nearly-incestuous attempt of Miranda's foster brother Caliban. This anti-erotic fury, and Prospero's scorn of all physicality, combine to silence any potential desires of his own. But I think we must consider if these attitudes represent skilful ploys of denial, a benefit of projection.

In the three Romance plays preceding *The Tempest* almost all of the errant males (all except the story-book villains Antiochus and Cloten) are 'ignorant' of their family relationships with the women they desire. Displacement of unconscious wish into apparent 'accident' is not available in *The Tempest* because of the centrality of Prospero's magian omniscience. (The exclusion of Romance 'accident' from *The Tempest* is indeed the most daring of its many deviations from the mode of Shakespeare's other last plays.[11]) But there is still of course, in another sense, an 'accident' in the play: the accident of the unusual situation of Prospero and Miranda. Their isolated life on a desert island may bring to mind the Biblical account of Lot and his daughters, or other legends and true stories of shipwreck and similar disasters leading to paternal incest. Such associations lead directly to a suspicion of an incest theme for some readers. For example R. E. Gajdusek begins a complex psychoanalytic perception with: 'there is an incestuous base to the image of a father alone on an isle with his daughter for many years . . .' (p. 158).

Let us trace the possible ramifications of this proposed 'image' in the play. As we have suggested, the closeness of Prospero and asexual Ariel implies the sexual side of Prospero is severely repressed; this indeed could be in order to prevent incest. Yet not only his own, but all physicality is scorned by Prospero, especially that of his 'poisonous slave' Caliban, and later of the substitute 'log-man' Ferdinand.

Language highlighting Prospero's dismissive attitude to the body occurs in his first encounter with vigorous Ferdinand. The Prince violently objects to being called a 'traitor' (here we may remember how the identical charge was much better resisted by Pericles when it was made in identical circumstances by good King Simonides). Prospero's retort to this is: 'What! I say,/ My foot my tutor?' (I,ii,470–1). This ejaculation resembles a proverb of the age: 'Do not make the foot the head' (Tilley, F562, p. 232). But it is particularly pointed because of the circumstance in which Prospero's sneering identifies a lowly bodily part with Ferdinand. What part this really is is suggested by Prospero's immediately following threat: 'I can . . . make thy weapon drop'. 'My foot' may thus represent the phallus, following the symbolism wherein '"down below" in dreams often relates to the genitals' (Freud, 1900a, p. 410).

Prospero's most explicit contempt for sexuality is seen of course in his extreme hatred of frankly lustful Caliban. That this hatred may reflect unconscious jealousy is indicated by the fact that Prospero metes out identical harsh treatment to innocent Ferdinand and to guilty Caliban; both sexual contenders for Miranda are condemned to log-carrying and imprisonment.

The play suggests that Prospero finds servile grotesqueness in all physical activity. He imposes needed tasks on a scorned 'rabble'[12] of spirits, or by dint of dire threats on Caliban or Ariel, and on Ferdinand who suffers log-carrying as undeserved *punishment* (IV,i,1). Punishment for what, we may ask? And how, when Shakespeare's Pericles is praised for haling ropes, is Ferdinand's labour degrading?

I believe the answer lies in how the log-carrying, which represents for Prospero something degrading yet unfortunately necessary (I,ii,312–15), represents in the play sexual arousal. We may note that Prospero explicitly bans Cupid and Venus from the unconsummated marriage masque (IV,i,94–101), although a young engaged couple have need of strong desire. It is left to Miranda herself to remind us of the importance of sex. Sexually equivocal talk on the part of virginal heroines is no rarity in Shakespeare, but none express libido so explicitly as her comments on Ferdinand's 'log'. She says of it: 'when this burns/ 'Twill weep for having wearied you', leading on to talk of 'striving' and 'discharging' and her desire – 'pray give me that;/ I'll carry it to the pile'(III,i,18–24).

I will next argue that by means of projective identification Prospero first locates all lust for Miranda in log-carrying slaves. But after Ferdinand's acceptance as her suitor the value of despised 'log carrying' has to change. Then Prospero is obliged to acknowledge his own denied desires, in order truly to relinquish them. The 'thing of darkness' that he takes back in and acknowledges as *his* is an internal object. It is the Caliban–monster that he has created by splitting off unwanted parts of himself and thrusting them out by projective identification.

5

To allow Ferdinand his manhood, and Miranda her womanhood, Prospero must readjust his own outlook very significantly. He begins this process in earnest at the exact moment when, while striving to entertain Prince Ferdinand, he suddenly 'remembers' his rebelled slave Caliban. A connection is thus made, through Prospero's thinking, between the Ferdinand and Caliban sub-plots which are otherwise kept entirely separate.

At this crucial moment of 'remembering' Prospero dismisses the marriage masque, an event that is the only unexpected turn in the play. For once Prospero seems off-guard and out of control.

When he suddenly stops the performance with the aside 'I had forgot that foul conspiracy/ Of the beast Caliban and his confederates' (IV,i,139–40), Prospero's emotion may be signalled by the Folio stage direction: 'Prospero *starts sodainly and speakes, after which to a strange hollow and confused noyse,* [the dancers] *heauily vanish*'. Prospero, like his nymphs and reapers, may be sorrowful ('heavy'), and like his music ('noise') strangely confused. We too may be confused. Why does Prospero suddenly retract his wedding gift to Ferdinand and Miranda? Is this is in some way connected with his prior denigration of the masque as a 'vanity' or trifle to be performed by a 'rabble' of spirits? And in what way is this action connected with 'the beast Caliban'?

I believe that Prospero's sudden recollection of lustful and rebellious Caliban represents the beginning of his encounter at last with his denied incestuous wishes. These are aroused from their defensive enclosure by the ceremony representing his counter-wish for Miranda to marry Ferdinand. The collision of his wishes overwhelms the ceremony, but also initiates an eruption of the emotions that sweep the play to its finish.

When he ends the masque Prospero's emotions are certainly exceptionally dynamic. First psychic pain arises in him, so that Miranda comments to Ferdinand: 'Never till this day/ Saw I him touch'd with anger, so distemper'd' (IV,i,144–5). Yet this pain makes him gentle, and immediately after there is an unprecedented good temper in his tone to Miranda and Ferdinand. This leads on to his poetic set piece, 'Our revels now are ended . . .', which conveys several feelings in succession, expressing a complex state. Thereafter Prospero participates in the most vigorous actions of the play, in which he 'meets with' Caliban and, I would say, meets his own denied impulses, so that he can accept the marriage.

C. L. Barber succinctly captured the emergent tone here when he contrasted Theseus' 'proud scepticism' in *A Midsummer-Night's Dream* with Prospero's 'humble scepticism' in *The Tempest* (1959, p. 161). Prospero's evolving humility allows him for the first time to acknowledge personal limitations without being scornfully dismissive. This he does when he describes the insubstantiality of his revels in an elegiac tone untouched by the former scornful superiority with which he called them a 'trick' to be played by a 'rabble', a 'vanity of mine Art' ('vanity' meaning either 'trifling thing' or 'product of self-conceit') supplied because 'they expect it from me' (IV,i,35–41).

It is also unprecedented to see Prospero extend the least civility to Ferdinand, and now he offers him true courtesy, reversing his admitted (IV,i,1–31) former austere treatment of him, and excusing his boastfulness and demandingness concerning Miranda. Prospero now addresses Ferdinand as 'my son', and transforms the tartness formerly heard in his salutation 'sir'. Thus, without using magic or 'spirits' as intermediaries, Prospero makes direct apologies and personal amends.

Prospero's new tone shows him beginning to fulfill his earlier stated intention to encourage the 'Fair encounter/ Of two most rare affections' (III,i,74-5). Formerly, under the guise of making 'a trial', Prospero showed less than full acceptance, perhaps expressing more truth than he knew in remarking, 'So glad of this as they I cannot be' (III,i,92).

The famous 'revels' speech seems finer still if we compare with it Prospero's former use of language. Now fluent poetry replaces the dinning repetition and halting rhetoric heard in the establishing scene. I believe that Prospero's new clarity shows he is overcoming the consequences of former splitting and projection, his isolating bitterness and disgust; now he really wants to be understood.

The start of the 'revels' speech is a plangent lament about the dream-like insubstantiality of life. But this scepticism may be truly humble, for it can be understood as a farewell to familiar, cherished, but unsatisfactory illusions. So it may express what Melanie Klein calls the 'pining' for a truer awareness that precedes the reality-embracing 'depressive position' (1940, pp. 151, 163).

Later in the same speech Prospero moves on from verbal plangency and theatrical metaphors to a new intimacy of tone in which he reveals to Ferdinand his present humbled state of mind:

> Sir, I am vex'd;
> Bear with my weakness; my old brain is troubled:
> Be not disturbed with my infirmity.
>
> (IV,i,158-60)

Here, by acknowledging weakness, age, and infirmity, Prospero shows new moral strength. A true spiritual alchemist, he works upon himself as he works on others.

This then is how I would understand Prospero's vital gain in self-knowledge. To choose freely and completely to let his daughter grow up, Prospero must painfully confront hateful incestuous drives which he shares with his rival Caliban. He attempts to ratify her engagement with a masque, but regards this art work with defensive scorn. During the masque's celebration of fruitfulness and life's continuing he becomes restive because he feels bereft of importance, jealous and excluded. Next comes his aside, 'I had forgot . . . Caliban'. This begins a process of struggle and 'remembering' concluding near the play's end with: 'Set Caliban and his companions free', 'This thing of darkness I acknowledge mine' and 'Every third thought shall be my grave'.

Gajdusek holds that Prospero comes to confront the 'third facet of the goddess': 'the acknowledgment of his three children – the liberation of daughter, and monster-son, and spirit . . . [is for Prospero] a profound ritual acceptance of death' (1974, p. 156). Certainly he at last abjures his unconscious wish to live forever and command the full affections of a young woman, equally his and King Lear's initial folly. But we must reflect on the fact that for fully twelve years living with Miranda has been the best part of being alive for Prospero. The re-acquisition of a dukedom (subsidiary to his new son-in-law's) will hardly compensate him for her loss. Only love can motivate his willing renunciation.

I would like to make a last detailed point about the masque. Aristocratic casting had a prime allegorical function in actual court masquing and it was directly contrary to the genre to use a 'rabble' to play divinities. In a court masque of Shakespeare's time a rabble of merely professional acrobats and dancers would be used only for the disfigured anti-masque.[13]

So it seems that an anti-masque element is 'out of place' in Prospero's production, as it is in *The Tempest* itself. It extends beyond the Caliban–Trinculo–Stephano sub-plot, for such men as King Alonso and the self-proclaimed 'prime duke' Prospero himself must descend to strange cavortings before they can make reparation to all their damaged, split-off, projected internal objects.

6

Melanie Klein observed that psychic splitting if unchecked may lead to false reparative urges, producing manic, careless and ineffectual gestures of repair (see Klein, 1940, p. 153; Segal, 1980, p. 148). Perhaps Prospero's attitude to the spirits giving his masque, whom he calls a 'rabble' and the 'meaner fellows' of Ariel (IV,i,35), suggests manic reparation which allows him to feel superior to or contemptuous of his inner objects. But he rejects this 'bad art'. By more costly means than using sterile triumphant display he at last achieves acceptance of personal limitations, silence in the face of intractabilities, and painful renunciation. Thus he is able to acknowledge denied parts of himself, taking them back and healing his psychic splitting.

The importance of psychic splitting at the beginning of *The Tempest* has been argued on the basis of the play's imagery alone. Gajdusek refers to 'psychological schism (the good and bad brother, the good and bad father, Naples and Milan), a schism given explicit and basic form in the very first scene and in the tempest of self-created forces when [we hear] the cry "we split, we split"' (p. 153). He adds that 'The freckling or dappling [of Caliban] suggests that intermixture of light and dark, spirit and flesh, human and bestial which was the primitive synthesis' (p. 155). These are ingenious readings.[14] But the first elides the impact of the terror of death at sea, and the second ignores the tone of Prospero's scornful and nauseous description of Caliban, 'A freckled whelp hag-born – not honour'd with/ A human shape' (I,ii,283). By ignoring dramatic and emotional contexts psychodynamic readings of Shakespeare's verbal images run a similar risk to that of clinical psychoanalytic interpretations which ignore contexts of free associations and moods. These are the risks of being formulaic, tendentious, reductive, and inaccurate.

Thus for example I do not think Prospero's hate-filled description of the 'freckled whelp' Caliban indicates any sort of synthesis at all. On the contrary it serves as a benchmark of disgust against which we may measure his later description of him near the end of the play, when Prospero says tartly that Caliban 'is as disproportion'd in his manners/ As in his shape' (V,i,290–1). This is not complimentary, but compared with his earlier wild abuse ('thou poisonous slave', 'filth that thou art') it shows more control of thought and phrasing, evidence of a more balanced view.

At last Prospero says he may forgive Caliban, and the 'monster' replies with his first use of an abstract noun – which is 'grace' to boot! Like Prospero himself, Caliban makes gains in judgement: 'What a thrice-double ass/ Was I, to take this drunkard for a god,/

And worship this dull fool!' (V,i,295–7) Thus the distance between Caliban and Prospero narrows. Prospero, by accepting that he has Caliban-like drives himself, sees that Caliban is not so disgusting, while Caliban begins to develop the ability to endure frustration and limit.

Convergence with humanity is also implied when Ariel shows imaginative compassion for human weaknesses (V,i,18–20).[15] Following this Ariel serves more willingly, and Prospero is no longer harsh to him.

These changes are, in general, from Auden's 'dreadful appetite' for the 'fluent satisfaction of our will', to willingness. Thus Caliban's last lines begin: 'Ay that I will'. Prospero also shows surprising willingness when, despite the threatening tones of his earlier demands for pre-marital abstinence, he invites Ferdinand and Miranda to enjoy each other's company:

If you be pleas'd: retire into my cell,
And there repose: a turn or two I'll walk,
To still my beating mind.

(IV,i,161–3)

This gives them, instead of further demonstrations of omnipotent magic, privacy and his trust.

Exactly at the moment when Prospero trusts the lovers to moderate their passions, he himself encounters his own greatest passions. Just as Miranda has (I,ii,176), and Alonso will (V,i,246), Prospero now strenuously contends with a 'beating mind', suffering to find self-knowledge. His fourth act 'walk' is no theatrical ploy to get Prospero off stage; indeed he continues present for the rest of the play. Rather it physically signifies his mental distress.

As soon as Prospero is pacing in distress Ariel arrives saying 'Thy thoughts I cleave to'. He announces that he too has just 'thought' of Caliban while 'present[ing] Ceres'. Ariel's and Prospero's 'thoughts', arising in the midst of the masque of peace and plenty, ironically lead to the most physically violent episodes of the play, when they 'meet with Caliban'. At this point Caliban and company are already misled, trapped and outcast, resembling unwanted projected-out parts of Prospero's self. They are 'I' th'filthy-mantled pool beyond' Prospero's formerly ascetic 'cell' – now used for wooing. Dredged out of the pool, degraded and smelling 'all horse-piss', they are next presented with bait or 'stale'[16] in the form of flashy clothing. Prospero provides this 'trumpery' to tempt their shallow usurping social pretensions. Caliban does not fall for civilized bait, does not want to steal or 'dote . . . on such luggage', for his mind is focused on 'murther'. Then the three conspirators are harried with dogs. Prospero participates in an imaginative riot, an anti-masque rout, when his musically-voiced pack terrifies the characters representative of the 'low' appetites that have terrified him. At the end of the fourth act he touches the height of his mania: 'At this hour/ Lies at my mercy all mine enemies . . .' (IV,i,262–3).

The myth of Actaeon may come to mind. Because of Actaeon's intrusion into her virgin privacy Diana made him into a stag harried and torn apart by his own hounds. Thus his lust gave rise to loss of humanity, to terror and dismemberment. (One of those hounds is named 'Tempest' in Ovid's account of the myth, well known to Shakespeare (Rouse, vol. 3, p. 262).) Particularly because Caliban and company have designs on Miranda, they are also hounded. But finally Prospero resists the worst splitting, and refrains from actually tearing apart Caliban, Stephano, Trinculo, and himself.

Rather Prospero restricts himself to making frightening impressions through stinks, sounds, wild sights and, most powerfully, imagination. So he avoids becoming like the names of two of his own avenging hounds, 'Fury' and 'Tyrant'. By working his ends through sensory illusions only, he allows each of his island's visitors their autonomous reaction to the images he presents. This autonomy is symbolized by the independence of the multiple sub-plots of *The Tempest*. John Russell Brown explains how Prospero's ubiquity unifies parts of the play without making it mechanical:

> The characters from the wreck have their own concerns and, with the exception of Ferdinand, do not meet Prospero until the last scene of all. He controls their fortunes and actions, and even their moral awareness, but desires and actions are their own, right through the play. Prospero is affected by the feelings of others, especially his daughter's happiness . . . (p. 30)

I wonder only if the word 'controls' may be too strong applied to 'moral awareness'. Awareness can not be really moral if it is controlled by another; in my view Prospero *enables* possibilities of a moral awareness which may or may not appear.

Prospero produces this enabling, I suggest, through the creation of an illusory setting offering an abnormally free alternative to the everyday world. The drunken 'Cacaliban' bawls 'Freedom, highday!', and holiday illusions release for all new possibilities and freedom of choice in the abatement of custom. This produces extreme situations, confined by the mage only within the bounds of physical safety. To these extremes the characters respond in ways that stretch and test them, and they often suffer. But such sufferings may be repaid by an enlargement of life.

In direct contrast to his brother's method of 'granting' and 'trashing' greedy wishes, Prospero removes all his countrymen from their customary hopes and stations, and presents to each a fluid field in which their own fantasies can flourish. In the language of modern psychology we could say that Antonio uses behaviourist techniques, modifying responses by means of rewards and punishments. Prospero contrastingly offers on his island a safely supervised, highly fluid psychodynamic freedom. Although this is a possibly punishing freedom, it allows his captives to effect their own changes.

Prospero's magic acts are acceptable because he uses white magic, and conjures only in perceptions. Thus he calls for music to release the 'mourning' and 'distracted' nobles – to 'work mine end upon their senses' (V,i,53). Working upon their senses means presenting art and illusion to stimulate but not to control.[17] Use is made of 'lower' senses when Stephano, Trinculo, and Caliban go 'dancing up to th'chins, that the foul lake/ O'erstunk their feet'. But they stumble there themselves following Ariel's animal noises which are enchanting music to their drunkenness. They follow 'as they smelt music' in a riot of guilt and terror; like Actaeon they are harried by something of their own.

Caliban's drenching encounter with 'civilization' is not merely a degradation. Although he is degraded from a cheerfully lustful 'natural man' to a foot-licking servant of servants, he learns from the experience, and makes new distinctions. He comes to appreciate that he is wiser than Trinculo, calling him a 'pied ninny' and 'scurvy patch'. In rivalry he beseeches King Stephano to 'take his bottle from him: when that's gone,/ He shall drink nought but brine; for I'll not show him/ Where the quick freshes are' (III,ii,64–6). Surely enough, being deprived of his loved bottle would devastate the dipsomaniac jester.

But this is not just a joke. The Kleinian understanding of how love and change as well as hate and entrapment are anchored in the pleasures and frustrations of the archaic oral phase of development explains why in *The Tempest* we often meet images of satisfactory feeding and of deprivation or spoiling of food or drink. Thus Miranda remembers in the 'dark backward and abysm of time' the 'women that attended me', Prospero admits 'By Providence divine,/ Some food we had, and some fresh water', and we have the masque of fruitful Ceres. We have also the Boatswain's 'must our mouths be cold?' alluding to death, and repeated bitter threatenings such as 'Sea-water shalt thou drink', 'He shall drink nought but brine'. 'Red-hot' immoderate drinking is followed by loss of drink ('Ay, but to lose our bottles in the [filthy] pool . . .'; 'There is not only disgrace and dishonour in that, monster, but an infinite loss' (IV,i,208–10)) in the destined downfall of the clowns. Psychic reality also demands an oral element in the destinies of the highborn set. Oral frustration, according to Klein, is the prototypic source of the splitting which may or may not lead to growth (1946, p. 184; 1957, *passim* and esp. pp. 43–6 and 86–91). Thus King Alonso and his companions are driven to distraction when their banquet is taken from them by a censuring Harpy. Following this experience some but not all of them confront their guilt and gain in humanity.

Deprivation of nutrition represents for all, high and low, a loss of identity, love, and community. This is best expressed by direct childlike Caliban. After the rape attempt on Miranda Caliban is no longer petted and fed, and spitefully insists he will eat alone when it pleases him. But, recalling his own 'dark backward and abysm of time', this seems to him a bitter replacement for his original good object relation (with Prospero) which offered drink and food-with-love:

I must eat my dinner.
This island's mine, by Sycorax my mother,
Which thou tak'st from me. When thou cam'st first,
Thou strok'st me, and made much of me; wouldst give me
Water with berries in't . . .

(I,ii,332–6)

Exactly as in infantile phantasies of 'bad part objects' described by
Melanie Klein, frustrating sources of nutrition in *The Tempest*
become biting, poisonous and retaliatory monsters when tainted by
split-off guilt (1957, pp. 29 and 85). After the courtier's banquet is
denied them by the Harpy, 'their great guilt,/ Like poison given to
work a great time after/ Now 'gins to bite the spirits' (III,iii,104–6).
Almost all react, but King Alonso suffers the worst because he has
failed to achieve the high moral standard his rank demands. He runs
from the banquet persuaded that his sins have caused the death of
his son; his punishment is due entirely to his own guilty conscience.

Thus Prospero's enemies 'are all knit up'. Yet they are knit with
pains that can redeem them, for oral terrors are a necessary part of
a Kleinian fundamental sequence of growth progressing from
frustration to hatred, aggression, guilt, and remorse, and finally to
better understanding of self and others. Prospero's magic island
allows individuals to grow by providing scope for encounters with
hate-filled, spiteful and terrifying split-off part objects as well as with
unrealized potentials for good. The tendencies which emerge
include perfidiousness and folly in courtiers, greed and folly in the
clowns, insecurity and loss of faith in the King, virility in Ferdinand,
erotic love in Miranda, and so forth. But none I think learns more
or changes more than Prospero.

The evidence for this transformation is in the changed quality of
Prospero's speeches, and, tellingly, of his silences. At first his
silences serve to cover up his own irresponsibility, while he
vehemently insists on the lack of kinship between himself and his
despised enemies. His own lapses are covered by the noise of his
outrage; paradoxically he is least communicating when he most
insists on being heard. Later he begins to show very different sorts
of silence, indicating strength, tolerance and sensitivity, rather
than, as formerly, his moral cowardice.

Thus Prospero says nothing concerning Miranda's disobedience to him when she tells Ferdinand her name. He appears to accept as part of her natural growing away from him her self-admitted brief forgetfulness of her 'dear father' and his 'hest' (III,i,36–7,53). Prospero is also silent concerning Ferdinand's weak boasts about his prior mistresses (III,i,37–48), although hearing these may partly motivate his strong insistence on Miranda's and Ferdinand's sexual restraint. Ever-increasing tolerance finally allows Prospero to give space to Ferdinand and Miranda, first in his cell, and then on the public stage where they replace him as the main focus of attention and amazement.

In the difficult circumstance of confronting his old enemies Prospero casts off his former fulminating and shows strength and restraint. Thus he gives a delicate pardon to repentant Alonso before it is half asked for: 'There, sir, stop: / Let us not burthen our remembrance' with/ A heaviness that's gone' (V,i,198–200). A most interesting new reticence also governs Prospero's relations with Sebastian and Antonio, to whom he says aside:

> But you, my brace of lords, were I so minded,
> I here could pluck his highness' frown upon you,
> And justify you traitors: at this time
> I will tell no tales.
>
> (V,i,126–9)

Here Prospero's omniscience, upon which Sebastian comments 'The devil speaks in him', is used for the first time with non-magical effectiveness. His hints threatening exposure of the plot to assassinate Alonso allow Prospero to enforce from Antonio the return of the dukedom: 'I . . . require/ My dukedom of thee, which, perforce, I know,/ Thou must restore' (V,i,132–4). These effective menaces are not delivered in tones of devilish triumph, nor in tones of retributive bitterness, but in tones of *usable* anger; they indicate practical aggression rather than paralyzing fury.

Yet of anger there is plenty, as we hear in Prospero's last remark to Antonio, who still seems unmoved:

For you, most wicked sir, whom to call brother
Would even infect my mouth, I do forgive
Thy rankest fault, – *all of them* . . .

(V,i,130–3, italics added)

But this pardon is also practical, buying more even than a dukedom. It also helps prepare a safer world for Miranda and Ferdinand to return to, giving some hope for peace and forgiveness rather than retribution and feud.

So finally only willing penitence is sought from those who struck Prospero 'with their high wrongs . . . to the quick' (V,i,25). By feeling the depth of his own baseness Prospero becomes able to 'stomach' the society of men, to forgive even the impenitent Antonio, and to release Miranda into the world. Prospero cannot perfect that world, nor make it perfectly safe for Miranda. It is often suggested that Prospero has only partial success and leaves some of the courtiers unimpressed (see Auden, 'The Sea and the Mirror'). But he forgives all of them, because in allowing them to discover their own guilt his power has reached its limit.

The play may suggest that the farthest limits of Prospero's power are the limits of the tiny isle, for we hear how unforceful Prospero was before arriving there, and how he will become a mere mortal man after leaving. The setting for his omnipotence is moreover a place of only temporary illusion, as is a playhouse.[18] The association is reciprocal, for 'the unities' which are more strictly adhered to in *The Tempest* than in any other Shakespeare play suggest that the isle is coextensive with the theatre, while the theatre metaphors used by Prospero, together with Ariel's theatrical practices, suggest the isle is itself a theatre. But although similarly circumscribed in place and time, neither the isle nor the theatre need be inconsequential. Prospero's 'project', if it succeeds at all, will extend beyond his 'bare isle' to Italy, while the effect of reading or viewing *The Tempest* may also reach to where we live. Artistic illusions, like Prospero's magic Art, are only misleadings of sense and perception. Yet they may have lasting powers, because what they speak of are the symbolic objects of unconscious mental life that determine all our moods, actions and development. Art can help us to live by helping us to symbolize richly, and to judge rightly the correspondence between outer experience and inner symbol.

Such judgement is called for by Prospero's epilogue. Its simple tetrameter couplets contrast sharply with the plangent blank verse concerning his illusory 'revels'; the style alerts us that the things now considered are not phantasmagoria.

The epilogue of *The Tempest* in a sense dissolves the play's pageant by making it real, by gathering its audience as real beings into the theatrical transaction. There is a kind of 'taking out' of *The Tempest*'s audience that shares the Jacobean masque convention of finally requesting the audience's willing participation. Although this request resembles a conventional theatrical bid for applause rather than the masque's bid for dancing, in one sense at least *The Tempest* originally went beyond court masque in terms of participation. Shakespeare's commercial playhouse did not impose polite etiquette, and so whether or not to participate was a genuine and humbling free choice of the audience in their 'real lives'.

Real on a deeper plane is the 'deceiver' referred to in the epilogue, who we may agree is no mythical shape melting into 'thin air' but a permanent part of humanity, a part of all of us. A personal connection between the viewer and the play's dilemma is urged by the final couplet: 'As you from crimes would pardon'd be/ Let your indulgence set me free'. If we applaud after hearing this then we acknowledge by our act of acceptance that we too require forgiving. The magic island contains, finally, not only medicine for courtiers and for clowns, but for all.

NOTES

1. Traditionally *The Tempest* is taken to be the latest written Shakespeare play. Stephen Orgel raises the possibility that *The Winter's Tale* was written slightly later (1987, pp. 63–4). Shakespeare almost certainly contributed parts of *Henry VIII* and *Two Noble Kinsmen* later than 1611.
2. Indeed Kermode (1963, p. 42) overstates this view: 'Prospero is clearly in charge of the whole action, so there is no genuine uncertainty . . . This is in some ways impoverishing.'
3. The trend goes much further. D. L. Hirst for instance cites Jan Kott's belief that *The Tempest* 'represents Prospero's (and Shakespeare's)

final disillusionment' (p. 28). Hirst then offers these criteria for 'good' (!) drama: 'To bully, to terrify, to make the guilty repent, to regain his dukedom, are actions an actor can *play*; to forgive is passive and will not sustain a performance' (p. 57). Hirst then calls for Action, as crude as violent, to avoid 'nebulous dominating concern which leads to the worst sort of interpretations'. But I am sure that in phenomenological terms *to forgive*, for instance, is the inverse of being passive.

4. Some but not all of these simply denigrate Shakespeare as a proponent of a dying culture, and campaign to see his work 'marginalized' (see Evans, M., p. 251).

5. Prospero's admission is interpreted by Stephen Greenblatt as instancing 'the containment of a subversive force by the authority that has created that force in the first place' (p. 29). In this alternative revisionist reading Caliban and his reactions are in a more subtle way the properties of Prospero, but once again Prospero possesses his slave.

6. The over-emphasizing of discourses of power in Shakespeare is not new. As early as 1927 Wyndham Lewis, having claimed the superiority of Machiavelli to Shakespeare, went on to praise the 'machiavellian vein' of Ernest Renan's Shakespearian extrapolation in his play *Caliban* (p. 282). Lewis appreciated especially Renan's lines beginning 'In reality men only respect those who grind them into the dust and kill them . . .', reflecting Lewis's and Renan's authoritarian politics, which would probably be anathema to most revisionists. Yet it seems to me that Paul Brown in a way shares this view by maintaining that 'the production of narrative, in [*The Tempest*], is always related to questions of power' and that 'Prospero's narrative demands of its subjects that they should accede to *his* vision of the past' (p. 59). I hope to establish that this image of Prospero grinding down the free visions of others conveys just the opposite of what occurs in *The Tempest*.

7. But it may be noted that Renaissance commonplaces about heroic neo-Platonism are often mocked by Shakespeare as hollow poses. Insincerity taints vaunted intentions to pursue the 'contemplative mode' in *Love's Labour's Lost*, *The Taming of the Shrew*, *Richard II* and *Measure for Measure*.

8. Pepys saw Dryden's and Davenant's version of 1670 because *The Tempest* 'had been assigned the peculiar property of Davenant's company' (Summers, 1922, p. xli). This version is described as 'prurient' by Harry Levin (p. 230), but to me *The Tempest; or The Enchanted Isle* (in Summers, pp. 1–103) seems more risible than ribald. It crudely amplifies certain aspects of Shakespeare's text, giving to Caliban a lusty incestuous sister, to Miranda an ignorant sex-mad

sister, and making Prospero finally need Caliban to act as a hangman to execute Ferdinand. These same elements receive an even more burlesque treatment in T. Duffett's 1675 *The Mock-Tempest; or the Enchanted Castle* (in Summers, pp. 105-74).

9. Colman (p. 221) says there is one other instance, in *Timon of Athens* (IV,iii,163), which I doubt. But there may be non-misogynist menstrual implications not noted by him in Olivia's remark in *Twelfth Night*, ''tis not that time of moon with me to make one in so skipping a dialogue' (I,v,201-3).

10. Such intensities prohibit strictly allegorical readings of Caliban and Ariel, for instance as the vegetive and sensitive souls of faculty psychology (see Davidson, 1963). In *The Tempest* as in Dante's *Inferno* the impression of a true-seeming psychology is paradoxically heightened by the fantastic setting; Caliban, Ariel and Prospero seem 'real toads' in an 'imaginary garden'. The doubleness of verisimilitude and symbolism in the play supports its doublings of inner and outer, choice and rebellion, need and neediness, love and pain.

11. Bonamy Dobrée argues that therefore *The Tempest* does not equal the other last plays because the theme of forgiveness has become mechanical, even a bit 'nasty' (pp. 26-31). But I think forgiveness is still the central issue and is more interesting morally because it does not depend on chance and error.

12. The Arden footnote which states that the word 'rabble' was 'not at this stage of development contemptuous' (Kermode, 1961, p. 95) is incorrect. The *Oxford English Dictionary* shows the word was precisely that from 1529. Contempt is found also in numerous uses by Shakespeare.

13. The explicit use of a disorderly anti-masque was common by 1609 (Orgel, 1968, p. 144). Bonamy Dobrée (p. 16) holds that Prospero's masque is 'a somewhat grim and sterile vision' while Philip Edwards (1968, p. 142) thinks it 'a thing of immense beauty'. It can be both in our reading, as its failure is part of Prospero's reparative dynamic.

14. I do not think them vitiated by Dover Wilson's concept that nothing should be analysed in a Shakespeare play that could not have been noticed by its first night's audience (pp. 3-4). Surely Shakespeare may have expected some of his audience to attend the same play many times (as slightly later Samuel Pepys did *The Tempest*).

15. Convergence of another sort is implied by Ariel's use of language. Despite Coleridge's often repeated comment that his language is more delicate than Caliban's, Ariel robustly refers to belching or vomiting (III,iii,56) and to stinking feet (IV,i,184).

16. Shakespeare's 'stale' is a complex word. Here it means first a decoy. But 'horse urine', an important second meaning, is reflected in Octavius Caesar's Roman praise of Antony: 'Thou didst drink/ The stale of horses and the guilded puddle/ Which beasts would cough at' (*Antony and Cleopatra* I,iv,61–3). Note the tipsy dignity of Trinculo's complaint 'Monster, I do smell all horse-piss; at which my nose is in great indignation' (IV,i,199–200). So 'stale' in *The Tempest* probably suggests the urine used vindictively by Prospero. Melanie Klein connects urethral-sadistic impulses with primitive phantasies of projecting 'harmful excrements, expelled in hatred, split-off parts of the ego . . .' (1946, p. 183). But note that Caliban does not want to take up the worthless bait or stale, so does not accept Prospero's attempt to locate in him denied parts of himself through such a Kleinian 'projective identification'.

17. Although Prospero threatens to 'peg' Ariel in a cloven oak tree on the island (bettering Sycorax's pine), such grievous torture is never carried out. I think the threat discloses, rather, the barely averted danger in Prospero's schizoid tendencies which threaten to pin his spirit to the sequestered island.

18. I have tried (Sokol, 1985) to demonstrate that Shakespeare sometimes portrays temporary illusions indeed intended to result in permanent change.

8 A BIBLIOGRAPHY OF PSYCHOLOGICAL AND PSYCHOANALYTIC SHAKESPEARE CRITICISM, 1979–1989

CHRISTINE LEVEY

There appears to be a symbiotic relationship between material on Shakespeare and psychoanalysis. On the one hand literary scholars turn to psychoanalytical models as a tool in interpreting the works of Shakespeare, and on the other psychoanalysts often use Shakespearean examples to illustrate their theories. Freud himself did this of course.

Psychoanalysis not being an easily delineated subject, and psychodynamic thinking often overlapping other areas of psychology, I have included items dealing with questions of guilt, conflict, identity, separation, dreams, ambivalence, stereotyping, gender difference and so forth. The ten years' work considered here reflects a growing interest in a feminist psychoanalysis taking into account issues of patriarchy, sexual identity and gender studies.

I have taken 1979 as the starting date for this bibliography because David Willbern's excellent bibliography (no. 393 below) reviews the literature of the previous fourteen years, and explains how to delve back further.

My sources include: the *Shakespeare Quarterly* annual bibliography; the *MLA Bibliography*; *Psychological Abstracts*; and references cited in books and articles. I have used new information technology such as on-line bibliographical databases and CD ROM as well as the usual method of searching through printed sources. Despite all this I'm sure I must have dropped some references along the way, for which I apologize.

I have excluded abstracts, book reviews, dissertations and works not in the English language. I have also excluded work that was previously published outside my date parameters, even if it was reprinted within them.

The bibliography is arranged alphabetically by author and date, and is numbered consecutively. There is an index from the works of Shakespeare to the numbered citations. To avoid overloading the index I have referenced only the Shakespeare works treated at some length in the listed items. Likewise I have not cross-referenced books that address all or nearly all of Shakespeare's works. I have taken the date of an article to be the date of the publication in which it appears.

Place of publication is London unless otherwise stated.

1. Abrams, Richard H. (1986) 'Leontes's enemy: madness in *The Winter's Tale*', in William Coyle, ed. *Aspects of Fantasy: Selected Essays from the 2nd International Conference on the Fantastic in Literature and Film*. Westport, CT and London: Greenwood Press, 1986, pp. 155–62.

2. Adelman, Janet (1985) 'Male bonding in Shakespeare's comedies', in Erickson and Kahn (1985), pp. 73–103.

3. —— (1985) '"This is and is not Cressid": the characterization of Cressida', in Shirley N. Garner, Claire Kahane and Madelou Spreugnether, eds *The (M)other Tongue: Essays in Feminist Psychoanalytic Interpretation*. Ithaca, NY: Cornell Univ. Press, 1985, pp. 119–141.

4. —— (1987) '"Born of woman": fantasies of maternal power in *Macbeth*', in Garber (1987), *Cannibals . . .* , pp. 90–121.

5. —— (1989) 'Bed tricks: on marriage as the end of comedy in *All's Well That Ends Well* and *Measure for Measure*', in Holland (1989), pp. 151–74.

6. Allman, Eileen J. (1980) *Player-King and Adversary: Two Faces of Play in Shakespeare*. Baton Rouge, LA: Louisiana State Univ. Press.

7. Altieri, Charles (1984) 'Criticism as the situating of performances: or what Wallace Stevens has to tell us about *Othello*', in Victor A. Kramer, ed. *American Critics at Work: Examinations of Contemporary Literary Theories*. Troy, NY: Whitston, 1984, pp. 265-95.

8. Anderson, Sexton G. and Lauderdale, Margaret D. (1985) 'Understanding personality: Shakespeare, Jung and Myers-Briggs', *J. of Counseling and Development* 63: 313-14.

9. Andresen-Thom, Martha (1982) 'Shrew-taming and other rituals of aggression: baiting and bonding on the stage and in the wild', *Women's Studies* 9: 121-43.

10. Andrews, John F., ed. (1985) *William Shakespeare: His World, His Work, His Influence*, 3 vols. New York: Charles Scribner's Sons.

11. Ardolino, Frank A. (1983) 'Severed and brazen heads: headhunting in Elizabethan drama', *J. of Evolutionary Psychology* 4: 169-81.

12. Asp, Carolyn (1981) ' "Be bloody, bold and resolute": tragic action and sexual stereotyping in *Macbeth*', *Studies in Philology* 25: 153-69.

13. —— (1986) 'The clamor of Eros: Freud, aging and *King Lear*', in Kathleen Woodward and Murray M. Schwartz, eds *Memory and Desire: Aging - Literature - Psychoanalysis*. Bloomington, IN: Indiana Univ. Press, 1986, pp. 192-204.

14. —— (1986) 'Subjectivity, desire and female friendship in *All's Well That Ends Well*' (Special issue: 'Feminism and Psychoanalysis'), *Literature and Psychology* 32: 48-63.

15. —— (1989) '*Love's Labour's Lost*: language and the deferral of desire', *Literature and Psychology* 35: 1-21

16. Bamber, Linda (1982) *Comic Women, Tragic Men: A Study of Gender and Genre in Shakespeare*. Stanford, CA: Stanford Univ. Press.

17. Barber, C. L. (1980) 'The family in Shakespeare's development: tragedy and sacredness', in Schwartz and Kahn (1980), pp. 188-202.

18. Barber, C. L. and Wheeler, Richard P. (1986) *The Whole Journey: Shakespeare's Power of Development*. Berkeley, CA: Univ. Calif. Press.

19. Bark, Nigel M. (1985) 'Did Shakespeare know schizophrenia? The case of Poor Mad Tom in *King Lear*', *Br. J. of Psychiatry* 146: 436–8.

20. Barricelli, Jean-Pierre and Gibaldi, Joseph, eds (1982) *Interrelations of Literature*. New York: Modern Language Assoc. of America.

21. Belsey, Catherine (1985) 'Disrupting sexual difference: meaning and gender in the comedies', in Drakakis (1985), pp. 166–90.

22. Bentley, Greg (1984) 'Melancholy, madness, and syphilis in *Hamlet*', *Hamlet Studies* (University of Delhi) 6: 75–80.

23. Berek, Peter (1988) 'Text, gender, and genre in *The Taming of the Shrew*', in Charney (1988), pp. 91–104.

24. Beresford, Thomas (1982) 'Playing and the two traditions: clinical psychiatry and literary criticism', *Southern Review* 18: 259–79.

25. Berger, Harry Jr (1979) '*King Lear*: The Lear family romance', *The Centennial Review* 23: 348–76.

26. —— (1981) 'Marriage and mercifixation in *The Merchant of Venice*: the casket scene revisited', *Shakespeare Quarterly* 32: 155–62.

27. —— (1982) 'Text against performance in Shakespeare: the example of *Macbeth*', *Genre* 15: 49–79.

28. —— (1985) 'Psychoanalyzing the Shakespeare text: the first three scenes of the Henriad', in Parker and Hartman (1985), pp. 210–19.

29. —— (1985) 'Text against performance: the Gloucester family romance', in Erickson and Kahn (1985), pp. 210–29.

30. Bergeron, David M. (1983) 'Sexuality in *Cymbeline*', *Essays in Literature* 10: 159–68.

31. Bernthal, Craig A. (1985) '"Self" examination and readiness in *Hamlet*', *Hamlet Studies* (University of Delhi) 7: 38–51.

32. Berry, Edward I. (1979) 'Prospero's "brave spirit"', *Studies in Philology* 76: 36–48.

33. —— (1980) 'Rosalynde and Rosalind', *Shakespeare Quarterly* 31: 42–52.

34. Berry, Patricia (1982) 'Hamlet's poisoned ear', *Spring: An Annual*, pp. 195–211.

35. Berry, Ralph (1981) *Shakespearean Structures*. Macmillan.

36. Bevington, David (1984) 'Shakespeare's development: *Measure for Measure* and *Othello*', *Emotions and Behavior Monographs* 1: 277-96.

37. Billingheimer, Rachel V. (1986) 'Psychological and political trends in "To be, or not to be": stage and film Hamlets of the twentieth century', *Literature in Performance* 7: 27-35.

38. Birenbaum, Harvey (1983) 'A view from the Rialto: two psychologies in *The Merchant of Venice*', *San Jose Studies* 9: 68-82.

39. —— (1988) 'Between the mirror and the face: symbolic reality in *Richard II*', in Homan (1988), pp. 58-75.

40. Blechner, Mark J. (1988) '*King Lear*, King Leir, and incest wishes', *Am. Imago* 45: 309-25.

41. Blum, Harold P. (1986) 'Psychoanalytic studies and *Macbeth*: shared fantasy and reciprocal identification', *Psychoanal. Study Child* 41: 585-99.

42. Bock, Philip K. (1984) *Shakespeare and Elizabethan Culture: An Anthropological View*. New York: Schocken.

43. —— (1987) '"Neither two nor one": dual unity in *The Phoenix and Turtle*', *J. of Psychoanalytic Anthropology* 10: 251-67.

44. Boni, John (1982) 'From medieval to renaissance: paradigm shifts and artistic problems in English renaissance drama', *J. of the Rocky Mountain Medieval and Renaissance Assoc.* 3: 45-63.

45. Boose, Lynda E. (1982) 'The father and the bride in Shakespeare', *PMLA* 97: 325-47.

46. —— (1986) 'An approach through theme: marriage and the family', in Robert H. Ray, ed. *Shakespeare's Approaches to Teaching King Lear*. New York: Modern Language Assoc. of America, 1986, pp. 59-68.

47. Brown, Carolyn E. (1986) 'Erotic religious flagellation and Shakespeare's *Measure for Measure*', *English Literary Renaissance* 16: 139-65.

48. —— (1986) '*Measure for Measure*: Isabella's beating fantasies', *Am. Imago* 43: 67-80.

49. —— (1989) '*Measure for Measure*: Duke Vincentio's "crabbed" desires', *Literature and Psychology* 35: 66-88.

50. Bruss, Neal H. (1981) 'Lacan and literature: imaginary objects and social order', *Massachusetts Review* 22: 62–92.

51. Byles, Joan Mary (1979) 'Narcissism and idealism in *Troilus and Cressida, Othello* and the *Winter's Tale*', *Am. Imago* 36: 80–93.

52. —— (1982) '*Macbeth*: imagery of destruction', *Am. Imago* 39: 149–64.

53. —— (1989) 'The problem of the self and the other in the language of Ophelia, Desdemona and Cordelia', *Am. Imago* 46: 37–59.

54. Bynum, W. F. and Neve, Michael (1986) '*Hamlet* on the couch', *American Scientist* 74: 390–96.

55. Calderwood, James L. (1984) 'Speech and self in *Othello*', *Shakespeare Quarterly* 38: 293–303.

56. —— (1986) *If It Were Done: Macbeth and the Tragic Action*. Amherst, MA: Univ. Mass. Press.

57. —— (1987) *Shakespeare and the Denial of Death*. Amherst, MA: Univ. Mass. Press.

58. —— (1988) 'Immortal money: *The Merchant of Venice*', in Homan (1988), pp. 27–42.

59. Carducci, Jane (1987) 'Shakespeare's *Coriolanus*: "Could I find out/The woman's part in me"', *Literature and Psychology* 33: 11–20.

60. Carr, Stephen L. and Knapp, Peggy A. (1981) 'Seeing through *Macbeth*', *PMLA* 96: 837–47.

61. Cartelli, Thomas (1987) 'Shakespeare's Merchant, Marlowe's Jew: the problem of cultural difference', *Shakespeare Studies* 20: 255–60.

62. Cath, Stanley H. (1988) 'Caesar and his barren relationship with Rome', *Psychohistory Review* 16: 259–82.

63. Cavell, Stanley (1983) '"Who does the wolf love?": reading *Coriolanus*', *Representations* 1: 1–20.

64. —— (1985) '"Who does the wolf love?": *Coriolanus* and the interpretations of politics', in Parker and Hartman (1985), pp. 245–72.

65. Charney, Maurice (1980) *Shakespearean Comedy*. New York: New York Literary Forum.

66. —— (1985) 'Contemporary issues in Shakespearean interpretation', in Andrews (1985), vol. 3, pp. 889-911.

67. —— (1987) 'Analogy and infinite regress in *Hamlet*', in Charney and Reppen (1987), pp. 156-67.

68. —— (1988) *"Bad" Shakespeare*. Rutherford, NJ: Fairleigh Dickinson Univ. Press/London: Assoc. Univ. Presses.

69. Charney, Maurice and Reppen, Joseph, eds (1987) *Psychoanalytic Approaches to Literature and Film*. Assoc. Univ. Presses.

70. Cheung, King-Kok (1984) 'Shakespeare and Kierkegaard: "dread" in *Macbeth*', *Shakespeare Quarterly* 35: 430-39.

71. Cluck, Nancy A. (1985) 'Shakespearean studies in shame', *Shakespeare Quarterly* 36: 141-51.

72. Cohen, Walter (1985) *Drama of a Nation: Public Theater in Renaissance England and Spain*. Ithaca, NY: Cornell Univ. Press.

73. Colman, E. A. M. (1986) 'Squibb academic lecture: Shakespeare and DSM III', *Australian and New Zealand J. of Psychiatry* 20: 30-36.

74. Cook, Carol (1986) ' "The sign and semblance of her honor": reading gender difference in *Much Ado About Nothing*', *PMLA* 10: 186-202.

75. Corrigan, Timothy (1982) *Coleridge, Language and Criticism*. Athens, GA: Univ. Georgia Press.

76. —— (1982) 'Naturalization and psychology in Coleridge's Shakespeare criticism, 1800-1812', in Corrigan (1982), pp. 77-120.

77. Coursen, H. R. (1980) 'The death of Cordelia: a Jungian approach', *Hebrew University Studies in Lit.* 8: 1-12.

78. —— (1984) ' "Age is unnecessary": a Jungian approach to *King Lear*', *The Upstart Crow* 5: 75-92.

79. —— (1985) 'A Jungian approach to characterization: *Macbeth*', in Erickson and Kahn (1985), pp. 230-44.

80. —— (1986) *The Compensatory Psyche: A Jungian Approach to Shakespeare*. Lanham, NY and London: Univ. Press of America.

81. Cunliffe, Helen (1988) '"The story of the night told over": D. W. Winnicott's theory of play and *A Midsummer Night's Dream*', *Ideas and Production* 8: 37–50.

82. Czerniecki, Krystian (1988) 'The jest digested: perspectives on history in *Henry V*', in Jonathan Culler, ed. *On Puns: The Foundations of Letters*. Oxford: Blackwell, 1988, pp. 62–82.

83. Daalder, Joost (1988) 'Shakespeare's attitude to gender in *Macbeth*', *AUMLA: J. of the Australasian Universities Language and Literature Assoc.* 70: 366–85.

84. Dalsimer, K. (1985) *Female Adolescence: Psychoanalytic Reflections on Works of Literature*. New Haven, CT: Yale Univ. Press.

85. Davis, Derek Russell (1982) 'Hurt minds', in John Russell Brown, ed. *Focus on Macbeth*. Routledge & Kegan Paul, 1982, pp. 210–28.

86. Dayton, Paige V. (1988) 'The making of a mysogynist', *J. of Evolutionary Psychology* 9: 346–51.

87. Dickey, Stephen (1986) 'Language and role in *Pericles*', *English Literary Renaissance* 16: 550–66.

88. Dollimore, Jonathan and Sinfield, Alan, eds (1985) *Political Shakespeare: New Essays in Cultural Materialism*. Manchester: Manchester Univ. Press.

89. Donaldson, Peter (1987) 'Olivier, *Hamlet* and Freud', *Cinema J.* 26: 22–48.

90. Dougan, James D. (1987) 'Reinforcement in the sixteenth century: was the bard a behaviorist?', *Behavior Analyst* 10: 189–96.

91. Drakakis, John, ed. (1985) *Alternative Shakespeares*. Methuen.

92. Dreher, Diane Elizabeth (1986) *Domination and Defiance: Fathers and Daughters in Shakespeare*. Lexington, KY: Univ. Press of Kentucky.

93. Driscoll, James P. (1980) 'The Shakespearean metastance: the perspective of *The Tempest*', in Harry R. Garvin, ed. *Shakespeare: Contemporary Critical Approaches*. Lewisburg, PA: Bucknell Univ. Press/London: Assoc. Univ. Presses, 1980, pp. 154–69.

94. —— (1983) *Identity in Shakespearean Drama*. Lewisburg, PA.: Bucknell Univ. Press/London: Assoc. Univ. Presses.

95. DuBois, Page (1985) 'A disturbance of syntax at the gates of Rome', *Stanford Literature Review* 2: 185-208.

96. Dubrow, Heather (1987) *Captive Victors: Shakespeare's Narrative Poems and Sonnets.* Ithaca, NY: Cornell Univ. Press.

97. Dundes, Alan (1980) '"To love my father all": a psychoanalytic study of the folktale source of *King Lear*', in Alan Dundes, *Interpreting Folklore.* Bloomington, IN: Indiana Univ. Press, 1980, pp. 211-22.

98. Dunn, Allen (1988) 'The Indian boy's dream wherein every mother's son rehearses his part: Shakespeare's *A Midsummer Night's Dream*', *Shakespeare Studies* 20: 15-32.

99. Engle, Lars (1989) 'Afloat in thick deeps: Shakespeare's sonnets on certainty', *PMLA* 104: 832-43.

100. Erickson, Peter (1981) 'The failure of relationship between men and women in *Love's Labor's Lost*', *Women's Studies* 9: 65-81.

101. —— (1982) 'Patriarchal structures in *The Winter's Tale*', *PMLA* 97: 819-29.

102. —— (1985) 'In memory of C. L. Barber: "The man working in his works"', in Erickson and Kahn (1985), pp. 303-22.

103. —— (1985) *Patriarchal Structures in Shakespeare's Drama.* Berkeley, CA: Univ. Calif. Press.

104. —— (1985) 'Shakespeare and the "author-function"', in Erickson and Kahn (1985), pp. 245-55.

105. Erickson, Peter and Kahn, Coppélia, eds (1985) *Shakespeare's Rough Magic: Renaissance Essays in Honor of C. L. Barber.* Newark, DE: Univ. Delaware Press/London: Assoc. Univ. Presses.

106. Erlich, Avi (1985) 'Neither to give nor to receive: narcissism in *Timon of Athens*', in Saul N. Brody and Harold Schechter, eds *CUNY English Forum*, vol. 1. New York: AMS Press.

107. Evans, Malcolm (1985) 'Deconstructing Shakespeare's comedies', in Drakakis (1985), pp. 67-94.

108. Faas, Ekbert (1988) *Retreat into the Mind: Victorian Poetry and the Rise of Psychiatry.* Princeton, NJ: Princeton Univ. Press.

109. Faber M. D. (1979) 'The painted breast: a psychological study of Melville's Pierre', *Psychoanal. Rev.* 66: 519-51.

110. —— (1985) *'Antony and Cleopatra*: the empire of the self', *Psychoanal. Rev.* 72: 71–104.

111. Farrell, Kirby (1983) 'Self-effacement and autonomy in Shakespeare', *Shakespeare Studies* 16: 75–99.

112. —— (1989) 'Love, death, and patriarchy in *Romeo and Juliet*', in Holland (1989), pp. 86–102.

113. Feder, Lillian (1980) *Madness in Literature*. Princeton, NJ: Princeton Univ. Press.

114. Ferguson, Margaret W. (1985) '*Hamlet*: letters and spirits', in Parker and Hartman (1985), pp. 292–309.

115. Ferguson, Margaret W., Quilligan, Maureen and Vickers, Nancy J. eds (1986) *Rewriting the Renaissance: The Discourses of Sexual Difference in Early Modern Europe*. Chicago, IL: Univ. Chicago Press.

116. Ferry, Anne (1983) *The 'Inward' Language: Sonnets of Wyatt, Sidney, Shakespeare, Donne*. Chicago, IL: Univ. Chicago Press.

117. Fiedler, Leslie A. (1985) 'Shakespeare's commodity-comedy: a meditation on the preface to the 1609 Quarto of *Troilus and Cressida*', in Erickson and Khan (1985), pp. 50–60.

118. Fineman, Joel (1985) 'The turn of the shrew', in Parker and Hartman (1985), pp. 138–59.

119. —— (1986) *Shakespeare's Perjured Eye: The Invention of Poetic Subjectivity in the Sonnets*. Berkeley, CA: Univ. Calif. Press.

120. Fleming, Keith (1982) '*Hamlet* and Oedipus today: Jones and Lacan', *Hamlet Studies* (University of Delhi) 4: 54–71.

121. Frattaroli, Elio J. (1987) 'On the validity of treating Shakespeare's characters as if they were real people', *Psychoanalysis and Contemporary Thought* 10: 407–37.

122. Freedman, Barbara (1980) 'Egeon's debt: self-division and self-redemption in *The Comedy of Errors*', *English Literary Renaissance* 10: 360–83.

123. —— (1980) 'Errors in comedy: a psychoanalytic theory of farce', in Charney (1980), pp. 233–43.

124. —— (1981) 'Falstaff's punishment: buffoonery as defensive posture in *The Merry Wives of Windsor*', *Shakespeare Studies* 14: 163–74.

125. —— (1987) 'Separation and fusion in *Twelfth Night*', in Charney and Reppen (1987), pp. 96-119.

126. —— (1989) 'Misrecognizing Shakespeare', in Holland (1989), pp. 244-60.

127. French, Marilyn (1982) *Shakespeare's Division of Experience*. Jonathan Cape.

128. Frost, David (1987) 'Constructing Hamlet's mind', *Sydney Studies in English* 12: 3-20.

129. Frye, Roland Mushat (1982) 'Prince Hamlet and the protestant confessional', *Theology Today* 39: 27-38.

130. Garber, Marjorie (1981) *Coming of Age in Shakespeare*. Methuen.

131. —— (1986) ' "What's past is prologue": temporality and prophecy in Shakespeare's history plays', in Barbara K. Lewalski, ed. *Renaissance Genres: Essays on Theory, History and Interpretation*. Cambridge, MA: Harvard Univ. Press, 1986, pp. 301-31.

132. —— (1987) *Cannibals, Witches and Divorce: Estranging the Renaissance*. Baltimore, MD: John Hopkins Univ. Press.

133. —— (1987) *Shakespeare's Ghost Writers: Literature as Uncanny Causality*. Methuen.

134. Gardiner, Judith K. (1985) 'Mind mother: psychoanalysis and feminism', in Gayle Greene and Coppélia Kahn, eds *Making a Difference: Feminist Literary Criticism*. Methuen, 1985, pp. 113-45.

135. Garner, Shirley N. (1981) '*A Midsummer Night's Dream*: "Jack shall have Jill;/Nought shall go ill"', *Women's Studies* 9: 47-63.

136. —— (1984) 'Shylock: "his stones, his daughter, and his ducats"', *The Upstart Crow* 5: 35-49.

137. —— (1988) '*The Taming of the Shrew*: inside or outside of the joke?', in Charney (1988), pp. 105-19.

138. —— (1989) 'Male bonding and the myth of women's deception in Shakespeare's plays', in Holland (1989), pp. 135-50.

139. Ghosh, Gauri P. (1981) 'Shakespeare and the problem plays: alteration of a negative vision', *J. of the Dept. of English* (Calcutta University) 17: 34-63.

140. Gillespie, Gerald (1981) 'Romantic Oedipus', in Gerhart Hoffmeister, ed. *Goethezeit: Studien zur Erkenntnis und Rezeption Goethes und seiner Zeitgenossen. Festschrift für Stuart Atkins.* Bern: Franke, 1981, pp. 331–45.

141. Girard, René (1979) 'Myth and ritual in Shakespeare: *A Midsummer Night's Dream*', in Josué V. Harari, ed. *Textual Strategies: Perspectives in Post-structuralist Criticism.* Ithaca, NY: Cornell Univ. Press, 1979, pp. 189–212.

142. —— (1980) 'Shakespeare's theory of mythology', in Wendell M. Aycock and Theodore M. Klein, eds *Classical Mythology in Twentieth Century Thought and Literature.* Proceedings of the Comparative Literature Symposium, Texas Tech. University, vol. 11. Lubbock, TX: Texas Tech. Press. 1980, pp. 107–24.

143. —— (1985) 'The politics of desire in *Troilus and Cressida*', in Parker and Hartman (1985), pp. 188–209.

144. Gohlke, Madelon (1980) '"And when I love thee not": women and the psychic integrity of the tragic hero', *Hebrew University Studies in Literature* 8: 44–65.

145. —— (1980) '"I wooed thee with my sword": Shakespeare's tragic paradigms', in Lenz (1980), pp. 150–70.

146. —— (1982) '"All that is spoke is marred": language and consciousness in *Othello*', *Women's Studies* 9: 157–76.

147. Goldberg, Carl (1985) 'What ails Antonio? The nature of evil in psychiatric disorders', *J. of Psychology and Judaism* 9: 68–85.

148. —— (1989) 'The shame of *Hamlet* and Oedipus', *Psychoanal. Rev.* 76: 581–603.

149. Goldberg, Jonathan (1985) 'Shakespearean inscriptions: the voicing of power', in Parker and Hartman (1985), pp. 116–37.

150. Goldman, Michael (1981) 'Characterizing *Coriolanus*', *Shakespeare Survey* 34: 73–84.

151. Gomez, Efrain A. (1986) 'Some psychoanalytic thoughts about *King Lear*, Dante, and Don Quixote', *J. of the Am. Acad. of Psychoanal.* 14: 545–56.

152. Gornick, Lisa K. (1987) 'Freud and the creative writer', *Psychoanalysis and Contemporary Thought* 10: 103–27.

153. Graham, Ilse (1988) '"O treason of the blood": reverberations of *Othello* through the German drama of the eighteenth century', in Roger Bayer, ed. *Das Shakespeare-bild in Europa zwischen Aufklärung und Romantik*. Bern: Peter Lang, 1988, pp. 118-42.

154. Gray, Garry (1985) 'Iago's metamorphosis', *CLA Journal* 28: 393-403.

155. Green, André (1986) 'On Hamlet's madness and the unsaid', *Hebrew University Studies in Literature* 14: 18-39.

156. Greenberg, Samuel I. (1985) 'Shylock in *The Merchant of Venice*', *Am. J. Psychoanal.* 45: 160-65.

157. Greenblatt, Stephen J. (1980) 'Improvisation and power', in Edward W. Said, ed. *Literature and Society: Selected Papers from the English Institute 1978*. Baltimore, MD: John Hopkins Univ. Press, 1980, pp. 57-99.

158. —— (1980) *Renaissance Self-fashioning: From More to Shakespeare*. Chicago, IL: Univ. Chicago Press.

159. —— (1982) 'The cultivation of anxiety: *King Lear* and his heirs', *Raritan* 2: 92-114.

160. —— (1985) 'Invisible bullets: renaissance authority and its subversion, *Henry IV and Henry V*', in Dollimore and Sinfield (1985), pp. 18-47.

161. Greene, Gayle (1979) '"This that you call love": sexual and social tragedy in *Othello*', *J. of Women's Studies in Literature* 1: 16-32.

162. Greene, James J. (1984) '*Macbeth*: masculinity as murder', *Am. Imago* 41: 155-80.

163. Groen, Jan (1985) 'Women in Shakespeare with particular reference to Lady Macbeth', *Int. Rev. Psycho-Anal.* 12: 469-78.

164. Grudin, Robert (1979) *Mighty Opposites: Shakespeare and Renaissance Contrariety*. Berkeley, CA: Univ. Calif. Press.

165. Halverson, John (1988) '*Hamlet*: ethos and transcendence', *Anglia* 106: 44-73.

166. Handelman, Susan (1979) '*Timon of Athens*: the rage of disillusion', *Am. Imago* 36: 45-68.

167. Hanly, Charles (1986) 'Lear and his daughters', *Int. Rev. Psycho-Anal.* 13: 211-20.

168. Harding, D. W. (1979) 'Father and daughter in Shakespeare's last plays', The Arthur Skemp Memorial Lecture (University of Bristol), *Times Literary Supplement* 30 November 1979, pp. 59–61.

169. Hartman, Geoffrey (1981) *Saving the Text: Literature/Derrida/Philosophy*. Baltimore, MD: John Hopkins Univ. Press.

170. —— (1985) 'Shakespeare's poetical character in *Twelfth Night*', in Parker and Hartman (1985), pp. 37–53.

171. Hartman, Vicki S. (1983) '*A Midsummer Night's Dream*: a gentle concord to the oedipal problem', *Am. Imago* 40: 355–69.

172. Hawkins, Sherman (1989) 'Aggression and the project of the histories', in Holland (1989), pp. 41–65.

173. Hayles, Nancy K. (1979) 'Sexual disguise in *As You Like It* and *Twelfth Night*', *Shakespeare Survey* 32: 63–72.

174. —— (1980) 'Sexual disguise in *Cymbeline*', *Modern Language Quarterly* 41: 231–47.

175. Hays, Janice (1980) 'Those "soft and delicate desires": *Much Ado* and the distrust of women', in Lenz (1980), pp. 79–99.

176. Hellenga, Robert R. (1981) 'Elizabethan dramatic conventions and Elizabethan reality', *Renaissance Drama* 12: 27–49.

177. Henke, James T. (1987) 'The "schizoid world", and a Shakespearean cure: an overview', *J. of Evolutionary Psychology* 8: 238–49.

178. Hess, Noel (1987) '*King Lear* and some anxieties of old age', *British J. of Medical Psychology* 60: 209–15.

179. Hildebrand, H. Peter (1986) 'The Caledonian tragedy', *Int. Rev. Psycho-Anal.* 13: 39–49.

180. —— (1988) 'The other side of the wall: a psychoanalytic study of creativity in later life', *Int. Rev. Psycho-Anal.* 15: 353–63.

181. Hillman, Richard (1986) '*Hamlet* and death: a recasting of the play within the player', *Essays in Literature* 13: 201–18.

182   Hinely, Jan Lawson (1980) 'Bond priorities in *The Merchant of Venice*', *Studies in English Literature* 20: 217–39.

183. —— (1987) 'Expounding the dream: shaping fantasies in *A Midsummer Night's Dream*', in Charney and Reppen (1987), pp. 120–38.

184.   Hogan, Patrick C. (1979) '*King Lear*: splitting and its epistemic agon', *Am. Imago* 36: 32-44.

185.   —— (1983) '*Macbeth*: authority and progenitorship', *Am. Imago* 40: 385-95.

186.   Holbrook, David (1986) 'Cambridge entrance: a baffling examination paper', *English: The Journal of the English Association* 35: 123-36.

187.   Holland, Norman N. (1980) 'Hermia's dream', in Schwartz and Kahn (1980), pp. 1-20.

188.   —— (1982) *Laughing: A Psychology of Humor*. Ithaca, NY: Cornell Univ. Press.

189.   —— (1984) 'Freud, physics and literature', *J. of the Am. Acad. of Psychoanal.* 12: 301-20.

190.   —— (1989) 'Sons and substitutions: Shakespeare's phallic fantasy', in Holland (1989), pp. 66-85.

191.   Holland, Norman N., Homan, Sidney and Paris, Bernard J., eds (1989) *Shakespeare's Personality*. Berkeley, CA: Univ. Calif. Press.

192.   Holloway, Julia B. (1985) 'Strawberries and mulberries: Ulysses and *Othello*', in William M. Calder III, Ulrich K. Goldsmith and Phyllis B. Kenevan, eds *Hypatia: Essays in Classics, Comparative Literature, and Philosophy. Presented to Hazel E. Barnes on her 70th Birthday*. Boulder, CO: Colorado Associated Univ. Press, 1985, pp. 125-36.

193.   Homan, Sidney, ed. (1988) *Shakespeare and the Triple Play: From Study to Stage to Classroom*. Lewisburg, PA: Bucknell Univ. Press.

194.   Hooks, Roberta M. (1987) 'Shakespeare's *Anthony and Cleopatra*: power and submission', *Am. Imago* 44: 37-49.

195.   Horwich, Richard (1988) *Shakespeare's Dilemmas*. New York: Peter Lang.

196.   Humphries, Jefferson (1983) 'Seeing through Lear's blindness: Blanchot, Freud, Saussure and Derrida', *Mosaic* 16: 29-43.

197.   Hunt, John (1988) 'A thing of nothing: the catastrophic body in *Hamlet*', *Shakespeare Quarterly* 39: 27-44.

198. Hunter, Dianne (1988) 'Doubling, mythic difference, and the scapegoating of female power in *Macbeth*' (Special issue: 'The persistence of myth: psychoanalytic and structuralist perspectives'), *Psychoanal. Rev.* 75: 129–52.

199. Jardine, Lisa (1983) *Still Harping on Daughters: Women and Drama in the Age of Shakespeare.* 2nd edn. Hemel Hempstead, Herts.: Harvester.

200. Jowitt, J. A. and Taylor, R. K. S. eds (1982) *Self and Society in Shakespeare's Troilus and Cressida and Measure for Measure.* Bradford: University of Leeds Centre for Adult Education.

201. Kahn, Coppélia (1981) *Man's Estate: Masculine Identity in Shakespeare.* Berkeley, CA: Univ. Calif. Press.

202. —— (1985) 'The cuckoo's note: male friendship, and cuckoldry in the *Merchant of Venice*', in Erickson and Kahn (1985), pp. 104–12.

203. —— (1986) 'The absent mother in *King Lear*', in Ferguson (1986), pp. 33–49.

204. —— (1987) '"Magic of bounty": *Timon of Athens*, Jacobean patronage and maternal power', *Shakespeare Quarterly* 38: 34–57.

205. Kanzer, Mark (1979) 'Shakespeare's dog images – hidden keys to *Julius Caesar*', *Am. Imago* 36: 2–31.

206. Kehler, Dorothea (1985) 'King of tears: mortality in *Richard II*', *Rocky Mountain Review of Language and Literature* 39: 7–18.

207. Kernberg, Otto F. (1980) 'Adolescent sexuality in the light of group processes', *Psychoanal. Q.* 49: 27–47.

208. Kerrigan, John (1981) 'Hieronimo, *Hamlet* and remembrance', *Essays in Criticism* 31: 105–26.

209. Kerrigan, William (1980) 'Psychoanalysis unbound', *New Literary History* 12: 199–206.

210. —— (1989) 'The personal Shakespeare: three clues', in Holland (1989), pp. 175–190.

211. Kestenbaum, Clarice J. (1983) 'Fathers and daughters: the father's contribution to feminine identification in girls as depicted in fairy tales and myths', *Am. J. Psychoanal.* 43: 119–27.

212. Keyes, Laura (1988) 'Hamlet's fat', in Homan (1988), pp. 89–104.

213. Kiell, Norman (1982) *Psychoanalysis, Psychology and Literature: A Bibliography*, 2 vols. 2nd edn. Metuchen, NJ: Scarecrow Press.

214. Kimbrough, Robert (1982) 'Androgyny seen through Shakespeare's disguise', *Shakespeare Quarterly* 33: 17-33.

215. —— (1983) '*Macbeth*: the prisoner of gender', *Shakespeare Studies* 16: 175-90.

216. King, Walter N. (1982) *Hamlet's Search for Meaning*. Athens, GA: Univ. Georgia Press.

217. Kirsch, Arthur C. (1981) *Shakespeare and the Experience of Love*. Cambridge: Cambridge Univ. Press.

218. —— (1984) 'Macbeth's suicide', *ELH* 51: 269-96.

219. Kleinberg, Seymour (1983) '*The Merchant of Venice*: the homosexual as anti-Semite in nascent capitalism', *J. of Homosexuality* 8: 113-26.

220. Knapp, Peggy A. (1980) '*Hamlet* and Daniel (and Freud and Marx)', *Massachusetts Review* 21: 487-501.

221. Knights, L. C. (1982) 'Shakespeare: King Lear and the great tragedies', in Boris Ford, ed. *The New Pelican Guide to English Literature*, vol. 2, *The Age of Shakespeare*. Rev. and expanded edn. Harmondsworth and New York: Penguin, 1982, pp. 327-56.

222. Konstan, David (1983) 'A dramatic history of misanthropes', *Comparative Drama* 17: 97-123.

223. Koskenniemi, Inna (1983) 'On some physiological terms used for characterization in English renaissance drama', in E. G. Stanley and Douglas Gray, eds *Five Hundred Years of Words and Sounds: A Festschrift for Eric Dobson*. Cambridge: D. S. Brewer, 1983, pp. 92-9.

224. Kranz, David L. (1982) 'Shakespeare's new idea of Rome', in P. A. Ramsey, ed. *Rome in the Renaissance: The City and the Myth*. Papers of the Thirteenth Annual Conference of the Center for Medieval and Early Renaissance Studies. Binghamton, NY: Medieval and Renaissance Studies, 1982, pp. 371-80.

225. Krieger, Elliott R. (1979) *A Marxist Study of Shakespeare's Comedies*. Macmillan.

226.   Kristeva, Julia (1987) *Tales of Love*. New York: Columbia Univ.
       Press.

227.   Krohn, Janis (1986) 'Addressing the oedipal dilemma in *Macbeth*',
       Psychoanal. Rev. 73: 333–47.

228.   —— (1986) 'The dangers of love in *Antony and Cleopatra*', *Int. Rev.
       Psycho-Anal.* 13: 89–96.

229.   Kuhns, Richard (1983) *Psychoanalytic Theory of Art: A Philosophy
       of Art on Developmental Principles*. New York: Columbia Univ.
       Press.

230.   La Belle, Jenijoy (1980) '"A strange infirmity": Lady Macbeth's
       amenorrhea', *Shakespeare Quarterly* 31: 381–86.

231.   Lake, James H. (1988) '*Othello* and the comforts of love', *Am. Imago*
       45: 327–35.

232.   Lande, Maydee G. (1986) '*The Winter's Tale*: a question of motive',
       Am. Imago 43: 51–65.

233.   Laurent, Camille Pierre (1984) 'Dog, fiend and christian, or Shylock's
       conversion', *Cahiers Elisabethans* 26: 15–27.

234.   Lenz, Carolyn Ruth Swift, Greene, Gayle and Neely, Carol Thomas,
       eds (1980) *The Woman's Part: Feminist Criticism of Shakespeare*.
       Urbana, IL: Univ. Illinois Press.

235.   Leonard, Nancy S. (1979) 'The persons of the comic in Shakespeare
       and Jonson', *Research Opportunities in Renaissance Drama* 22:
       11–15.

236.   Levenson, Jill L. (1981) 'Dramatists at (meta) play: Shakespeare's
       Hamlet, II, ii, ll. 410–591 and Pirandello's *Henry IV*', *Modern
       Drama* 24: 330–37.

237.   Levin, Harry (1982) 'Two scenes from Macbeth', in Philip H. Highfill
       Jr, ed. *Shakespeare's Craft: Eight Lectures*. The Tupper Lectures on
       Shakespeare. Carbondale, IL: Southern Illinois Univ. Press for the
       George Washington University, 1982, pp. 48–68.

238.   Levin, Richard A. (1980) '*All's Well That Ends Well* and "all seems
       well"', *Shakespeare Studies* 13: 131–44.

239.   —— (1985) *Love and Society in Shakespearean Comedy: A Study
       of Dramatic Form and Content*. Newark, DE: Univ. Delaware
       Press/London: Assoc. Univ. Presses.

240.　———— (1985) 'The new refutation of Shakespeare', *Modern Philology* 83: 123–41.

241.　———— (1988) 'Feminist thematics and Shakespearean tragedy', *PMLA* 103: 125–38.

242.　Lewis, Catherine R. (1985) 'Poet, friend and poetry: the idealized image of love in Shakespeare's sonnets', *Am. J. Psychoanal.* 45: 176–90.

243.　Lifson, Martha Ronk (1988) 'Learning by talking: conversation in *As You Like It*', *Shakespeare Survey*, 40: 91–105.

244.　Livingston, Howard (1980) '*Hamlet*, Ernest Jones, and the critics', *Hamlet Studies* (University of Delhi) 2: 25–33.

245.　Lordi, Robert J. (1982) '*Macbeth* and his "dearest partner of greatness", Lady Macbeth', *The Upstart Crow* 4: 94–106.

246.　Lukacher, Ned (1986) *Primal Scenes: Literature, Philosophy, Psychoanalysis*. Ithaca, NY: Cornell Univ. Press.

247.　MacCary, W. Thomas (1985) *Friends and Lovers: The Phenomenology of Desire in Shakespearean Comedy*. New York: Columbia Univ. Press.

248.　McDonald, Russ (1988) 'Fear of farce', in Charney (1988), pp. 77–90.

249.　McFarland, Thomas (1981) 'The image of the family in *King Lear*', in Lawrence Danson, ed. *On King Lear*. Princeton, NJ: Princeton Univ. Press, 1981, pp. 91–118.

250.　McLuskie, Kathleen (1985) 'The patriarchal bard: feminist criticism and Shakespeare: *King Lear* and *Measure for Measure*', in Dollimore and Sinfield (1985), pp. 88–108.

251.　Mahon, Eugene J. (1989) 'A note on "The theme of the three caskets"', *Psychoanal. Study Child* 44: 325–30.

252.　Mahon, John W. and Pendleton, Thomas A., eds (1987) '*Fanned and Winnowed Opinions': Shakespearean Essays Presented to Harold Jenkins*. Methuen.

253.　Mahony, Patrick (1979) 'Shakespeare's sonnet, number 20: its symbolic gestalt', *Am. Imago* 36: 69–79.

254.　Marchant, Robert (1984) *A Picture of Shakespeare's Tragedies*. Retford, Notts.: Brynmill Press.

255.   Markert, John (1981) 'Shakespeare's neurotic persona: sonnets 71–74', *J. of Evolutionary Psychology* 2: 101–11.

256.   Mills, Paul (1982) 'Brothers and enemies in *Measure for Measure*', in Jowitt and Taylor (1982), pp. 96–109.

257.   Mitchell, Giles R. and Wright, Eugene P. (1983) 'Hotspur's poor memory', *South Central Bulletin* 43: 121–23.

258.   Montrose, Louis Adrian (1981) '"The place of a brother" in *As You Like It*: social process and comic form', *Shakespeare Quarterly* 32: 28–54.

259.   —— (1983) '"Shaping fantasies": figurations of gender and power in Elizabethan culture', *Representations* 1: 61–94.

260.   —— (1986) '*A Midsummer Night's Dream* and the shaping fantasies of Elizabethan culture: gender, power, form', in Ferguson (1986), pp. 65–87.

261.   Mooney, Michael E. (1985) '"Edgar I nothing am": "Figuren-position" in *King Lear*', *Shakespeare Survey* 38: 153–66.

262.   Muller, John P. (1980) 'Psychosis and mourning in Lacan's *Hamlet*', *New Literary History* 12: 147–65.

263.   Muslin, Hyman L. (1981) '*King Lear*: images of the self in old age', *J. of Mental Imagery* 5: 143–55.

264.   —— (1982) '*Romeo and Juliet*: the tragic self in adolescence', *Adolescent Psychiatry* 10: 106–17.

265.   —— (1984) 'Shakespeare and the psychology of the self: the case of *Othello*', in Paul E. Stepansky and Arnold Goldberg, eds *Kohut's Legacy: Contributions to Self Psychology*. Hillsdale, NJ: Analytic Press, 1984, pp. 215–31.

266.   —— (1988) '*Macbeth*: the self of evil', *Psychoanalytic Psychology* 5: 357–68.

267.   Nardo, Anna K. (1983) '*Hamlet*, a man to double business bound', *Shakespeare Quarterly* 34: 181–99.

268.   Natoli, Joseph and Rusch, Frederik L. (1984) *Psychocriticism: An Annotated Bibliography*. Westport, CT and London: Greenwood Press.

269. Neely, Carol Thomas (1980) 'Women and men in *Othello*: "What should such a fool/Do with so good a woman?"', in Lenz (1988), pp. 211–39.

270. —— (1985) 'Broken nuptials in Shakespeare's comedies', in Erickson and Kahn (1985), pp. 61–72.

271. —— (1985) *Broken Nuptials in Shakespeare's Plays*. New Haven, CT: Yale Univ. Press.

272. —— (1987) 'Feminist criticism and teaching Shakespeare', *ADE Bulletin* 87: 15–18.

273. Neiditz, Minerva (1979) 'Primary process mentation and the structure of *Timon of Athens*', *Hartford Studies in Literature* 11: 24–35.

274. Netzer, Carol (1982) 'Annals of psychoanalysis: Ella Freeman Sharpe', *Psychoanal. Rev.* 69: 207–19.

275. Nevo, Ruth (1980) *Comic Transformations in Shakespeare*. Methuen.

276. —— (1980) 'Shakespeare's comic remedies', in Charney (1980), pp. 3–15.

277. —— (1987) '*Measure for Measure*: mirror for mirror', *Shakespeare Survey* 40: 107–22.

278. —— (1987) 'Motive and meaning in *All's Well That Ends Well*', in Mahon and Pendleton (1987), pp. 26–51.

279. —— (1987) *Shakespeare's Other Language*. Methuen.

280. Newman, Karen (1982) 'Writing the "talking cure": psychoanalysis and literature', *Poetics Today* 3: 173–82.

281. Novy, Marianne (1984) *Love's Argument: Gender Relations in Shakespeare*. Chapel Hill, NC: Univ. of North Carolina Press.

282. —— (1989) 'Shakespeare and the bonds of brotherhood', in Holland (1989), pp. 103–15.

283. Oliver, T. (1984) 'Equivocal rhetoric in *Othello*', *Notes and Queries* 31: 203–5.

284. Oremland, Jerome D. (1983) 'Death and transformation in *Hamlet*', *Psychoanal. Inquiry* 3: 485–512.

285. Orgel, Stephen (1984) 'Prospero's wife', *Representations* 8: 1–13.

286. Padel, John (1981) *New Poems by Shakespeare: Order and Meaning Restored to the Sonnets*. Herbert Press.

287. —— (1985) 'Was Shakespeare happy with his patron? One psychoanalytic view of the relationship', *Psychoanal. Psychotherapy* 1: 25–42.

288. —— (1989) 'Shakespeare's sonnet 20: some limits to psychoanalytic interpretation', *Int. Rev. Psycho-Anal.* 16: 171–8.

289. Palombo, Stanley R. (1983) 'The genius of the dream', *Am. J. Psychoanal.* 43: 301–13.

290. Paolucci, Anne (1980) 'The expressionistic redemption of the "absurd": Shakespeare's *Hamlet* and Pirandello's *Enrico IV*', *Hamlet Studies* (University of Delhi) 2: 34–41.

291. Paris, Bernard J. (1980) 'Bargains with fate: a psychological approach to Shakespeare's major tragedies', *Aligarh J. of English Studies* 5: 144–61.

292. —— (1981) 'A Horneyan approach to Shakespeare', *Shakespeare Newsletter* 31: 14.

293. —— (1981) 'The inner conflicts of *Measure for Measure*: a psychological approach', *Centennial Review* 25: 266–76.

294. —— (1982) 'Bargains with fate: the case of *Macbeth*', *Am. J. Psychoanal.* 42: 7–20.

295. —— (1983) '*Richard III*: Shakespeare's first great mimetic character', *Aligarh J. of English Studies* 8: 40–67.

296. —— (1984) '"His scorn I approve": the self-effacing Desdemona', *Am. J. Psychoanal.* 44: 413–24.

297. —— (1984) 'Iago's motives: a Horneyan analysis', *Revue Belge de Philologie et d'Histoire* 62: 504–20.

298. —— (1987) 'Brutus, Cassius and Caesar: an interdestructive triangle', in Charney and Reppen (1987), pp. 139–55.

299. —— (1989) 'The not so noble Antonio: a Horneyan analysis of Shakespeare's *Merchant of Venice*', *Am. J. Psychoanal.* 49: 189–200.

300. —— (1989) '*The Tempest*: Shakespeare's ideal solution', in Holland (1989), pp. 206–25.

301. Parker, Patricia and Hartman, Geoffrey H., eds (1985) *Shakespeare and the Question of Theory*. Methuen.

302. Pequigney, Joseph (1985) *Such Is My Love: A Study of Shakespeare's Sonnets*. Chicago, IL: Univ. Chicago Press.

303. Peterson, Corinna (1987) 'To be or not to be: a study of ambivalence', *J. of Analyt. Psychol.* 32: 79–92.

304. Phillips, John A. S. (1980) 'Why does Hamlet delay? – Hamlet's subtle revenge', *Anglia* 98: 34–50.

305. Pierloot, Roland A. (1988) 'Impersonal objects in morbid jealousy', *Int. Rev. Psycho-Anal.* 15: 293–306.

306. Pollock, George H. and Gedo, John E., eds (1984) *Psychoanalyis: The Vital Issues*, vol.2, *Clinical Psychoanalysis and its Applications*. New York: International Universities Press.

307. Quillian, William H. (1983) *Hamlet and the New Poetic: James Joyce and T.S. Eliot*. Ann Arbor, MI: UMI Research Press.

308. Rabkin, Norman (1981) *Shakespeare and the Problem of Meaning*. Chicago, IL: Univ. Chicago Press.

309. Regan, Mariann Sanders (1982) *Love Words: The Self and the Text in Medieval and Renaissance Poetry*. Ithaca, NY: Cornell Univ. Press.

310. Richard, Jeremy (1986) '"The thing I am": Parolles, the comedic villain and tragic consciousness', *Shakespeare Studies* 18: 145–59.

311. Ridge, George Ross and Njoku, Benedict Chiaka (1983) *The Christian Tragic Hero in French and English Literature*. Atlantic Highlands, NJ: Humanities Press.

312. Roberts, David (1980) *The Indirections of Desire: Hamlet in Goethe's Wilhelm Meister*. Heidelberg: Winter.

313. Robertson, Hugh (1982) '*Troilus and Cressida* and *Measure for Measure* in their age: Shakespeare's thought in its context', in Jowitt and Taylor, eds (1982), pp. 3–26.

314. Robertson, Ritchie (1985) 'Shakespearean comedy and romantic psychology in Hoffman's *Kater Murr*', *Studies in Romanticism* 24: 201–22.

315. Rogers, Robert (1982) 'Hamlet's tongue', *Psychoanal. Rev.* 69: 533–55.

316.   —— (1987) 'General system theory and literary texts. Part 1: The reading process: from diversity to equifinality', *J. of Lit. Semantics* 16: 94–112.

317.   Rose, Jacqueline (1985) 'Sexuality in the reading of Shakespeare: *Hamlet* and *Measure for Measure*', in Drakakis (1985), pp. 95–118.

318.   —— (1986) '*Hamlet* – the Mona Lisa of literature', *Critical Quarterly* 28: 35–49.

319.   Rosenberg, Marvin (1988) 'Culture, character, and conscience in Shakespeare', in Homan (1988), pp. 138–49.

320.   Rubinstein, Frankie (1984) *A Dictionary of Shakespeare's Sexual Puns and Their Significance*. Macmillan.

321.   —— (1986) 'Shakespeare's dream-stuff: a forerunner of Freud's "dream-material"', *Am. Imago* 43: 335–55.

322.   —— (1988) 'Persistent sexual symbolism: Shakespeare and Freud', *Literature and Psychology*, 34: 1–26.

323.   Rudnytsky, Peter L. (1985) 'The purloined handkerchief in *Othello*', in Joseph Reppen and Maurice Charney, eds *The Psychoanalytic Study of Literature*. Hillsdale, NJ: Analytic Press, 1985, pp. 169–90.

324.   Schaum, Melita (1984) 'The social dynamics: separation, liminality and reaggregation in *King Lear*', *Aligarh J. of English Studies* 9: 148–54.

325.   Scheiner, William (1985) 'Justifying the unjustifiable: the Dover cliff scene in *King Lear*', *Shakespeare Quarterly* 36: 337–43.

326.   Schleiner, Winfried (1987) 'Prospero as a renaissance therapist', *Literature and Medicine* 6: 54–60.

327.   Schuman, Elliot P. (1983) 'The madness of Shakespeare's *King Lear*: retributive or restitutive?', *Modern Psychoanalysis* 8: 81–91.

328.   Schwartz, Mary C. (1984) 'A family romance: loving, losing and reuniting in *King Lear*', *Family Therapy Networker* 8: 42–6.

329.   Schwartz, Murray M. (1983) 'Anger, wounds, and the forms of theater in *King Richard II*: notes for a psychoanalytic interpretation', in Peggy A. Knapp, ed. *Assays: Critical Approaches to Medieval and Renaissance Texts*, vol. 2. Pittsburgh, PA: Univ. Pittsburgh Press, 1983, pp. 115–29.

330. Schwartz, Murray M. and Kahn, Coppélia (1980) *Representing Shakespeare*. Baltimore, MD: John Hopkins Univ. Press.

331. Segal, Ora (1986) 'Joyce's interpretation of dreams', *Hebrew University Studies in Literature* 14: 106–33.

332. Shainess, Natalie (1984) 'Shakespeare's *Timon of Athens*: the progress from naiveté to cynicism', *J. Am. Acad. of Psychoanal.* 12: 425–40.

333. Shakman, Michael L. (1986) '*The Tempest*', *Am. Imago* 43: 81–96.

334. Showalter, Elaine (1985) 'Representing Ophelia: women, madness, and the responsibilities of feminist criticism', in Parker and Hartman (1985), pp. 77–94.

335. Silver, David (1983) 'The Dark Lady: sibling loss and mourning in the Shakespearean sonnets', *Psychoanal. Inquiry* 3: 513–27.

336. Silverman, Kaja (1979) '*Hamlet* and the common theme of the fathers', *Enclitic* 3: 106–21.

337. Simon, Bennett (1984) '"With cunning delays and ever-mounting excitement" or, what thickens the plot in tragedy and in psychoanalysis', in Pollock and Gedo (1984), pp. 387–437.

338. —— (1988) *Tragic Drama and the Family: Psychoanalytic Studies from Aeschylus to Beckett*. New Haven, CT: Yale Univ. Press.

339. Sinaiko, Herman L. (1984) 'Tragedy and psychoanalysis', in Pollock and Gedo (1984), pp. 437–62.

340. Sinason, Valerie (1988) '*Richard III*, Hephaestus and Echo: sexuality and mental/multiple handicap', *J. of Child Psychotherapy* 14: 93–105.

341. Skura, Meredith Anne (1980) 'Interpreting Posthumus' dream from above and below: families, psychoanalysts, and literary critics', in Schwartz and Kahn (1980), pp. 203–16.

342. —— (1981) *The Literary Use of the Psychoanalytic Process*. New Haven, CT: Yale Univ. Press.

343. —— (1985) 'Shakespeare's psychology: characterization in Shakespeare', in Andrews (1985), vol. 2, pp. 571–87.

344. Slights, Camille (1980) 'In defense of Jessica: the runaway daughter in the *Merchant of Venice*', *Shakespeare Quarterly* 31: 357–68.

345. Snow, Edward A. (1980) 'Sexual anxiety and the male order of things in *Othello*', *English Literary Renaissance* 10: 384–412.

346. —— (1985) 'Language and sexual difference in *Romeo and Juliet*', in Erickson and Kahn (1985), pp. 168–92.

347. Snyder, Susan (1979) *The Comic Matrix of Shakespeare's Tragedies: Romeo and Juliet, Hamlet, Othello, and King Lear.* Princeton, NJ: Princeton Univ. Press.

348. —— (1982) '*King Lear* and the psychology of dying', *Shakespeare Quarterly* 33: 449–60.

349. Soellner, Rolf (1982) 'Shakespeare's Lucrece and the Garnier–Pembroke connection', *Shakespeare Studies* 15: 1–20.

350. Speziale-Bagliacca, Roberto (1980) 'Lear, Cordelia, Kent, and the fool: a psychological interpretation', *Int. Rev. Psycho-Anal.* 7: 413–28.

351. Spicer, Harold (1983) 'Hamlet's "mole of nature"', *Ball State University Forum* 24: 61–72.

352. Splitter, Rudolph (1982) 'Language, sexual conflict and "symbiosis anxiety" in *Othello*', *Mosaic* 15: 17–26.

353. Sprengnether, Madelon (1986) 'Annihilating intimacy in *Coriolanus*', in Mary Beth Rose, ed. *Women in the Middle Ages and Renaissance: Literary and Historical Perspectives.* Syracuse, NY: Syracuse Univ. Press, 1986, pp. 89–111.

354. —— (1989) 'The boy actor and femininity in *Antony and Cleopatra*', in Holland (1989), pp. 191–205.

355. Stachniewski, John (1988) 'Calvinist psychology in *Macbeth*', *Shakespeare Studies* 20: 169–89.

356. States, Bert O. (1985) 'The horses of *Macbeth*', *Kenyon Review* 7: 52–66.

357. Stern, Jeffrey (1987) 'The sins of the fathers: "Prince Hal's conflict" reconsidered', *Emotions and Behavior Monographs* 4: 487–502.

358. Sternlight, Sanford (1982) '*Hamlet* – the actor as prince', *Hamlet Studies* (University of Delhi) 4: 19–32.

359. Stockholder, Kay (1982) 'Worlds in dream and drama: a psychoanalytic theory of literary representation', *Dalhousie Review* 62: 374–96.

360.   —— (1987) '*Macbeth*: a dream of love', *Am. Imago* 44: 85–105.

361.   Strauch, Edward H. (1980) 'The scope and limits of the Freudian approach to literature', *Aligarh J. of English Studies* 5: 125–43.

362.   —— (1982) 'Implications of Jung's archetypal approach for literary study', *Aligarh J. of English Studies* 7: 1–17.

363.   Stuart, Simon (1979) *New Phoenix Wings: Reparation in Literature*. Routledge & Kegan Paul.

364.   Sundelson, David (1980) 'So rare a wonder'd father: Prospero's *Tempest*', in Schwartz and Kahn (1980), pp. 33–53.

365.   —— (1981) 'The dynamics of marriage in the *Merchant of Venice*', *Humanities in Society* 4: 245–62.

366.   —— (1981) 'Misogyny and rule in *Measure for Measure*', *Women's Studies* 9: 83–91.

367.   —— (1983) *Shakespeare's Restorations of the Father*. New Brunswick, NJ: Rutgers Univ. Press.

368.   Sunohara, Masahiko (1984) '*King Lear* as a tragedy of love, with special regard to passive love', *Shakespeare Studies* (Japan) 20 (for 1981–82): 59–89.

369.   Taft, Edmund M. IV (1986) 'Love and death in *Twelfth Night*', *Iowa State J. of Research* 60: 407–16.

370.   Taylor, Gary (1985) *To Analyze Delight: A Hedonist Criticism of Shakespeare*. Newark, DE: Univ. Delaware Press.

371.   Tennenhouse, Leonard (1980) 'The counterfeit order of *The Merchant of Venice*', in Schwartz and Kahn (1980), pp. 54–69.

372.   Tobin, J. J. M. (1981) '*Hamlet* and Christ's teares over Jerusalem', *Aligarh J. of English Studies* 6: 158–67.

373.   Traub, Valerie (1988) 'Jewels, statues and corpses: containment of female erotic power in Shakespeare's plays', *Shakespeare Studies* 20: 215–38.

374.   Tucker, Kenneth (1984) 'Psychetypes and Shakespeare's *Antony and Cleopatra*', *J. of Evolutionary Psychology* 5: 176–81.

375.   Verhoeff, Han (1984) 'Does Oedipus have his complex?', *Style* 18: 261–83.

376. Vey-Miller, Marguerite M. and Miller, Ronald J. (1985) 'Degrees of psychopathology in *Hamlet*', *Hamlet Studies* (University of Delhi) 7: 81–7.

377. Wall, John N. (1979) 'Shakespeare's aural art: the metaphor of the ear in *Othello*', *Shakespeare Quarterly* 30: 358–66.

378. Warner, William Beatty (1986) *Chance and the Text of Experience: Freud, Nietzsche, and Shakespeare's Hamlet*. Ithaca, NY: Cornell Univ. Press.

379. Watson, Robert N. (1984) *Shakespeare and the Hazards of Ambition*. Cambridge, MA: Harvard Univ. Press.

380. Weimann, Robert (1985) 'Mimesis in *Hamlet*', in Parker and Hartman (1985), pp. 275–91.

381. Weiser, David K. (1982) 'Essays in definition: Shakespeare's sonnets 21, 23 and 25', *Cahiers Elisabethans* 22: 3–14.

382. Westlund, Joseph (1984) *Shakespeare's Reparative Comedies: A Psychoanalytic View of the Middle Plays*. Chicago, IL: Univ. Chicago Press.

383. —— (1987) 'What comedy can do for us: reparation and idealization in Shakespeare's comedies', in Charney and Reppen (1987), pp. 83–95.

384. Wexler, Joyce (1988) 'A wife lost and/or found', *The Upstart Crow* 8: 106–17.

385. Wheeler, Richard P. (1981) *Shakespeare's Development and the Problem Comedies: Turn and Counter-turn*. Berkeley, CA: Univ. Calif. Press.

386. —— (1985) '"And my loud crying still": *The Sonnets, The Merchant of Venice*, and *Othello*', in Erickson and Kahn (1985), pp. 193–209.

387. —— (1987) 'Psychoanalytic criticism and teaching Shakespeare', *ADE Bulletin* 87: 19–23.

388. —— (1988) 'Introduction' in C. L. Barber, *Creating Elizabethan Tragedy: The Theater of Marlowe and Kyd*. Chicago, IL: Univ. Chicago Press, 1988, pp. 1–44.

389. White, John (1983) 'Liberation and the unity of opposites in *Romeo and Juliet*', *Revision* 6: 79–80.

390. Wilcher, Robert (1982) 'The art of the comic duologue in three plays by Shakespeare', *Shakespeare Survey* 35: 87-100.

391. Wilkins, Robert (1989) 'The king and his fool', *J. of Family Therapy* 11: 181-95.

392. Willbern, David (1979) 'Paranoia, criticism and Malvolio', *Hartford Studies in Literature* 11: 1-23.

393. —— (1980) 'A bibliography of psychoanalytic and psychological writings on Shakespeare: 1964-1978', in Schwartz and Kahn (1980), pp. 264-88.

394. —— (1980) 'Shakespeare's nothing', in Schwartz and Kahn (1980), pp. 244-63.

395. —— (1986) 'Phantasmagoric *Macbeth*', *English Literary Renaissance* 16: 520-49.

396. —— (1989) 'What is Shakespeare?' in Holland (1989), pp. 226-43.

397. Williamson, Marilyn L. (1982) 'Doubling women's anger, and genre', *Women's Studies* 9: 107-19.

398. Wilson, Anne (1983) *Magical Thought in Creative Writing: The Distinctive Roles of Fantasy and Imagination in Fiction*. Stroud, Glos.: Thimble Press.

399. Wilson, Douglas B. (1983) 'The commerce of desire: Freudian narcissism in Chaucer's *Troilus and Criseyde* and Shakespeare's *Troilus and Cressida*', *English Language Notes* 21: 11-22.

400. Wilson, Rob (1987) '*Othello*: jealousy as mimetic contagion', *Am. Imago* 44: 213-33.

401. Wolf, Ernest S. (1980) 'Psychoanalytic psychology of the self and literature', *New Literary History* 12: 41-60.

402. Wright, Elizabeth (1984) *Psychoanalytic Criticism: Theory in Practice*. Methuen.

403. Zak, William F. (1984) *Sovereign Shame: A Study of King Lear*. Lewisburg, PA: Bucknell Univ. Press/ London: Assoc. Univ. Presses.

REFERENCES

Place of publication is London unless otherwise stated.

Adams, R. M. (1953) '*Trompe-l'oeil* in Shakespeare and Keats', *Sewanee Review* 61: 238-55

Adelman, J. (1985) ' "This is and is not Cressid": the characterization of Cressida', in S. Nelson Garner, C. Kahane, M. Sprengnether, eds *The(M)other Tongue: Essays in Feminist Psychoanalytic Interpretation*. Ithaca, NY and London: Cornell Univ. Press, pp. 119-41.

Alvarez, A. (1955) 'William Shakespeare: *The Phoenix and the Turtle*', in J. Wain, ed. *Interpretations*. Routledge & Kegan Paul, pp. 1-16.

Andreas-Salomé, L. (1962) 'The dual orientation of narcissism', *Psychoanal. Q.* 31: 1-30.

Arendt, H. (1977) *Eichmann in Jerusalem*. Harmondsworth: Penguin.

Auden, W. H. (1945) 'The Sea and the Mirror: a commentary on Shakespeare's *The Tempest*', in *The Collected Poetry*. New York: Random House, pp. 351-404.

Axton, M. (1977) *The Queen's Two Bodies*. Royal Historical Society.

Bachelard, G. (1964) *The Poetics of Space*, trans. M. Jolas. Boston, MA: Beacon.

Barber, C. L. (1959) *Shakespeare's Festive Comedy*. Cleveland, OH: Meridian, 1963.

—— (1969) ' "Thou that beget'st him that did thee beget": transformation in *Pericles* and *The Winter's Tale*', *Shakespeare Survey* 22: 59-67.

Barker, G. A. (1963) 'Themes and variations in *Pericles*', *English Studies* 41: 401-14.

Barron, D. B. (1960) ' "The babe that milks": an organic study of *Macbeth*', *Am. Imago* 17: 133-61.

Berger, H. Jr (1985a) 'Text against performance: the Gloucester family romance', in P. Erickson and C. Kahn, eds *Shakespeare's Rough Magic*. Newark, DE: Univ. Delaware Press, pp. 210-29.

—— (1985b) 'Psychoanalyzing the Shakespeare text: the first three scenes of the *Henriad*', in P. Parker and G. Hartman, eds *Shakespeare and the Question of Theory*. Methuen, pp. 210-29.

Bernstein, D. (1983) 'The female superego: a different perspective', *Int. J. Psycho-Anal.* 64: 187-201.

Bethell, S. L. (1944) *Shakespeare and the Popular Dramatic Tradition*. Staples Press.

Bettelheim, B. (1976) *The Uses of Enchantment*. New York: Knopf.

Bion, W. R. (1957) 'Attacks on linking', in Spillius (1988), vol. 1, pp. 87–101.

Bock, P. K. (1984) *Shakespeare and Elizabethan Culture*. New York: Schocken.

Bradbrook, M. (1984) *On Shakespeare*. Brighton: Harvester.

Brockbank, P. (1966) '*The Tempest*: conventions of art and empire', in J. R. Brown and B. Harris, eds *Stratford-upon-Avon Studies 8: Later Shakespeare*. Arnold, 1974, pp. 183–201.

Brockbank, P., ed. (1985) *Players of Shakespeare*. Cambridge: Cambridge Univ. Press.

Brooks, P. (1980) 'Repetition, repression, and return', *New Literary History* 11: 503–26.

—— (1987) 'The idea of a psychoanalytical literary criticism', *Critical Inquiry* 13: 334–48.

Brown, J. R. (1969) *Shakespeare: The Tempest*. Edward Arnold.

Brown, P. (1985) '"This thing of darkness I acknowledge mine": *The Tempest* and the discourse of colonialism', in J. Dollimore and A. Sinfield, eds *Political Shakespeare*. Manchester: Manchester Univ. Press, pp. 48–71.

Bullough, G. (1975) *Narrative and Dramatic Sources of Shakespeare*, vol. 8. Routledge.

Buxton, J. (1980) 'Two dead birds: a note on *The Phoenix and Turtle*', in J. Carey, ed. *English Renaissance Studies Presented to Dame Helen Gardner*. Oxford: Clarendon Press, pp. 44–55.

Chasseguet-Smirgel, J. (1964) 'Feminine guilt and the Oedipus complex', in Chasseguet-Smirgel, ed. *Female Sexuality*, Maresfield Library, 1985, pp. 94–134.

Chodorow, N. (1978) *The Reproduction of Mothering: Psychoanalysis and the Reproduction of Gender*. Berkeley, CA: Univ. Calif. Press.

Cohn, N. (1957) *The Pursuit of the Millennium*. Secker & Warburg.

Cole, E. T. (1987) *Troilus and Cressida: Performance Programme*. Stratford, Ontario: Commercial Print-Craft.

Colie, R. (1966) *Paradox Epidemica*. Princeton, NJ: Princeton Univ. Press.

Colman, E. A. M. (1974) *The Dramatic Use of Bawdry in Shakespeare*. Longman.

Cook, J. (1980) *Women in Shakespeare*. Harrap.

Davidson, F. (1963) '*The Tempest*: an interpretation', *J. of English and German Philology* 62: 501–17.

Dobrée, B. (1952) '*The Tempest*', *Essays and Studies* 5: 26–31.

Donne, J. *The Elegies and The Songs and Sonnets*, Helen Gardner, ed. Oxford: Clarendon Press, 1965.

Dover Wilson, J. (1943) *The Fortunes of Falstaff*. Cambridge: Cambridge Univ. Press, 1953.

Edwards, P. (1968) *Shakespeare and the Confines of Art*. Methuen.

Edwards, P. ed. (1976) *Pericles*. Harmondsworth: Penguin.

Evans, G. B., ed. (1974) *The Riverside Shakespeare*. Boston, MA: Houghton Mifflin.

Evans, M. (1986) *Signifying Nothing*. Brighton: Harvester.

Ewbank, I.-S. (1980) ' "My name is Marina" ' in I.-S. Ewbank, P. Edwards and G. K. Hunter, eds *Shakespeare's Styles*. Cambridge: Cambridge Univ. Press, pp. 95–111.

Faber, M. D. (1985) '*Antony and Cleopatra*: the empire of self', *Psychoanal. Rev.* 72: 71–104.

Felperin, H. (1964) 'Keats and Shakespeare: two new sources', *English Language Notes* 2: 105–9.

Fenichel, O. (1937) 'The scoptophilic instinct and identification', *Int. J. Psycho-Anal.* 18: 6–34.

Ferguson, J. C. (1928) *Mythology of All Races*, vol. 8, *China*. Boston, MA: Marshall Jones.

Fiedler, L. (1973) *The Stranger in Shakespeare*. Paladin, 1974.

Fineman, J. (1977) 'Fratricide and cuckoldry: Shakespeare's doubles', *Psychoanal. Rev.* 64: 409–53.

Frattaroli, E. J. (1987) 'On the validity of treating Shakespeare's characters as if they were real people', *Psychoanalysis and Contemporary Thought* 10: 407–37.

Freud, S. (1900a) *The Interpretation of Dreams*, in James Strachey, ed. *The Standard Edition of the Complete Psychological Works of Sigmund Freud*, 24 vols. Hogarth, 1953–1973, vols 4–5.

—— (1900b) *The Interpretation of Dreams*, in A. Richards, ed. *Pelican Freud Library*, based on *S.E.* Harmondsworth: Penguin, 1976–, vol. 4.

—— (1901) *The Psychopathology of Everyday Life*. P.F.L. 5.

—— (1909) 'Family romances', *S.E.* 9, pp. 235–41.

—— (1923) *The Ego and the Id*. P.F.L. 11.

—— (1925) 'Some psychological consequences of the anatomical distinction between the sexes', *S.E.* 19, pp. 243–58.

Frye, N. (1983) *The Myth of Deliverance*. Toronto: Univ. Toronto Press.

Furdi, A. (1984) 'The play with a play within the play', Ph. D. dissertation, Hebrew University.

Gajdusek, R. E. (1974) 'Death, incest and the triple bond', *Am. Imago* 31: 109–58.

Garber, M. (1981) *Coming of Age in Shakespeare*. Methuen.

—— (1987) *Shakespeare's Ghost Writers*. Methuen.

Gilligan, C. (1982) *In a Different Voice*. Cambridge, MA: Harvard Univ. Press.

Goolden, P. (1955) 'Antiochus's riddle in Gower and Shakespeare', *Review of English Studies*, n.s. 6, 23: 245–51.

Gornick, L. K. (1987) 'Freud and the creative writer', *Psychoanalysis and Contemporary Thought* 10: 103–27.

Graves, R. (1955) *The Greek Myths*. Harmondsworth: Penguin.

Green, A. (1979) *The Tragic Effect: The Oedipus Complex in Tragedy*, trans. A. Sheridan. New York: Cambridge Univ. Press.

—— (1980) 'The unbinding process', *New Literary History* 12: 11–39.

Greenblatt, S. (1985) 'Invisible bullets', in J. Dollimore and A. Sinfield, eds *Political Shakespeare*. Manchester: Manchester Univ. Press, pp. 18–47.

Grosart, A. B. (1878) *Robert Chester's 'Love's Martyr, or Rosalins Complaint' 1601*. New Shakespeare Society, Series 8, No. 2.

Guntrip, H. (1968) *Schizoid Phenomena, Object-Relations, and the Self*. Hogarth and The Institute of Psycho-Analysis.

Hamilton, J. W. (1969) 'Object loss, dreaming, and creativity', *Psychoanal. Study Child* 24: 488–531.

Hartman, G., ed. (1978) *Psychoanalysis and the Question of the Text*. Baltimore, MD: Johns Hopkins Univ. Press.

Hawkes, T. (1973) *Shakespeare's Talking Animals*. Edward Arnold.

Henryson, R. *Testament of Cresseid*, ed. Denton Fox. Thomas Nelson & Sons, 1967.

Herman, N. (1989) *Too Long a Child: The Mother–Daughter Dyad*. Free Association Books.

Hirsh, E. D. Jr (1967) *Validity in Interpretation*. New Haven, CT: Yale Univ. Press.

Hirst, D. L. (1984) *The Tempest: Text and Performance*. Macmillan.

Hobson, A. (1972) *Full Circle: Shakespeare and Moral Development*. Chatto & Windus.

Hoeniger, F. D., ed. (1963) *Pericles*. The Arden Shakespeare. Methuen, 1977.

Holland, N. (1966) *Psychoanalysis and Shakespeare*. New York: McGraw-Hill.

—— (1975) *The Dynamics of Literary Response*. New York: Norton.

Honigman, E. A. J. (1985) *Shakespeare's Lost Years*. Manchester: Manchester Univ. Press.

Isaacs, S. (1948) 'The nature and function of phantasy', *Int. J. Psycho-Anal.* 29: 73–97.

James, D. G. (1967) *The Dream of Prospero*. Oxford: Clarendon Press.

Jones, E. (1935) 'Early female sexuality', *Int. J. Psycho-Anal.* 16: 263–73.

—— (1949) *Hamlet and Oedipus*. New York: Norton.

—— (1953,1955,1957) *Sigmund Freud: Life and Work*, 3 vols. Hogarth.

Kahn, C. (1980) 'The providential tempest and the Shakespearean family', in Schwartz and Kahn (1980), pp. 217–43.

Kantorowicz, E. H. (1957) *The King's Two Bodies: A Study in Medieval Political Theology*. Princeton, NJ: Princeton Univ. Press.

Kermode, F., ed. (1954) *The Tempest*. The Arden Shakespeare. Methuen, 1961.

Kermode, F. (1963) *William Shakespeare: The Final Plays*. Longman.

Kirsch, A. (1978) 'The polarization of erotic love in *Othello*', *Modern Language Review* 73: 21–40.

Klein, M. (1929) 'Infantile anxiety situations reflected in a work of art and in the creative impulse', in J. Mitchell, ed. *The Selected Melanie Klein*. Harmondsworth: Penguin, 1986, pp. 84–94.

—— (1930) 'The importance of symbol formation in the development of the ego', in Mitchell (1986), pp. 95–111.

—— (1931) 'A contribution to the theory of intellectual inhibition', in R. E. Money-Kyrle, ed. *Love, Guilt and Reparation and Other Works, 1921–1945*. Hogarth and The Institute of Psycho-Analysis, 1975, pp. 236–47.

—— (1935) 'A contribution to the psychogenesis of manic depressive states', in Mitchell (1986), pp. 116–45.

—— (1940) 'Mourning and its relation to manic-depressive states', in Mitchell (1986), pp. 146–74.

—— (1946) 'Notes on some schizoid mechanisms', in Mitchell (1986), pp. 176–200.

—— (1952) 'The origins of transference', in Mitchell (1986), pp. 201–10.

—— (1957) *Envy and Gratitude: A Study of Unconscious Sources*. Tavistock.

Knights, L. C. (1946) 'How many children had Lady Macbeth?', in Knights (1960) *Explorations*. Macmillan, pp. 48–61.

Lacan, J. (1966) *Ecrits*, trans. A. Sheridan. New York: Norton, 1977.

—— (1968) 'The mirror phase as formative of the function of the I', *New Left Review* 51: 71–7.

—— (1972) 'Seminar on *The Purloined Letter*', trans. J. Mehlman, *Yale French Studies* 48: 39–72.

Langbaum, R., ed. (1964) *The Tempest*. New York: Signet.

Laplanche, J. and Pontalis, J.-B. (1967) *The Language of Psychoanalysis*. Hogarth, 1973.

Levin, H. (1976) *Shakespeare and the Revolution of the Times*. New York: Oxford Univ. Press.

Lewis, C. S. (1954) *English Literature in the Sixteenth Century*. New York: Oxford Univ. Press.

Lewis, W. (1927) *The Lion and the Fox*. Grant Richards.

Loewald, H. (1980) *Papers on Psychoanalysis*. New Haven, CT: Yale Univ. Press.

Lussier, A. (1985) 'The core conflict: superego – ideal ego. An essay on the structural point of view'.   Paper presented to the Toronto Psychoanalytic Society.

Mahler, M. F., Pine, F. and Bergman, A. (1975) *The Psychological Birth of the Human Infant*. New York: Basic.

Mahood, M. M., ed. (1987) *The Merchant of Venice*. The New Cambridge Shakespeare. Cambridge: Cambridge Univ. Press.

Mancia, M. and Meltzer, D. (1981) 'Ego-ideal functions and the psychoanalytical process', *Int. J. Psycho-Anal.* 62: 243–49.

Matchett, W. (1965) *"The Phoenix and the Turtle", Shakespeare's Poem and "Love's Martyr"*. Mouton.

Miller, F. J. (1916) *The Metamorphoses of Ovid*. Loeb Classical Library. Cambridge, MA: Harvard Univ. Press.

Miller, J. (1986) *Subsequent Performances*. Faber.

Mitchell, J., ed. (1986) *The Selected Melanie Klein*. Harmondsworth: Penguin.

Money-Kyrle, R. E., ed. (1975) Klein, M. *Love, Guilt and Reparation and Other Works,1921–1945*. Hogarth and The Institute of Psycho-Analysis.

Muller, W. M. (1918) *Mythology of All Races*, vol. 12, *Egypt*. Boston, MA: Marshall Jones.

Nathan, N. (1956) '*Pericles* and *Jonah*', *Notes and Queries* 201: 10–11.

Nevo, R. (1980) *Comic Transformations in Shakespeare*. Methuen.

Nuttall, A. D. (1967) *Two Concepts of Allegory: A Study of Shakespeare's The Tempest*. Routledge & Kegan Paul.

—— (1983) *A New Mimesis*. Methuen.

Orgel, S. (1968) 'To make boards speak: Inigo Jones's stage and the Jonsonian masque', *Renaissance Drama* 1: 121–52.

Orgel, S. ed. (1987) *The Tempest*. Oxford: Clarendon Press.

Padel, J. (1981) *New Poems by Shakespeare: Order and Meaning Restored to the Sonnets*. Herbert Press.

—— (1985) 'Was Shakespeare happy with his patron?', *Psychoanal. Psychotherapy* 1: 25–42.

—— (1989) 'Shakespeare's Sonnet 20: some limits to psychoanalytic interpretation', *Int. Rev. Psycho-Anal.* 12: 273–83.

Palmer, D. J., ed. (1968) *Shakespeare: The Tempest*. Macmillan Casebook Series. Macmillan.

Partridge, E. (1947) *Shakespeare's Bawdy*. Routledge & Kegan Paul, 1956.

Pepys, S. *The Shorter Pepys*. Selected from the diary of Samuel Pepys, ed. Robert Latham. Bell & Hyman, 1985.

Piers, G. and Singer, M. B. (1971) *Shame and Guilt*. New York: Norton.

Plaut, E. and Hutchinson, F. (1986) 'The role of puberty in female psychosexual development', *Int. Rev. Psycho-Anal.* 13: 417–32.

Prince, F. T., ed. (1960) *The Poems*. The Arden Shakespeare. Methuen.

Reid, S. A. (1970) 'A psychoanalytic reading of *Troilus and Cressida* and *Measure for Measure*', *Psychoanal. Rev.* 57: 262–82.

Riesenberg Malcolm, R. (1981) 'Melanie Klein: achievements and problems', in R. Langs, ed. *The Yearbook of Psychoanalysis and Psychotherapy*. New York: Gardner Press, 1987, vol. 2, pp. 306–21.

Robson, K. S. (1967) 'The role of eye-to-eye contact in maternal–infant attachment', *J. of Child Psychology and Psychiatry* 8: 13–25.

Rogers, R. (1970) *A Psychoanalytical Study of the Double in Literature*. Detroit, MI: Wayne State Univ. Press.

Rothenberg, A. B. (1973) 'Infantile fantasies in Shakespearean metaphor: (I) the fear of being smothered', *Psychoanalytic Review* 60,2: 205–22.

Rouse, W. H. D. (1904) *Shakespeare's Ovid, Being Arthur Golding's Translation of the Metamorphoses*. Centaur, 1961.

Schafer, R. (1968) *Aspects of Internalization*. New York: International Universities Press.

Schanzer, E., ed. (1965) *Pericles*. New York: Signet.

Schwartz, M. and Kahn, C., eds (1980) *Representing Shakespeare*. Baltimore, MD: Johns Hopkins Univ. Press.

Scott, W. C. M (1987) 'Making the best of a sad job'. Paper presented at the British Psychoanalytical Society.

Segal, H. (1980) *Melanie Klein*. New York: Penguin Modern Masters, 1981.

Skura, Meredith (1980a) 'Revisions and rereadings in dreams and allegories', in J. H. Smith, ed. *The Literary Freud*. New Haven, CT: Yale Univ. Press, pp. 345–79.

—— (1980b) 'Interpreting Posthumus' dream from above and below: families, psychoanalysts, and literary critics', in Schwartz and Kahn (1980), pp. 203–16.

Slap, J. W. (1966) 'On sarcasm', *Psychoanal. Q.* 25: 98–108.

Smith, H. (1974) Preface to *Pericles* in G. B. Evans, ed. *The Riverside Shakespeare*. Boston, MA: Houghton Mifflin, pp. 1479–82.

Sokol, B. J. (1980) 'Numerology in Fulke Greville's *Caelica*', *Notes and Queries* 27: 328–9.

—— (1985) 'A Spenserian idea in *The Taming of the Shrew*', *English Studies* 66: 308–15.

Spillius, E. B., ed. (1988) *Melanie Klein Today*, 2 vols. Routledge.

Summers, M. (1922) *Shakespeare Adaptions*. Cape, 1932.

Tayler, E. (1990) 'Remarks as Honored Scholar at the Milton Society Dinner, Washington, D. C. 12/28/89', *Milton Quarterly* 24: 44-6.

Tilley, M. P. (1950) *A Dictionary of Proverbs in English in the Sixteenth and Seventeenth Century*. Ann Arbor, MI: Univ. Michigan Press.

Traversi, D. T. (1969) *An Approach to Shakespeare*. New York: Doubleday Anchor.

Turner, V. (1957) *Schism and Continuity in an African Society*. Manchester: Manchester Univ. Press.

—— (1969) *The Ritual Process: Structure and Anti-structure*. Routledge & Kegan Paul.

—— (1974) *Dramas, Fields and Metaphors*. Ithaca, NY: Cornell Univ. Press.

—— (1977) 'Variations on a theme of liminality', in S. F. Moore and B. G. Meyerhoff, eds *Secular Ritual*. Amsterdam: Van Gorcum, pp. 36-52.

Wheeler, R. P. (1972) 'Poetry and fantasy in Shakespeare's Sonnets 88-96. *Literature and Psychology* 22: 121-62.

Wilders, J. (1988) *New Prefaces to Shakespeare*. Oxford: Blackwell.

Willbern, D. (1978) 'A bibliography of psychoanalytic and psychological writings on Shakespeare', in Schwartz and Kahn (1980), pp. 264-88.

—— (1980) 'Shakespeare's nothing', in Schwartz and Kahn (1980), pp. 244-63.

Wilson Knight, G. (1932) *The Shakespearian Tempest*. Oxford Univ. Press.

—— (1947) *The Crown of Life*. Oxford Univ. Press.

—— (1955) *The Mutual Flame*. Methuen.

—— (1980) 'Caliban as a red man', in I. S. Ewbank, P. Edwards and G. K. Hunter, eds *Shakespeare's Styles*. Cambridge: Cambridge Univ. Press, pp. 205-20.

Winnicott, D. W. (1971) *Playing and Reality*. Harmondsworth: Pelican, 1985.

—— (1988) *Human Nature*. New York: Schocken.

Wollheim, R. (1984) *The Thread of Life*. Cambridge: Cambridge Univ. Press.

Yeats, W. B. (1899) 'Notes to *The Wind Among the Reeds*', in A. N. Jeffares, *A Commentary on the Collected Poems of W. B. Yeats*. Stanford, CA: Stanford Univ. Press, 1968.

—— (1932) 'Notes to *Fighting the Waves*', in R. K. Alspach, ed. *The Variorum Edition of the Plays of W. B. Yeats*. Macmillan, 1966.

INDEX

This first edition of
The Undiscover'd Country:
New Essays on Psychoanalysis and Shakespeare
was finished in March 1993.

The book was commissioned by Robert M. Young,
copy-edited and proofread by Anita Kermode,
and produced by Ann Scott for
Free Association Books